*Pr*

# ACE FR



*an*

# NO REGRETS

"Even by standards of '70s hard rock excess, original KISS guitarist Ace Frehley was out of this world. In this breezy, buzzy, and debauched memoir, the Spaceman takes readers on a rocket ride through his ups and downs with his bandmates, musical career, private life, and booze-and-drug binges that would make the guys in Mötley Crüe beg for a day to recover."

—*Houston Press*

"Kiss fans will clamor over this book of brain droppings from the one, and only, member of the band to have more personality than his made-up character. . . . Ace Frehley remains a true icon of rock and his take on his life is one wild ride. . . . There have been many books written about the band but none so human as this. . . . Candid."

—*Classic Rock Revisited*

"A side of the band's story that has heretofore gone largely undocumented."

—*Buffalo News*

"The book's insightful early chapters provide a glimpse of Ace as a fan and student of rock rather than just inaccessible, fabulously wealthy practitioner—even after joining KISS. . . . *No Regrets* is a breezy read, tracing the path of one of rock's most iconic—and certainly most colorful—guitarists."

—*The Cleveland Sound*

"When KISS took the pop-music world by storm in their '70s prime, lead guitarist Ace Frehley, the Spaceman, was fully committed to living the dream as best expressed in the shout-along chorus of the costumed rockers' breakthrough single, 'Rock and Roll All Nite'. . . . He's sober now and telling all."

—*The Arizona Republic*

"A captivating read that details Frehley's musical success and his dangerous, drug- and alcohol-fueled lifestyle that left him lucky to be alive."

—*Ridgewood Patch*

"KISS fan or not, it's a fun read. Frehley's voice comes through, and his sense of humor shines through."

—*Phoenix New Times*

"*No Regrets* is at its richest when depicting Frehley's formative years as a rebel without a press agent. . . . The drug stories are recounted with [a] familiar mixture of abject humiliation and vaudevillian zeal."

—*Orlando Weekly*

"Frehley has had plenty of triumphant rock star moments in his career."

—MTV Hive

"An interesting read chronicling the rocker's time with KISS."

—*Huffington Post*

"As one of the original members of KISS, flamboyant guitarist Ace Frehley was instrumental in not only putting the band on the rock 'n' roll map, but also turning them into a household name around the world. In *No Regrets*, Frehley looks back at the band's humble beginnings."

—MSNBC.com

# NO REGRETS

# ACE FREHLEY

WITH JOE LAYDEN & JOHN OSTROSKY

# NO REGRETS

A Rock 'n' Roll Memoir

Gallery Books / VH1 Books

New York London Toronto Sydney New Delhi

Gallery Books
A Division of Simon & Schuster, Inc.
1230 Avenue of the Americas
New York, NY 10020



First Gallery Books trade paper edition June 2012



Designed by Joy O'Meara

Manufactured in the United States of America

5 7 9 10 8 6

Library of Congress Cataloging-in-Publication Data is available.

ISBN 978-1-4516-1394-0
ISBN 978-1-4516-1395-7 (paperback)
ISBN 978-1-4516-1396-4 (ebook)

TO ALL THE ACE FREHLEY FANS

IN THE UNIVERSE

# CONTENTS


1 A Bronx Tale 1

2 Gangs of New York 9

3 Music in the Fifth Dimension 19

4 Movin' on Up 31

5 Are You Experienced? 45

6 Flash and Ability 63

7 KISS Comes to Life 79

8 Here's Looking at You, KISS 93

9 On the Road 107

10 Alive! 125

11 The KISS Hits the Fan 139

12 Going Solo 157

13 Fast Cars, Celebs, and Betty White 183

14 Apple Wine and Airplane Glue 209

CONTENTS

15 Smokey and the Bandit (Revisited) 223

16 Rocket Rides and Rehabs 237

17 Cough Syrup, Fish Sandwiches, and Voodoo 249

18 Return of the Bad Boys 261

19 Into the Void 275

Epilogue 295

A Special Thanks 299

Photo Insert Captions 301

# 1

# A BRONX TALE

When I was a kid I used to carry around this awful image in my head—a picture of three men tangled awkwardly in high-tension wires, fifty feet in the air, their lifeless bodies crisping in the midday sun.

The horror they endured was shared with me by my father, an electrical engineer who worked, among other places, at the U.S. Military Academy at West Point, New York, helping with the installation of a new power plant in the 1950s. Carl Frehley was a man of his times. He worked long hours, multiple jobs, did the best he could to provide a home for his wife and kids. Sometimes, on Sunday afternoons after church, he'd pile the whole family into a car and we'd drive north through the Bronx, into Westchester County, and eventually find ourselves on the banks of the Hudson River. Dad would take us on a tour of the West Point campus and grounds, introduce us to people, even take us into the control room of the electrical plant. I'm still not sure how he pulled that one off—getting security clearance for his whole family—but he did.

Dad would walk around, pointing out various sights, explaining the rhythm of his day and the work that he did, sometimes talking in the language of an engineer, a language that might as well have been Latin to me. Work was important, and I guess in some way he just wanted his kids to understand that; he wanted us to see this other part of his life.

One day, as we headed back to the car, my father paused and looked up at the electrical wires above, a net of steel and cable stretching across the autumn sky.

"You know, Paul," he said, "every day at work, we have a little contest before lunch."

I had no idea what he was talking about.

A contest? Before lunch?

Sounded like something we might have done at Grace Lutheran, where I went to elementary school in the Bronx.

"We draw straws to see who has to go out and pick up sandwiches for the whole crew. If you get the shortest straw, you're the delivery boy."

That was the beginning. From there, my father went on to tell us the story of the day he drew the short straw. While he was out picking up sandwiches, there was a terrible accident back on the job. Someone had accidentally thrown a switch, restoring power to an area where three men were working. Tragically, all three men were electrocuted instantly. When my father returned, he couldn't believe his eyes. The bodies of his coworkers were being peeled off the high-tension wires.

"Right up there," he said quietly, looking overhead. "That's where it happened."

He paused, put a hand on my shoulder.

"If I hadn't drawn the short straw that day, I'd have been up there in those wires, and I wouldn't be here right now."

I looked at the wires, then at my father. He smiled.

"Sometimes you get lucky."

Dad would repeat that story from time to time, just often enough to keep the nightmares flowing. That wasn't his intent, of course—he always related the tale in a whimsical "what if?" tone—but it was the outcome nonetheless. You tell a little kid that his old man was nearly fried to death, and you're sentencing him to a few years of sweaty, terror-filled nights beneath the sheets. I get his point now, though. You never know what life might bring . . . or when it might come to a screeching halt.

And it's best to act accordingly.

The Carl Frehley I knew (and it's important to note that I didn't know him all that well) was quiet and reserved, a model of middle-class decorum, maybe because he was so fucking tired all the time. My father was forty-seven years old by the time I came into this world, and I sometimes think he was actually deep into a second life at that point. The son of German and Dutch immigrants, he'd grown up in Bethlehem, Pennsylvania, finished three years of college, and had to leave school and go to work. Later on he moved to New York and married Esther Hecht, a pretty young girl seventeen years his junior. My mom had been raised on a farm in Norlina, North Carolina. My grandfather was from northern Germany—the island Rügen, to be precise. My grandmother was also German, but I'd always heard whispers of there being some American Indian blood in our family. It was boredom, more than anything else, that brought my mom to New York. Tired of life on the farm, she followed her older sister Ida north and lived with her for a while in Brooklyn.

Dad, meanwhile, came for the work.

There was always a little bit of mystery surrounding my dad, things he never shared; nooks and crannies of his past were always a taboo subject. He married late, started a family late, and settled into a comfortable domestic and professional routine. Every so often, though, there were glimpses of a different man, a different life.

My dad was an awesome bowler, for example. He never talked about being part of a bowling league or even how he learned the game. God knows he only bowled occasionally while I was growing up, but when he did, he nailed it. He had his own ball, his own shoes, and textbook form that helped him throw a couple of perfect games. He was also an amazing pool player, a fact I discovered while still in elementary school, when he taught me how to shoot. Dad could do things with a pool cue that only the pros could do, and when I look back on it now I realize he may have spent some time in a few shady places. He once told me that he had beaten the champion of West Virginia in a game of pool. I guess you have to be pretty good to beat the state champion of any sport.

"Hey, Dad. What's your high run?" I once asked him while we were shooting pool.

"One forty-nine," he said, without even looking up.

Holy shit . . .

I must have been only about ten years old at the time, and I didn't immediately grasp the enormity of that number, but I quickly realized it meant making 149 consecutive shots without missing.

That's ten fuckin' racks!

You have to know what you're doing to polish off that many balls without screwing up. And that little piece of information, coupled with the times I saw him execute trick shots and one-handed shots, made me wonder even more about his elusive past. Perhaps, when he was younger, he lived life in the fast lane and we had much more in common than one might think. Maybe, just maybe, Carl Frehley kicked some ass.

It's kinda fun to think so, anyway.

I grew up just off Mosholu Parkway in the Bronx, not far from the New York Botanical Garden and Bronx Zoo. It was a middle-class neighborhood of mixed ethnic backgrounds, consisting of mostly German, Irish, Jewish, and Italian families. Ours was pretty normal and loving, a fact I came to appreciate even more after I began hanging out with some serious badasses who were always trying to escape their violent and abusive home lives. Conversely, my dad never hit or abused me as a child, but I often wondered how much he really cared about me since we never did anything together one-on-one. Now as I think back, I realize more and more that he loved me, and that he did the best he could under the circumstances.

It's pretty hard to look at the Frehleys and suggest that my upbringing contributed in any way to my wild and crazy lifestyle and the insanity that was to ensue. Sure, my dad was a workaholic and never home, but there was always food on the table, and we all felt secure. My parents enjoyed a happy and affectionate marriage—I can still see them holding hands as they walked down the street, or kissing when Dad came home from work. They always seemed happy together, and there was very little fighting at home. We had relatives in Brooklyn and North Carolina, all on my mother's side, but I knew very little about my dad's side of the family. There were no photo albums or letters, no interesting stories or visits from aunts and uncles. Nothing. I knew he had a brother who had tragically drowned at age eight, but the rest was sketchy at best. When I tried to ask him for more details, my mom would intervene.

"Don't push your father," she'd say. "It's too painful for him."

So I'd let it go.

People who know me only as the Spaceman probably find this hard to believe, but I was raised in a family that stressed education and religion. My parents also understood the value of the arts and sciences. The way I'm fascinated with computers and guitars, my dad was fascinated with motors and electrical circuits, and he used to build his own batteries in the basement as a child. I know he was very good at what he did because in addition to his work at West Point, he also serviced the elevator motors in the Empire State Building, and was involved in designing the backup ignition system for the Apollo spacecraft for NASA. He had notebooks filled with formulas and sketches, projects he worked on until the wee hours of the morning.

So my parents emphasized learning, and two of their three children got the message. My sister, Nancy, who is eight years my senior, was a straight-A student who went on to get a master's degree in chemistry; she taught high school chemistry for a while before getting married to start a family. My brother, Charles, was an honors student as well. He studied classical guitar at New York University, where he finished tenth in his class.

Then there was me, Paul Frehley, the youngest of three kids and the black sheep to boot.

In the beginning I enjoyed school and team sports, but as I got older, my social life and music began taking precedence over my studies. I remember coming home with B's, C's, and D's on my report card and hearing my parents complain.

"Why can't you be more like Charlie and Nancy?"

I'd just throw up my hands. Between bands and girlfriends, who had time to study?

"You're wasting your life, Paul," my dad would say, shaking his head.

Once, just to prove a point, I told my parents that I'd study hard for a semester and prove I was just as bright as my brother and sister. And you know what? I got all A's and B's on the next report card. (Much later, it was the same sort of "I told you so" attitude that would compel me to challenge the other guys in KISS to an IQ test. Just for the record, I scored highest: 163, which is considered "genius.") Now, I know I drove my parents crazy, but God had other plans for me. It all stemmed from something I sensed at an early age: the desire to become a rock star and follow my dreams. Crazy as that sounds, I really believed it would happen.

You can partially credit my blind ambition to Mom and Dad! You see, if there was a common thread within our family, it was music. Thanks to the influence of our parents, all the Frehley kids played instruments. My father was an accomplished concert pianist: he could perform Chopin and Mozart effortlessly. My mom played the piano, too, and she enjoyed banging out a few tunes at family gatherings. Charlie and Nancy took piano lessons and performed at recitals as well. They eventually started fooling around with the guitar and formed a folk group, but that was never my cup of tea. From the beginning, I was drawn to rock 'n' roll and started figuring out songs by the Beatles and the Stones on my brother's acoustic guitar. One day, by chance, I picked up my friend's new electric guitar and checked it out. I plugged it in, turned the amp up to ten, and strummed a power chord.

I immediately fell in love. It was a life-changing event! I was only twelve, but I was totally hooked. Within a couple of years I had a Fender Tele and a Marshall amp in my bedroom, and I'd sold my soul to rock 'n' roll. There was no turning back.

My parents were not entirely unsupportive of my obsession (Dad even bought me my first electric guitar as a Christmas present), probably because it beat the alternative. There were worse vices, worse behavior, as I'd already demonstrated. See, at the same time that I was teaching myself guitar and forming my first band, I was also running with a pretty tough crowd. So while it may be true that the rock 'n' roll lifestyle nearly killed me as an adult, it's also true that without music, I might never have made it to adulthood in the first place.

I started hanging out with the toughest guys in the neighborhood when I was still in grammar school, playing poker, drinking, cutting school—generally just looking for trouble. At first I was uncomfortable with some of the things I had to do, but I learned pretty quickly that alcohol made everything a lot easier. I didn't like to fight, but fearlessness came with a few beers. Talking to girls was sometimes awkward, but with a little buzz I could charm them right out of their pants.

The first drink? I remember it well. Every drinker remembers his first drink, just as vividly as he remembers his first fuck. I was eleven years old and hanging out with my brother and his friend Jeffrey. Jeff's father had a small cabin on City Island in the Bronx, and we went there one Friday after school. The plan was to do some fishing and hang out. I loved fishing when I was a kid; I still do. And it was on that weekend that I discovered that beer went hand in hand with fishing. Jeff's dad had left a six-pack of Schaefer beer in the fridge, and we each had a can or two. Not exactly hard-core drinking, but enough to get me comfortably numb. I can remember exactly how it felt, smooth and dry. Pretty soon I felt kind of lightheaded and silly, and I couldn't stop laughing. Then I passed out. The next thing I remember is waking up in the morning with a slight headache and a dry mouth, but to be honest, I couldn't wait to do it again.

And I didn't wait. Not long, anyway.

The following weekend, we ended up going to a party with more beer and girls—older girls! I'd been attracted to girls for a while by now, but this was unexplored territory. Here I was, playing Spin the Bottle and Seven Minutes in Heaven with thirteen-year-olds, but after my first beer, all I can remember is thinking, *bring it on!*

I'd found girls and alcohol to be a great combination.

The rock 'n' roll would soon follow.

2

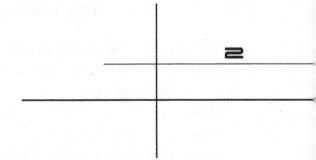

# GANGS OF NEW YORK

The social divide in my neighborhood was fairly clear: either you were a strong student with designs on college . . . or you weren't. My brother and sister fell into the first category; I fell into the second. Like a lot of kids drifting through school in the Bronx in the 1950s and early '60s, I sought friendship and camaraderie in a different circle, one populated by kids who favored leather jackets and jeans, and greased-up pompadours.

The transition occurred right around the time I went through puberty (doesn't it always?). Through much of elementary school I'd been an indifferent but harmless student, a kid who preferred sports to studying. I was taller than most of my friends, lanky and reasonably athletic, so most games came easily to me. I played shortstop in baseball, was cocaptain of my school's basketball team, and won a handful of medals in track and field. About the only game I didn't like was football. I was skinny as a kid, without an ounce of extra flesh. Good for playing basketball (and not a bad look for a guitar player, I might add), but not so great for football. One of the local cops talked me and some buddies into joining the Police Athletic League football team one year, and I can still remember the opening kickoff. The ball sailed right into my arms and I took off down the sideline, figuring I had the speed and moves to make a good return.

Wrong.

I never even saw the kid coming. He nailed me right in the chest and knocked the wind outta me! The ball went one way, my helmet went another. For several seconds I lay there gasping—I'd never had been hit like that, and I couldn't believe how much it hurt. It was scary as hell; from that point on, I realized football wasn't for me.

Truth is, much as I'd like to claim otherwise, I was not a particularly tough kid. That much was revealed not merely on the football field, but on the streets of the Bronx as well. I was a fun-loving kid who liked music and sports. I didn't fit neatly into the laid-back, studious group; neither did I fit neatly into the gang scene. The tough guys were always testing other kids, pushing people around, seeing how far they could go before they'd trigger a response. I hated that feeling of apprehension, having to worry about walking to the candy store, or coming home from school, not knowing who might be waiting around the next corner smoking cigarettes, listening to doo-wop music, and waiting for an opportunity to kick the shit out of some little kid.

Basically, for these guys, it was target practice.

And on more than one occasion, I was the target.

Admittedly, there were times I invited the attention (although that wasn't my intent). Like I said, I started early with girls, and when you were messing around with girls in my neighborhood it was wise to exercise some caution and common sense. Specifically, only an idiot would chase girls who were attached in one way or another to one of the local gangs.

Well, what the fuck? For a smart kid, I could be a real idiot. Stubborn, too. I'm a Taurus, after all.

Dominating the street scene in this part of the Bronx was the Ducky Gang, a collection of kids ranging in age from the early teens to the mid-twenties. Predominantly Irish, but with a sprinkling of Italian and German thrown in, the Duckies were a formidable group whose turf centered around the Twin Lakes (the "duck pond") section of the New York Botanical Garden. The Ducky Boys were born around the time I was in elementary school, and their rise paralleled my adolescence. Although they died out in the mid-1970s (only to be immortalized in the movie *The Wanderers*), they were the Kings of New York as far as I was concerned, and my fear of them was surpassed only by my desire to join their ranks. Not necessarily because I admired them or wanted to be part of a gang, but simply because I got tired of getting my ass kicked.

The moment of clarity came one afternoon while walking home from school, when I was about twelve or thirteen. I'd been hanging out with this pretty girl for a few weeks, chasing her on weekends, looking for her at parties, occasionally stealing a little make-out time. Well, I should have known better. The girl had already been claimed by one of the Ducky Boys, so protocol dictated that everyone else keep their distance.

She was, for all practical purposes, untouchable.

And I touched.

So there I was, strolling through the park, minding my own business, when all of a sudden this chick's boyfriend pops out from behind a tree and steps in front of me. I wasn't even sure how to react. The kid was a year or two older than me, a head taller, and probably twenty-five pounds heavier; a grown man, by comparison. I froze for a moment and tried to weigh my options.

Drop my schoolbooks and run like hell?

Exercise a little diplomacy? (I'd always been pretty nimble when it came to talking my way out of trouble.)

Down the road I'd learn the finer points of street fighting, the most important of which is this: always get off the first shot. But I was inexperienced and scared. Before I had a chance to react, the kid leaned forward and punched me in the face. I went down for the count.

I don't know how long I was unconscious, probably only a few seconds. But when I came to, with my head aching and my vision blurred, the kid was standing over me.

"Stay away from my girl," he said, "or I'll fuckin' kill you."

And then he went off, leaving me there alone, dizzy and disoriented, wondering whether any girl was worth so much trouble.

But, of course, they were. I've had a problem with females my entire life, and by that I mean, women have always gotten me into trouble. More accurately, I've gotten myself into trouble because of women. It's been a recurring theme of self-destruction, right up there with drugs and alcohol; from the time I learned how to use it, I've too often led with my dick, and I've taken a lot of punishment as a result.

There was, however, no reasoning with my adolescent mind (to say nothing of my adolescent hormones). Another guy would have gone home and jerked off to a *Playboy* magazine until he found a girl more suitable to his position in life. Not me. I liked the wilder chicks for a very good reason: they put out. That left me and my blue balls with basically two choices.

1) Find another girl.
2) Join the Duckies.

I chose option number two.

The Ducky Gang didn't accept just anyone. You had to prove yourself worthy by being put through an initiation that lasted for several weeks. For me, that turned out to be a good thing. The lag between my first expression of interest and the point of no return (full-blown gang membership) was so vast that I had time to develop other, less risky interests—like playing the guitar. For a while, though, I really wanted to be part of a gang and felt the need to be accepted.

We were known, unofficially, as the Junior Duckies. I loved being part of the gang and enjoyed the security they offered, even if it included some of the same guys who had been making my life miserable a few years before. For the Junior Duckies, gang life was mostly about mischief and messing around with girls. Every weekend we'd get together at the duck pond and drink beer, get all riled up, and go looking for trouble. That didn't take much effort, as the Duckies weren't the only gang in town. We'd wander down to the Bronx River Parkway, near the edge of Ducky turf, and if we found anyone venturing over the line we'd quickly engage in a rumble. These were less lethal in those days. While some of the older guys in the Ducky Gang carried knives and zip guns, we usually resorted to chains or baseball bats. For the Junior Duckies excitement came in the form of taking risks. We'd hitch rides on the backs of city buses and elevated trains, activities that usually caught the attention of the local cops and led to us being chased all over the neighborhood. Cheap thrills, I guess you'd say. When we weren't fighting or partying with the local chicks, in the winter we'd sometimes throw snowballs at patrol cars just to get a reaction. They'd hit the lights and give chase, and we'd scatter in all directions. Stupid? Sure. But it was exciting and lots of fun. A couple of times I got busted and ended up down at the Fifty-Second Precinct, where my parents would have to come and pick me up. After a while my mom used to worry whenever I left the house.

"Please be careful out there tonight, Paul," she'd say, wringing her hands.

But she never tried to stop me, and neither did my father. By the time I was fourteen, I was basically spinning out of control. I didn't want to stay home or do my homework, or even go to school, for that matter. I just wanted to hang out with my friends and party. I wanted it so bad that I was willing to go through a Junior Ducky initiation. Fighting was part of it, obviously; if the Duckies got in a fight, you were expected to be there, and to stand up for your buddies. Maybe you'd be assigned a target—some poor kid at school who had pissed off one of the Duckies—and your job was to lay him out. I'd been on the receiving end of those encounters; now I was being asked to dole out the punishment. Cowards, in any form, were not welcome. Sometimes, to prove you had balls, you were asked to do something dangerous.

Or stupid.

Or, in my case, both.

---

"Come on, Paul, get your skinny ass out there!"

We were standing near an overpass above Webster Avenue on a Saturday night, and below, the weekend traffic was busy. Here was the moment of truth. If I wanted to be part of the gang I'd have to show a willingness to put my life at risk. This time I was on my own.

"This is fucking nuts," I said.

And it was. They told me to crawl out on a catwalk under the bridge and then hang from a beam with my feet dangling over the highway. I guzzled a couple of beers to boost my confidence, but I was still scared. I took a deep breath and got down on my hands and knees. I was so nervous, I nearly pissed my pants, but my fear was outweighed by my need to be accepted. If I could just get through this insane ritual without killing myself, I'd finally be part of the toughest gang in my neighborhood. Then I'd have protection. No one would ever fuck with me again. For that, believe it or not, I was willing to risk my life.

A few moments later, I was hanging above the highway. I could hear my friends yelling and cheering, but I couldn't make out a word they were saying with the noise from the traffic below. I forced my eyes open and looked back to the edge of the bridge. They were waving me back in. I pulled my legs into my chest and crawled back to safety, where I was greeted with open arms.

I was finally in!

In the Bronx they referred to it as "beer muscles"—a phenomenon in which an otherwise low-key, fun-loving guy gets drunk and suddenly becomes willing to fight with anyone. That was me. If I had two or three beers I'd go up against anybody, because basically I had no fear. With each drink the inhibitions faded, and so did any concern over repercussions. Maybe that's why people would back down from me (well, that and the fact that I had the Duckies on my side). I was tall and skinny, and not really great with my fists, but when I drank I felt like a superhero. I'd fight anybody, with almost no provocation. I won a lot of fights just because I refused to back down. People tend to think you're a little crazy when you're that quick to fire, and who wants to fight a crazy guy?

Alcohol, mainly beer, made me a different person, and I kind of liked that person. He wasn't afraid of anything or anybody. Not only that, but he was smooth as silk when it came to dealing with girls. It all goes hand in hand. Women like guys who are confident, funny, cocky. A little bit dangerous. I was all of those things in a single package. And as my fascination with music intensified in the coming years, I discovered that while alcohol did not make me a better guitar player, it did make me a more outgoing performer. When I was younger, playing at school dances or church activities, I suffered from stage fright. But if I had a couple of drinks, the nervousness melted away. I was Jimmy Page and Jimi Hendrix, all rolled into one. I owned the fucking room!

Drinking was always part of what we did in the Junior Duckies. Some of my friends were also into sniffing glue. It was readily available, the perfect cheap high for a kid. I did glue only a few times as a kid (and once as an adult—more on that later), and frankly found the trips to be either completely uneventful or nightmarish. The bad one happened behind a gas station near Frisch Field (named after the great ballplayer Frankie Frisch, a Bronx native, I'm proud to say). I huddled up with a couple buddies, both experienced huffers, and we snipped the cap off a tube of glue and went to work.

Some of the details escape me, but I do remember an overwhelming feeling of paranoia and fear. I became convinced that I had died and gone to hell; I was completely detached from reality. To this day it remains one of the most frightening experiences I've ever had with drugs—and that's saying something.

For a while afterward I was thoroughly antidrug. I'd drink beer, of course, but that's about it. In fact, a couple of years would pass before I'd even try smoking pot. By that time I'd begun hanging out with other musicians, guys who weren't part of my gang, or any other gang, for that matter. More like hippies. All of a sudden I started changing my hairstyle—out with the pompadour, in with the longer, shaggier look. I became fascinated with the British Invasion—the Beatles and the Stones especially—and then I started gravitating toward other musicians who played the music I liked to play. Those guys, for the most part, weren't tough guys; they were peace-and-love guys and rockers.

And I had one foot in their world.

If not for music I'm sure I would have become a full-fledged gang member and ended up either dead or in jail. But music pulled me away from that. It literally saved my life. I started playing on weekends, rehearsing at night, and eventually the guys in the Ducky Gang turned their backs on me. Can't blame them, really. How much rejection can you take?

"Hey, Paul, come on. We're gonna break into a warehouse tonight."

"Sorry, man. Can't make it. Got a gig."

It was a natural progression, with me going in one direction, and them going in another. I started playing more, even making money from some of my shows, while they became involved in more serious shit and taking heavier drugs. Not that I didn't want to run with those guys, as well, but . . . hey, there's only so many hours in a day. Eventually you have to make a choice.

I chose the guitar.

Or maybe the guitar chose me.

At the age of sixteen I was playing in some decent bands and getting progressively better gigs. At some point along the line I decided that I didn't want to go to jail. I'd been around enough police stations and holding cells, and I'd met enough guys who had done serious time to know that I probably wouldn't have done real well in prison. I wasn't cut out for it. I wanted to play music; I wanted to be a rock star. So when the activities of the Ducky Boys escalated, I pulled back. The early stuff had been fairly benign. I mean, we were hot-wiring cars and going on joyrides, but it wasn't like we were taking them to chop shops. I was lucky, too. I never got caught at anything that serious as a kid. I remember one day waking up with a hangover and realizing that I'd dodged a proverbial bullet the night before. I'd stolen a car and driven all over the Bronx before ditching it by the side of the road.

That one would have been costly: drunk driving, grand larceny, speeding, and whatever else they wanted to throw at me.

Evidence to the contrary notwithstanding, I wasn't stupid. I started to see that some of my friends were taking ridiculous chances with their lives. Probably because they didn't give a shit. They didn't see anything better down the road. Some of them didn't care if they lived or died. My friend Walter, for example, went away to juvenile hall when we were in our mid-teens. Shortly after he got out, he stabbed some guy in a bar fight. Did five years for that one in a state penitentiary. One of my closest friends, Tommy McCalden, hung himself at Rikers Island jail when he was eighteen years old. Tommy's dad had been superintendent of my building when I was growing up, and we were in the Junior Duckies together. We'd drifted apart by the time he died, but I still remember being shaken by the news.

I didn't want to go down that road. I wanted more out of life.

I *expected* more.

# 3

# MUSIC IN THE FIFTH DIMENSION

When it came to school, I was always a bit of a square peg, forever trying (or not trying) to fit in where I knew I didn't belong. I just couldn't seem to work up much enthusiasm over academic pursuits. I probably didn't even belong in a traditional classroom setting. I would have been better off at a school that catered to kids with more creative interests, like art and music. During my school days, there were only a few interesting teachers that got my creative juices flowing, so I spent a lot of time figuring out creative ways to avoid going to school in the first place. As a result, I went to three high schools in four years. Got bounced from the first two, dropped out of the third.

I started out at Our Saviour Lutheran, the next natural stop in the education chain for kids who went to Grace Lutheran Elementary School. But I hated it from the beginning. Within a few weeks I was cutting classes; then I began cutting entire days. Got away with it for a while, too. The trick was that you had to show up for school in the morning, and then you could sneak out. One day, though, I deliberately missed the bus and went off to hang out with some of my buddies. Unfortunately, I had neglected to tell my brother, Charlie, what I had planned. Charlie was a straight arrow, driven to do well in school, and, like a lot of older siblings, prone to worrying about his little brother. So when he got to lunch that day and couldn't find me, he became really nervous. It wasn't like he was trying to get me in trouble; he was legitimately concerned that something bad had happened to me. So he went to the principal's office and told them that I wasn't sick, and asked them to find me.

Which they did.

By the end of the day I was sitting in the principal's office with my mother, enduring a verbal reprimand.

"You know, Paul," the principal said, "you have to take your high school years more seriously if you want to make something of your life."

"Yes, sir."

He gave me a stern look.

"If this sort of behavior continues, we'll have to let you go."

Let you go . . .

It sounded less like a threat than a reward.

Needless to say, it did continue, and they did let me go.

I didn't care. I hated Our Saviour Lutheran. I had to take two different buses to get there, couldn't stand the uniforms, and found myself drowning in discipline the moment I arrived each morning. By the time I was a freshman in high school I'd had my fill of parochial education. For some reason I had this idea that if I could just transfer to the public high school in my neighborhood, DeWitt Clinton, everything would be better. So that's what I did.

The culture shock was immediate and overwhelming. I had no clue as to how public schools worked. For nine years I'd attended nothing but parochial schools, and while I found them to be generally stifling and unsupportive, there was a certain level of comfort that comes with familiarity. Both Grace Lutheran School and Our Saviour Lutheran High School were small and intimate; you couldn't help but know almost everyone in your grade, as well as most of the faculty.

DeWitt Clinton?

This place was like a fucking metropolis by comparison. With a student body of more than four thousand, including every high school stereotype you can imagine, it was a monument to Darwinism. You figured out a way to fit in and survive, or you were chewed up and spit out. Fortunately, I already had a few friends at Clinton, which helped ease the transition. Clinton was also where I started hanging out more with musicians than with gang members. But I split time between the two factions for a while. Sometimes I think I would have made a good diplomat; I've always been pretty good at finessing situations, of playing the role of peacemaker rather than instigator (this was true even many years later, in KISS). I could handle myself in a fight, but I rarely went looking for a confrontation. I preferred the path of least resistance.

More than anything else, I wanted to have a good time.

Just as they had at Our Saviour Lutheran, classes at DeWitt Clinton had a way of interfering with my prime directive, and before long I was on a first-name basis with everyone in the principal's office. One day I decided to cut school. In itself, this was nothing out of the ordinary; I did it all the time. Usually I'd just hang out with friends, smoke some pot, have a few beers, play my guitar. Harmless, lazy, aimless shit.

On this particular day, however, there was a purpose attached to my truancy. I don't remember the precise date, but it was somewhere between March 25 and April 2, 1967. During that week the legendary New York disc jockey Murray the K promoted a series of daylong concerts at the RKO 58th Street Theatre in Manhattan. "Murray the K Presents Music in the 5th Dimension" (that a radio personality received top billing gives you an idea of just how much power Murray the K wielded in those days) was a breathtaking collection of talent and diverse musical styles. Headlining the event, if the posters were to be believed, were Mitch Ryder and Wilson Pickett. These were the biggest draws: Ryder, newly solo and playing without the Detroit Wheels; and Pickett, one of the all-time great soul singers.

And that was just the beginning.

If you look at that poster now, it reads like a Who's Who of rock 'n' roll greats: Simon & Garfunkel, the Young Rascals, Phil Ochs, the Blues Project (featuring Al Kooper), and the two bands I most wanted to see: the Who and the Cream. (Yeah, that's right, "the Cream." That's the way they were advertised.)

For a week straight these guys tore up the RKO, turning a midtown movie theater into a showcase for some of the greatest musicians in rock 'n' roll history. I had to be part of it. Since shows started at 10 A.M. and ran pretty much all afternoon, school was out of the question.

That show was a life-changer for me. I was a month shy of my sixteenth birthday and in the early stages of trying to form some sort of artistic identity. I loved messing around with the guitar, and I'd played in bands with my brother and some friends. On some level I knew that I wanted to be a professional musician, but it wasn't until that day, sitting near the front of the RKO Theatre, that it all became clear to me.

I wanted to be Pete Townshend.

I wanted to be Eric Clapton.

I wanted to be a guitar-slinging rock star.

Neither Cream nor the Who had ever performed in the United States prior to the Murray the K shows; in retrospect, it was an historic event. Not that I realized it at the time. To me it was just one hell of a show. I don't recall exactly how it happened, but at some point I wound up near the stage with a few of my buddies early in the day, talking with Murray the K himself. I just walked up to him and began chatting about the show. Everyone knew Mitch Ryder at the time, but Murray was more interested in talking about the Who and Cream.

"These guys are gonna be huge," Murray assured us. "Wait and see."

The Who had already released a couple of albums, including *My Generation*, but they were still primarily a British phenomenon; same thing with Cream, a power trio with Eric Clapton, Jack Bruce, and Ginger Baker. I was familiar with both bands, but I had no idea what I was in for that day. Watching Clapton handle the guitar so fluidly and effortlessly was mesmerizing. But what really got my attention was seeing the Who and the way they combined theatrics with incredible music and harmonies. Keith Moon fucking attacked the drum kit. And Townshend blew me away with his powerful chord work and showmanship. I was spellbound as they destroyed their instruments and left the smoke-filled stage in ruins!

It was raw, violent, and entertaining as hell.

These guys knew how to play and sing, and they knew how to put on a show.

I sat there (actually, I'm sure I was standing) in awe of the whole experience. I'd seen a lot of live music by this time, but not by any bands of this caliber. This was big-time rock 'n' roll, and I wanted to be part of it. I wanted the whole deal: the giant amps, the special effects, the chicks screaming my name from the front row. But the funny thing is, I don't recall feeling overwhelmed by it. I don't think I ever felt like it was beyond my reach, or that I was dreaming too big. Sure, I idolized other musicians along the way, and I probably would have been too tongue-tied to speak with Pete Townshend if I'd had the opportunity that day in New York. But even then there was a little voice in the back of my head saying, "You can do this. You will do this."

I never set my sights low. I've always believed most people are ruined by the limitations they put on themselves. I was never afraid to take that step, to see what I was capable of doing. Does luck play a role in success, particularly in a creative field? Sure it does. But if you don't have the balls to give it a shot, you're destined to fail.

Clapton?

Townshend?

Those guys had talent. They also had balls.

And though he wasn't nearly as well-known, so did Jim McCarty, the lead guitarist for Mitch Ryder's band. Funny the way things come full circle sometimes. That show served as my introduction to big-time professional rock 'n' roll, and it made an indelible impression. A few years later, when I was about eighteen or nineteen, I ended up jamming with McCarty at a mutual friend's house in the Bronx. Jim was in town, visiting our buddy, and they invited me over. Music was like that in the late 1960s, early '70s. Paths crossed in the weirdest ways. There were so many people starting bands and playing gigs all over the country. It was a brotherhood.

Years later (decades, actually), when I was out on the road with my solo project, Frehley's Comet, Jim McCarty's band was my opening act. We'd sit around backstage afterward, tossing down beers and swapping stories. I always thought Jim was one of the most underrated American guitar players, and to be sharing a stage with him after all those years was a real trip.

You just never know how things are going to turn out.

Far as I could tell, there was no three-strike rule at DeWitt Clinton High School. By the middle of my junior year I'd already been caught skipping on multiple occasions and been suspended two or three times. What can I tell you? I was an incorrigible kid. And they were turbulent times. The Vietnam War was raging, and the music scene was changing rapidly. I'm lucky that I didn't get in a lot more trouble than I did. I wasn't a criminal, though; I was just a gigantic pain in the ass to some . . . albeit with a sense of style. See, by the time I was sixteen, I'd traded in my leather jacket and jeans for knee-high boots and ruffled shirts, like the guys in the Kinks or Paul Revere and the Raiders. I posed like a rock star and carried myself like a rock star, even though I hadn't yet realized the work that was involved in actually becoming a rock star.

I just figured it had nothing to do with attending classes at DeWitt Clinton.

So one day my friend and I got some beer and pot, and hooked up with a couple of chicks. Again, nothing out of the ordinary, except one of the girls was lucky to have a mother who worked every day, so the family apartment was conveniently empty. By ten o'clock that morning our party was in high gear. We got drunk, paired off, fooled around, and generally had a much more interesting day than we would have had at school. But the chick's mom came home from work early that day and freaked out. She caught us with our pants down and beer bottles everywhere. I zipped up my pants and ran out of the apartment with my buddy, while the chick's mom was still screaming.

The next day she called the dean of students at DeWitt Clinton.

For the other kids involved this was not a particularly serious offense. But for me it was the straw that broke the camel's back. In addition to poor grades and a history of truancy, I was found guilty of poor judgment when it came to personal grooming. In the mid-1960s, in Europe, you could wear long hair and pass it off as nothing more than a fashion statement. But in the United States of America, at this particular point in time, wearing long hair meant something else entirely. It was a political statement, and threatened people in authority. To be perfectly candid, I was blissfully unaware of issues of any greater significance than how to get chicks out of their clothes. I was hardly a political dissident. Any hippie tendencies I might have exhibited were strictly a matter of convenience and lifestyle. I wanted to get laid, get drunk, get high, and play in a band. I wanted a certain look onstage, and by achieving that look I found myself getting bundled in with the war protesters and demonstrators.

"Get a haircut, Frehley," the dean would tell me.

"Come on, man. It's a free country. Stop hassling me."

And they did—by kicking me out of school. Now I was oh-for-two as a high school student, and my parents, not surprisingly, were beginning to lose their patience. Not so much my mom—I was her baby boy and she always had a soft spot for me, no matter how disruptive a force I might have become. Moms are like that. But my father by now was in his sixties and had neither the time nor the inclination to gently encourage me to clean up my act. As I said, Dad was usually a fairly benign and quiet presence in my life, but a second expulsion nearly drove him over the edge.

"Clean up your act," he said one day, "or get out of the house."

"Fine," I said. "I'm outta here."

It was quite a dramatic moment. I grabbed some clothes and my guitar and left the apartment, slamming the door behind me. There was just one problem: I had no place to go. Shit, I was sixteen years old, with no money and no job skills. I couldn't go live with any of my friends, because their parents would have tossed me out as well. Staring down the prospect of being homeless in New York, I was left with only one option: Duke's place.

Duke was a black guy who lived on Burnside Avenue in the Bronx. He was, to put it mildly, something of an unsavory character, though I didn't really see it that way at the time. Duke was a musician in his early twenties and spent an unusual amount of time hanging out with high school kids. His father was the superintendent of an apartment building and Duke had a little one-bedroom place to himself in the basement. So he was on his own, but not really on his own, since Mom and Dad were picking up the tab. I'd gotten to know him a little bit through my musical connections. Duke always wanted to be in a band, but he wasn't a musician, so his plan was to assemble a group to back him up while he manned the microphone. He couldn't pay me anything, but the offer was attractive nonetheless.

"Tell you what," Duke said. "Come and back me up and I'll let you use my place whenever you want. Bring your girlfriend, have some beer, smoke some pot. Whatever you feel like doing."

For a kid in his teens, this wasn't a bad deal. Duke and I would play at the Veterans Hospital on Kingsbridge Road in the Bronx and entertain the sick vets. Sometimes it would just be the two of us—me on guitar and Duke singing. Other times we'd get a bass or rhythm guitar player and a drummer as well. But it was Dukie's show all the way. He was such a character. The guy was built like Hercules, and yet he'd move around like Mick Jagger. After the show we'd go back to Duke's house and drink beer and hang out. The fridge was always filled, which was a bonus when you skipped school and brought a girl over.

Needless to say, this entire arrangement demonstrated incredibly bad judgment on Duke's part, and I suppose it was just a matter of time before it blew up in his face. The cops busted a party at Duke's apartment and pulled us all in for questioning. I can still remember seeing the father of one of the girls getting into a fight with Duke at the police station, screaming at him, "You leave my daughter alone or I'll fucking kill you!"

The cops kept us there for hours, questioning all of us about Dukie and our relationship with him. They seemed less concerned about whether he had provided alcohol to minors than with the nature of his friendship with a bunch of teenagers.

Duke was nuts, though—completely off the hook. If he was frightened by his brush with the cops, you never would have known it. The party went on, with plenty of alcohol and underage girls. Eventually Duke disappeared from the neighborhood. I heard he was in prison, serving time for exactly the type of behavior that had gotten him into trouble in the past. By this time, though, I had long since parted company with Duke. I lived with him for less than a month, after which I made peace with my parents and moved back into their home.

Truth is, they were worried sick about me, and from that point on we coexisted in relative tranquility. By that I mean, Mom and Dad stopped hassling me about my budding rock 'n' roll lifestyle and I tried not to give them too much cause for concern. On some level, I think, they realized I wasn't a bad kid. I just wasn't the kind of kid they wanted me to be. What shocked them the most was how much success I had with girls. I usually had multiple girlfriends. My father, of course, didn't get it at all.

"What the hell does she see in you?" he'd say, shaking his head.

My mother, meanwhile, couldn't believe that my girlfriends would stop by the house to clean my room! They'd make my bed, pick up my dirty clothes, and then hang out and wait for me to get home from school. I'd walk through the door and Mom would be standing there with a look of bewilderment on her face.

"Michelle is here."

"Oh yeah? Where is she?"

Mom would point to my bedroom door and shake her head.

I think she was probably shocked on multiple levels, but she tolerated it. Maybe because it meant less work for her.

I don't mean to brag, but I always did well with girls. I started fooling around when I was eleven or twelve and lost my virginity at fifteen. To me, girls weren't all that mysterious. I wasn't the best-looking guy in the world, but I never lacked for companionship, mainly because I knew how to talk to chicks and make them feel at ease. I was funny. I'd tell jokes, do magic tricks, and I could play guitar. What else do you need, man?

When I got a little older and started hanging out in bars and clubs, I developed a few strategies for picking up women. It's silly, but you know what always worked? I would wear a T-shirt and suit jacket, and in the breast pocket of the jacket I kept a little teddy bear with its arms poking out. I'd go up to a chick, obviously after I had a couple drinks, and I'd say, "Hey, you want to meet my friend?" Then I'd open up my jacket and I'd have this little teddy bear, waiting to say hello.

Sometimes this would cause a girl to roll her eyes and walk away, but more often than not, the response was, "Awwwww, how cute!"

And then I'd be in the door.

If you're at least halfway decent looking, and you're funny and outgoing, all you need is that one little icebreaker. But most guys are too scared to even give it a shot. They don't know how to initiate a conversation. We all have our insecurities, of course, and I sure had mine, but after a couple of drinks I could do anything, including hit on the hottest chick in the room. Eventually I got so good at talking to girls that I could set up my buddies as well, which is how I ended up with the nickname "Ace."

"You know, you are such an ace, man," one of them said one night, after I'd introduced him to a girl he'd been lusting after. "You really help us out with the chicks."

That was that. The nickname stuck.

It's a cliché that guys get into bands primarily to meet girls, but as with any cliché, there's more than a little truth to it. The first time I played a church dance, when I was fourteen years old, girls gathered around the stage, staring at me and the other guys in the band. It had nothing to do with me, really, and everything to do with the fact that I was up there onstage, playing the guitar. Girls were drawn to it, like bees to nectar. They couldn't help themselves.

Sometimes you didn't even need the guitar; you simply had to act the part.

I was about sixteen or seventeen when I was hanging out one day with some friends near Fordham University. It was a busy weekend afternoon, with lots of people milling about, including tons of pretty girls. I was wearing my ruffled shirt and jeans tucked into knee-high boots. My hair was shoulder length: the rock star look.

"Hey, do me a favor," I said to one of my friends. "I'm going to go over near that group of girls, and I want you to walk up to me and ask me for my autograph."

My buddy played it up beautifully, just walked into the crowd and thrust a pen and paper in front of me.

"Oh, man, thanks. I love your records!" Within seconds I was surrounded by pretty girls. They flirted, vied for attention, and coyly tried to figure out exactly who the hell I was, this rock 'n' roll star in their midst.

It was intoxicating. And it was so, so easy.

4

# MOVIN' ON UP

Like a basketball player in search of a pickup game, I bounced from band to band. All I wanted was a chance to keep playing, and to improve, and to stand up there onstage in front of as many people as possible. I couldn't tell you the exact number of bands I started or joined. More than a dozen, for sure. Maybe two dozen. Some never got beyond the first rehearsal; others endured for months. It wasn't unusual for me to be playing in two or three bands at once.

Playing with your first real band, though, is like having sex for the first time: it's sloppy, fast, and exciting, and it makes you want more. At the very least, you don't forget the experience. Just for the record, my first "official" sexual partner was an aggressive and amorous chick named Jenny. I was fifteen years old and dating her friend Michelle (who, with high cheekbones, sunken eyes, and long, ink-black hair, looked for all the world like Cher, which was pretty cool at the time). Michelle was cute and fun, but she wasn't interested in giving up her virginity to me, or to anyone else, for that matter. Jenny had different feelings on this issue, and she let me know one night when we were all together at a party.

"Give me a call," she said, pressing a small piece of paper containing her phone number into my palm.

I did, and the very next day we got together at her apartment. One of us knew precisely what they were doing, and it wasn't me. Jenny didn't complain, though, and neither did I. When you're a fifteen-year-old boy getting laid for the very first time, all you really want (or need) is a warm, inviting body, and Jenny was more than accommodating. My performance was irrelevant and best left unexamined. I got better—a lot better—as time went on.

The first band actually came a few years earlier, a few months after getting my first electric guitar. I was thirteen years old and the band was called the Four Roses. It included me and my brother, Charlie, both playing guitar, along with another of the Junior Duckies, my buddy Joey, on drums, and Charlie's friend Barry on bass. We played an assortment of rock and pop tunes, including the Beatles, Paul Revere and the Raiders, and Herman's Hermits (the first song I ever learned to play on guitar was "Mrs. Brown You've Got a Lovely Daughter").

We weren't particularly smooth or committed, but we were good enough to play a few sets at church functions and school dances. The band survived for less than a year, and along the way it became apparent to me that I was more serious, and maybe more talented, than most young guitar players. For one thing, I liked practicing. There wasn't much that would hold my attention when I was a kid, but playing guitar was different. I'd sit in my room for hours, listening to songs and trying to replicate them. I had no interest in taking lessons or learning to read music (and never did, by the way), but I was more than willing to sit there alone, endlessly studying and dissecting songs, trying to figure out chord progressions and solos.

In the beginning I played rhythm guitar while Charlie played lead. This made sense. He was older and more experienced, and, frankly, a better player. Charlie could read music. He was a student of the guitar. I was self-taught and undisciplined. Within about six months, however, a weird thing began to happen. When we'd get together and rehearse,

Charlie would invite me to play lead on certain songs. I'm not even sure why he did that—we never talked about it. Looking back, though, I think he probably realized that his little brother had talent, and for whatever reason he wanted to encourage that talent. I can see it now as a generous thing for him to have done. I mean, Charlie kicked ass on guitar. He had started playing a year and a half before me and he was exceptionally skilled. So I don't know . . . maybe he was just looking out for his kid brother.

I do know this much: not long after that, the lineup shifted, and Charlie moved over to bass and rhythm guitar. I became a lead guitar player, and for the most part I've been there ever since.

By the time I was seventeen I'd been kicked out of DeWitt Clinton and transferred to Roosevelt High School. While my academic career remained something of an embarrassment, I'd at least gravitated away from the tough guys in my immediate area and begun hanging out primarily with musicians. I was also meeting a lot of different girls, often from different neighborhoods. I had a girlfriend named Kathy in Yonkers for a while. We met at a dance and started hanging out. It was through Kathy, coincidentally, that I reconnected with a kid named Tom Doyle, who had grown up down the block from me. Tommy and I were good friends up until the age of ten or eleven, when he was hit by a car while playing in the street. It was a horribly traumatic event for him and his family, and for his buddies. Tommy and I saw each other pretty much every day, played stickball and basketball together, and then all of a sudden he was gone. No one talked about it very much. I knew he was in the hospital for a long time, but he never came back to the neighborhood. I'd forgotten all about Tommy when I ran into him one night while I was playing at a high school dance in Yonkers, with a band called the Magic People (trippy, huh?). Turned out he lived not far away; his family had moved to Yonkers shortly after Tommy got out of the hospital. Since then he'd become a serious hippie (if there was such a thing). Tommy had long hair and a beard, smoked a ton of pot, and played in a band. We talked for a while that night, reminisced about the old neighborhood, and promised to keep in touch. And we did. In fact, though I'd eventually lose touch with Tommy again (I know he wound up playing with acoustic hippie street rockers David Peel and the Lower East Side), for a while we became close friends. I'd regularly make the trip from the Bronx to Yonkers to hang out with Kathy and Tommy. It was a good step for me, if only because it helped take me out of the Bronx, and away from some of my old friends and partners in crime.

Although I couldn't quite explain it, I realized on some level that life in Yonkers had more potential. I knew instinctively that by moving northward, into Yonkers and Westchester County, and associating with people who seemed to have better lives than I did, then maybe my life would improve as well. Maybe there would be more opportunity. The differences were not glaring, but I could feel them nonetheless. Almost everyone in my neighborhood lived in apartments; in Yonkers and Westchester, a lot of people seemed to own houses. I've never been particularly motivated by greed (I wouldn't have walked away from KISS—twice!—if money meant all that much to me), and it wasn't like I grew up in poverty. But I did want more out of life, and I just got the sense that if I hung around with folks who were more successful than I was, maybe some of that good fortune would rub off. It wasn't exactly a scientific theory, but it proved to be valid. You couldn't help but notice, even back in the late 1960s, that the Bronx was not a destination. It was a place people generally tried to escape. As a teenager I saw it time and again: if you made enough money, you got the hell out of there. You moved north into Westchester, bought a little house with some land, maybe raised a family. Or if you really had cash, you moved south into Manhattan. And the reason for this, of course, was that the Bronx was slowly deteriorating. It was becoming poorer, tougher, and more dangerous. I knew all of this through firsthand experience. If not for music, I'd almost certainly have been sucked into the gang life for good, and things might well have turned out badly for me. As it happened, though, playing guitar allowed me to enter a completely different world.

Not that I didn't maintain some of my ties with the Ducky Gang, or at least with individual gang members. And for some reason they didn't mind my lack of commitment. It's kind of hard to explain, but the way I did things—the way I communicated with people—I could get away with a lot. You might say I was a politician . . . or a bullshit artist (I mean, really, what's the distinction?). In the same way that I could talk to girls, and juggle multiple girlfriends, I had a natural rapport with guys. Whether they were laid-back, pot-smoking guitar players or gun-toting gangsters, I could get along with them. I've always tried not to be abrasive with people. I'm the kind of person who can assess a situation and figure it out; I'm good at reading people. For a while, yeah, I had to be a bit evasive when it came to the Ducky Boys. If they wanted me to be involved in some sort of gang activity—something I knew would get me in deep shit—I'd just be cordial but noncommittal.

"Tuesday night? Yeah, probably, I'll be available. Give me a call, okay?"

And then of course I wouldn't be around to take the call. Honestly? I had no interest in the gang scene anymore. It had served its purpose. By the time I was sixteen or seventeen and had gotten some serious insight into where these guys were going, and how their lives were turning out, I wanted no part of it. The criminal activity grew progressively more intense and reckless. The violence and drug use escalated. Admittedly, by the time I was in my thirties I had drug problems that were as severe as any of these guys', but not when I was in high school. I could see them fooling around with heroin and cocaine, and it scared me. Guys were getting sent to prison; they were overdosing and dying. I saw nothing glamorous about it anymore. When I was thirteen or fourteen? Sure. I wanted and needed the protection of a gang. You do what you have to do in order to survive, right? Being part of the Duckies gave that to me. I liked the excitement and the camaraderie. But the deeper I waded, the more apprehensive I became.

Ultimately it came down to this: if you weren't around, well . . . you weren't around. After a while, I didn't have to make excuses anymore. Out of sight, out of mind.

We look for kindred spirits, and in my case that meant other musicians, in particular guitar players who wore their hair long and favored rock star fashion and blues-influenced rock 'n' roll (as opposed to, say, pop music). Those people were few and far between in the Bronx, but you could find them if you looked hard enough. For a while in high school I lived just a couple of blocks from a guy named Emil "Peppy" Thielhelm. He was more commonly known by one of his stage names, Peppy Magoo or Peppy Castro. Peppy played rhythm guitar and sang lead for the Blues Magoos, who were at the forefront of the 1960s psychedelic music movement. I'd seen the band play when they opened for the Who and Cream at the RKO (later that same year they had a Top 10 hit single with "(We Ain't) Got Nothin' Yet,") and I knew they were a New York band. But I didn't know at the time that Peppy lived practically down the street. When I found out, of course, I did my best to strike up an acquaintanceship, if not a friendship. Peppy was a cool guy who didn't mind hanging out with a younger kid and showing him a few tricks. I can vividly remember sitting in Peppy's basement, each of us with guitar in hand, him demonstrating bar chords and other more complicated maneuvers, and me soaking it all up.

And I remember going to Orchard Beach in Pelham Bay that summer, and lying on the sand, listening to the radio with my friends, getting all excited when "(We Ain't) Got Nothin' Yet" crackled through the speaker.

Holy shit! That's Peppy!

The Blues Magoos were out on a national tour, getting major Top 40 airplay. By any reasonable definition, they had hit the big time. It didn't last, unfortunately, but for a while they enjoyed a pretty good run of success and developed a vigorous cult following. I looked at their achievements not with envy or awe, but with a sense of encouragement. When I saw that Peppy could make it, and have a song on the radio (remember, this was the 1960s, a time when there was no greater validation for a musician than Top 40 airplay), it made it that much more believable to me . . . that much more attainable.

It was one thing to see Eric Clapton and Pete Townshend in concert, and to say, "I'd like to do that."

It was quite another to smoke pot and jam with a local boy like Peppy Castro, and then watch him release a hit single.

I wanted to be like Clapton and Townshend.

I knew I could be like Peppy.

But I learned from all of them. Concerts were like school to me. I'd study the guitar player—not just how his hands moved along the neck and strings, but also how he interacted with the audience. What would he do to get the crowd excited and involved? I realized early on that while virtuosity was important, showmanship also mattered. They were two pieces of the puzzle, and if either was missing, the picture wasn't always complete.

The groups that just stood there and played weren't always visually exciting. I felt theatrical rock was the way to go. That's why I was putting smoke bombs in my amplifiers when I was sixteen. I studied Pete Townshend extensively in my early years—the way he played chords and inversions, his songwriting and use of harmony, and of course, his live performances. Townshend, Page, Clapton, and Hendrix—I had some of the best teachers in the world. I like to say that I never took a guitar lesson, but really that's not quite accurate. I did take lessons—from the best. By studying their work and emulating their actions, I became the guitar player I am today. The fact that I don't read music is irrelevant. That's true of a lot of rock guitarists. If you love playing, you figure it out on your own. You put in the time. You study, and you practice till your fingers bleed.

What probably made it easier for me is that I grew up in a household where music was important. I had the natural talent and the dexterity.

It was inherent. And I was exposed to music my whole life. I'd hear my sister play scales and just pick it up, almost by osmosis. It was never that hard for me to figure out something on a record. I'd be jamming with my friends, and I'd hear them struggling to play something, and I'd say, "No, no, no. Watch, it's like this." And then I'd demonstrate. I don't want to say playing guitar was easy, because that implies a lack of effort. But there's no question that it came easier to me than it did to others. I remember that for a while in my mid- to late teens, when I was playing in one band or another, I almost felt guilty when I got paid for playing gigs. It didn't feel like work. I was having too much fun. After a while, though, I started to accept the notion that performing could also be profitable. And I began to think, Wow, imagine doing this full-time as a professional. Imagine the women, the money, the adulation.

Imagine being a rock star.

It was a no-brainer.

But I also figured I had to devote most of my time and energy to the pursuit of this goal. And so, midway through my senior year at Roosevelt, only a few credits shy of a degree, I dropped out of high school. Stupid, I know. I mean, who quits in their senior year? But I had absolutely no interest in school anymore. It was, in my mind anyway, a complete waste of time.

If not for Jeanette Trerotola, I'd probably still be a high school dropout.

We started dating when I was eighteen years old. It was, almost from the beginning, a turbulent and passionate relationship—we've always known how to push each other's buttons. Jeanette and I got to know each other through her cousin Jodie and Tom Doyle. Tommy had a rehearsal studio in Yonkers, and in the evenings it became a favorite hangout for a lot of local rockers. You could drop by most nights and jam for a while, and eventually the jam would turn into a party. I'd visit Tommy a couple of times a week, hang out all weekend, drink beer, smoke pot, and jam. Well, one night I went to a birthday party at this girl Lynn's house just down the street. I had been seeing Lynn and she was Jodie's best friend. At the party I was introduced to two girls from Ardsley, New York, which is in Westchester County. They were both high school seniors and stylishly dressed. It was obvious to me that they were more refined than some of the girls at the party. One of them was named Diane Fratta; the other was Jeanette Trerotola.

We spent a little time getting acquainted, but since I was with Lynn I had to hold back. Not long after that I broke up with Lynn and started dating Diane, who was Jeanette's best friend. I don't recall exactly why I gravitated toward Diane instead of Jeanette—it probably had something to do with the fact that she had this really cool, layered haircut that I'd seen on only a few chicks. Diane was cool, but she was also a little shy and laid-back; regardless I was attracted to her, and she was attracted to me. Unfortunately her parents were less than thrilled with the prospect of Diane dating a guitar-toting, jobless high school dropout from the Bronx.

Can't imagine why.

Once you grow up and have kids, of course, you develop a different perspective on this sort of thing. You want what's best for your children, and sometimes (maybe most of the time) the child wants something else. I can see now that Diane's parents weren't being mean by voicing their disapproval; they were just looking out for their daughter. But there wasn't a whole lot they could do to stop us from dating. Or, at least, I didn't think there was much they could do. As it turned out, I was wrong. The summer after Diane graduated from high school, her parents decided that it was time for a very long, distant summer vacation. The whole family went away, and I was left behind to lick my wounds.

What was a boy to do?

Well, Diane was gone . . . but her best friend was still in town.

We had been hanging out regularly with a group of friends at a bar called the Candlelight Inn in Westchester. I'd actually been setting Jeanette up with a few friends of mine when we double dated, but it never worked out. Jeanette was from an upper-middle-class Italian family, and her parents naturally didn't approve of any of the guys she brought home from the Bronx. They didn't approve of me, either, for obvious reasons. Jeanette was headstrong and fun to be around. We fell into a relationship almost by accident. It was strange. We'd already developed a bit of a friendship that revolved around mutual acquaintances. One thing led to another, and pretty soon we were involved in a fairly intense relationship.

Jeanette was a year younger than me, and we were from different worlds. I was of German descent and lived in the Bronx. She was an Italian girl from Westchester. Jeanette's grandfather, Joseph Trerotola, was an impressive man who served as vice president of the Teamsters Union; Joe T. was a powerful guy who could shut down JFK Airport with one phone call, and played golf with President Nixon and Jimmy Hoffa. He was not a man you wanted to piss off. Jeanette's father also worked for the Teamsters, as an organizer. Jeanette's grandfather and father lived in the Bronx for some time before moving to Westchester, so you'd think we might have connected on some level. But we didn't. Not in the beginning, anyway. They disapproved of me at first, and wondered why I didn't have a car and was unemployed. I told her dad one evening that I was going to be a successful rock star, but he just laughed and shook his head. Whatever the case, the last thing they wanted was for their daughter to fall in love with an unemployed musician from the Bronx, but there was no keeping us apart. Jeanette ignored her parents' wishes and our relationship became more and more serious.

In the beginning, Jeanette was a positive influence on me. (I don't know that I can honestly say the reverse is also true.) A solid student whose family encouraged education, Jeanette enrolled at Pace University's Westchester campus shortly after we began dating. And within a couple of months she had convinced me that dropping out was one of the biggest mistakes of my life.

"You know," she said one day, "you really ought to go back to school and get your diploma."

"Why? What do they know about being in a band or playing guitar? I'll learn more out here, on my own."

Jeanette didn't pressure me, but instead systematically broke down my defenses, poked holes in whatever argument I might have presented. Basically she said I was too smart a guy to be walking around without at least a high school degree. She was right, and if I'm completely honest, I'll admit that I was somewhat embarrassed about being viewed as a dropout (or, worse, someone who had flunked out). So I went back to school, taking classes at Roosevelt in the evening while working various jobs during the day and gigging on weekends. Since I was only a few credits short of a degree, it wasn't long before I had graduated. I went over to Roosevelt one afternoon, picked up my diploma, and then put in a call to my bass player Gene, who lived near Arthur Avenue, in the Italian section of the Bronx. Along with another friend named Neil, Gene and I had formed a short-lived band called King Kong (believe it or not, I had a bass player named Gene back in high school . . . who knew?).

"Hey, man, I'm a high school graduate!" I said to Gene.

"Good for you." He didn't seem terribly excited.

"Are you free? We have to celebrate."

"Now you're talking."

First thing we did was buy two bottles of Mad Dog—MD 20/20, one of the all-time great (meaning horrible but effective) bum wines. The "MD" actually stood for Mogen David, the distiller of this fine brew; "20/20" represented its potency (20 percent alcohol) and the number of ounces in the bottle. Mad Dog was, and still is, cheap, strong wine (although the alcohol content of present-day MD is a saner 13 percent). Horrific stuff, but a sure and quick buzz. Very popular at the time. We also picked up a six-pack of Colt 45, just to make sure the job was well done, and then fished a couple of empty boxes out of the trash near a post office on Fordham Road. The boxes were clean and adorned with stamps, and our plan was to put the beer and Mad Dog inside, and then smuggle the package into a local movie theater. If anyone asked, we'd say we were going to the post office after the movie.

"I don't think we're gonna get away with this," Gene said.

"Ah, bullshit," I said, examining the package. "Looks official enough. I don't think anyone will say a word."

They didn't. Gene and I bought our tickets and strolled casually through the lobby, even stopping to pick up some popcorn along the way. Then we went into the theater and took a couple of seats near the front. We cracked open the Mad Dog, popped a couple of cans of Colt 45, and started celebrating my newly minted academic credentials. Before long we were getting pretty loose—putting our feet up on the seats in front of us, tossing popcorn at the screen, carrying on a running dialogue with the movie, rolling empty beer cans down the aisle. This naturally had the effect of drawing attention our way, and pretty soon one of the ushers was standing over us, flashlight in hand.

"Gentlemen, you'll have to keep it down or I'm going to have to ask you to leave."

I laughed, tossed a handful of popcorn in his face.

"Fuck off, man."

The usher scurried away. Poor kid was just trying to do his job, and here we were, a couple of loud-mouthed drunks making his life miserable. On the long list of atonements I've made (or should have made) over the years, this one is probably near the bottom. I mean, there was no long-term damage. But still . . . the kid deserved better.

He came back a few moments later, again told us to lower our voices or face expulsion. This time I didn't say a word. Instead I jumped out of my seat, curled my hand into a fist, and clocked the kid right on the jaw.

"What the hell?" he said, rolling toward the screen. His flashlight cracked against a seat and went dark, but in the flickering shadow of the film I could see his hat turned sideways on his head. And I could see something else.

The kid was crying.

He scrambled to his feet and ran toward the lobby, shouting "Somebody call the cops!" as he bolted through the doors at the rear of the theater.

I looked around the theater. Everyone was staring at us. Then I turned to Gene.

"What do you think?"

"I think we should get the fuck out of here," he said. "I don't feel like getting arrested tonight."

We bolted for the nearest exit door at the front of the theater, adjacent to the screen, and sprinted down an alleyway before heading back to my place, which was only about five blocks away. Budding alcoholic that I was, I was careful to grab the Mad Dog and Colt 45 before we made our exit, which allowed us to spend the remainder of the evening getting loaded in my room. It wasn't until about an hour later that I realized I was missing something.

"Can you believe this?" I said to Gene.

"What?"

"I left my fucking diploma at the theater."

Gene started to laugh—a stupid, amused, drunken cackle.

"Oh, well. Guess you're still a dropout, man."

Now I was pissed—in more ways than one. Drunk, yeah, but also really angry about having lost my diploma, and about the whole embarrassing situation. I was supposed to be meeting Jeanette the following night, and I'd planned to show her my diploma. Silly as it might sound, I was kind of proud that I'd actually gone back to school and finished the job. And I knew she'd be proud of me for having done it. The diploma was merely a piece of paper, yes, but it represented something. And now I'd lost it.

Or maybe not.

"Come on," I said to Gene. "We're going back."

He looked at me like I was nuts.

"Back where?"

"To the theater. I have to find my diploma."

"Oh, you gotta be trippin', man."

By the time we got back, the building was dark and the front doors locked. This was one of those elegant old theaters, with heavy, oak-frame doors and brass handles. I pulled at the door for a moment to see if I could pop the lock. No chance. Gene was about to give up, figuring reasonably that we'd used up our allotment of stupid behavior for the day. Just as he began to walk away, however, I spotted a garbage can on the sidewalk. And not one of those cheap plastic kinds, either. A good old-fashioned metal canister, about three and a half feet high, two feet in diameter.

Perfect . . .

I could hear Gene laughing as I heaved the pail through the front door, sending shards of glass in all directions. For some reason there was a delay before the theater's security alarm kicked in, just enough time for me to sprint into the place and begin rummaging for my diploma. I combed through the seats located in the general vicinity of where we had been sitting (or where I thought we had been sitting—Mad Dog wreaks havoc on the memory), but I could find nothing at all.

And then the alarms began to sound.

"Come on!" Gene shouted from the lobby. "Let's hit the road!"

"Fuck! I can't find it!"

I ran back out the front door, slipping on a pile of broken glass and slicing my hand open in the process. Then I scrambled to my feet and sprinted away. As Gene and I rounded a corner, I could see a pair of cop cars pulling up in front of the theater, sirens wailing, lights flashing.

Too tired and drunk to talk, I smiled at Gene, even as we kept running. We ended up back at my place completely exhausted, and I had to wake up my mom to help clean out and bandage my hand (since I was too loaded to do it myself).

The following day, I went down to Roosevelt and picked up a replacement diploma. They wanted to know what had happened to the original.

"It was destroyed in a freak accident at the theater," I said.

Which was the truth . . . sort of.

5

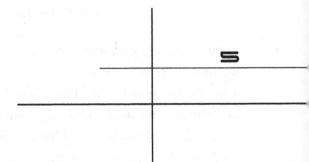

# ARE YOU EXPERIENCED?

**July 17, 1970**

In the wake of Woodstock, the entire music business was gripped with what could best be described as Festival Fever. Multi-act shows, sometimes lasting a few hours, stretching out over days, were all the rage. This being the height of the Vietnam War, themes of brotherhood and peace typically were attached to the proceedings, to give the whole thing an air of nobility. Really, though, it was the music that mattered.

That and the drugs.

And the sex.

The summer of 1969 had been a blast. I got into the hippie scene in a major way: drank a lot of wine, smoked a lot of pot, had sex with a half-dozen different girls. Everything was loose and easy and relatively safe. By the following summer, though, things seemed to have changed a bit. I noticed some of my friends had modified their habits when it came to dealing with mind-altering substances. Instead of just lighting up a joint, they'd drop some acid. A few had even started shooting dope. Heroin, frankly, scared the shit out of me. Always did. Even at the height of my drug use I stayed away from heroin, partly because I didn't like needles, but also because I honestly thought it might kill me. As for LSD, well, that was spooky shit as well. Probably had something to do with my bad glue trip and the scary psychosis that went along with it. I knew enough about acid to know that it could really fuck with your mind, and not just in the short term. I noticed that with some of my friends, if they had a couple of bad trips, the effects could linger for months, either in the form of flashbacks or depression. Then they'd start taking downers to ease the stress and anxiety that came with residual psychosis, or whatever you want to call it. All that mattered to me was this: if you dropped too much acid (and who the hell was to say how much was too much?) you had a reasonable chance of ending up in the nuthouse.

I didn't need that risk—my psychological state was fragile enough, as the U.S. Army had determined when I was classified 1-Y following a psychiatric evaluation at Fort Hamilton, in Brooklyn. That got me out of the draft, which was all well and good, but it certainly left some lingering doubts about my mental health.

So I never took LSD. Not intentionally, anyway. I may have been dosed a couple of times, however. I remember once in high school, for example, this kid named Alex who used to walk the hallways with a goofy smile on his face. A little heavy, with a bulbous nose and a face forever flushed red, he reminded me of Santa Claus. Handed out treats like St. Nick, as well.

"Try this, man," he said one day, offering me a joint.

"What is it?"

"Panama Red. Awesome shit."

I smoked it that afternoon with my friend Keith, and we tripped in a major way. I'm talking Day-Glo colors and kaleidoscopic visions. I don't know for sure if it was laced with acid, but if not, it was the strongest, strangest pot I've ever smoked. I didn't like the effect, and had no desire to seek it out intentionally. I didn't want to lose control. Two guys in one of my bands, Neil and John, tripped regularly. Me? I preferred alcohol. That I could handle (or so I rationalized). I knew that I was going to have a career in music someday, and I wanted a better life for myself. I saw guys tripping on acid, incapacitated months down the road, and it didn't make sense to me. I didn't think it was worth taking something with the chance I could end up with permanent brain damage or incapacitating mental illness (the irony, of course, is that eventually I wound up with both, despite abstaining from heroin and acid). It wasn't worth rolling the dice when I wanted to accomplish bigger things.

For better or worse, naïvely or not, that was my line in the sand.

Instinctively, I realized I had to remain clearheaded enough to take advantage of whatever opportunities came my way. There is a reason I chose the persona of the Spaceman when I joined KISS: I believe wholeheartedly in cosmic intervention; everything happens for a reason.

I was nineteen years old when I went to the New York Pop Festival, on Randall's Island in the East River, in the summer of 1970. This was yet another mini-Woodstock, with an amazingly eclectic lineup of musicians that included Mountain, Steppenwolf, Jethro Tull, Grand Funk Railroad, Richie Havens, Sly and the Family Stone, Dr. John, Van Morrison, and Eric Clapton.

Oh, and one other person.

Jimi Hendrix.

The whole thing was kind of surreal. You have to remember, for a kid like me, who used to walk around Roosevelt High with a copy of *Are You Experienced?* under his arm, seeing Hendrix was like a Catholic getting to meet the pope. Hendrix was nothing short of godlike. By the summer of 1970, unfortunately, Hendrix was nearing not only the end of his career, but the end of his life; within two months he'd be dead of a drug overdose. Still, on that day at Randall's Island (the last concert he'd ever perform in New York), he seemed at the peak of his powers—a living, breathing guitar hero.

I went to the show with some friends I used to hang out with at Poe Park, a little spot in the Bronx where Edgar Allan Poe lived out his final years, and where the Bohemian crowd around Fordham University used to gather. (I once organized a concert for one of my bands there.) But we separated shortly after we arrived. They were content to get high and listen to the music with the masses. I wanted to get closer. This had become a habit for me. Just as I'd managed to sidle up to Murray the K a few years earlier at the RKO Theatre, I suddenly found myself inching toward the stage at Randall's Island.

Maybe it was because I looked like a rock star, even if I wasn't one at the time. I was tall and skinny, with hair that went halfway down my back. I wore lemon yellow hot pants, a black T-shirt adorned with a snakeskin star, and checkered Vans sneakers. I fit in with the performers, more so than the crowd. As the day went on I kept my eyes on the entrance at the side of the stage, and I started to notice that some of the guys who had performed were walking out and watching other bands. In those days things were pretty laid-back. They didn't distribute official passes or laminates to the band members and road crew. If you belonged there, you just went about your business. Most people abided by the rules.

Not me.

I watched musicians walking in and out, in and out, offering nothing more than a nod or wave to security as they passed by. Then it dawned on me.

*Shit . . . I think I can get in there!*

So I walked up to the stage entrance, bold as hell, and looked one of the security guys right in the eye. He gave me a quick, visual once-over, head to toe, and nodded approvingly. I returned the gesture, didn't even smile (couldn't break character, after all), and walked on by.

Just like that, there I was, backstage at the New York Pop Festival.

Now I had a dilemma: Watch the show from the best seat in the house, right next to the speakers? Or hang out backstage and try to chat up my idols?

A little of both, maybe?

Next thing you know, I was sitting at a cafeteria table with John Kay, the lead singer, songwriter, and guitar player for Steppenwolf. We only talked for a few minutes, and it was cordial enough, but as John got up and walked away, he passed a security guard and pointed back at me. I couldn't quite hear him, but I could read his lips.

"Who is that fuckin' guy?"

Not wanting to attract attention to myself, I slipped out of the room, exited the backstage area, and took a more discreet position in a hallway between the stage and the dressing rooms. It was all very loose and informal (and let's be candid—a huge percentage of the people involved with the show, from performers to roadies, were high or stoned or tripping or drunk). I figured as long as I didn't cause any trouble, no one would bother to kick my ass out of there.

This proved to be true. I fit in so well that after about forty-five minutes of hanging out, somebody came over to me and said, "Hey, man, what band are you with?"

I shrugged my shoulders, tried to play it cool.

"I'm not with any band. I'm just hanging out."

The dude smiled a half-baked, pot-headed smile.

"You ever work as a roadie?"

"A few times."

This was true, if you considered setting up your own equipment to be roadie work.

"Cool," he said, gesturing for me to follow. "Let's go."

We walked down a hallway, through a curtain, and onto the stage, where I proceeded to set up drums for Mitch Mitchell, the vaunted drummer for the Jimi Hendrix Experience. I couldn't believe it! This was like a dream job, handling the equipment for one of the best drummers in the world, and doing it just a few feet from where Hendrix would be standing a short time later. I tried to maintain my composure, even as Hendrix's appearance drew near and the stage began to bustle with activity. I was working quietly with one of the band's "real" roadies, putting the kit together, when suddenly someone appeared at my side. A skinny white guy with a beard and a headband, he began tinkering with the kit, making subtle adjustments and occasionally tapping at the skins with his fingertips.

I figured he was just another member of the crew, until I heard the other roadie say, "Hey, Mitch. Which snare you want to use tonight?"

And then it dawned on me.

*Are you shitting me? I'm setting up Mitch Mitchell's drums . . . with Mitch Mitchell himself?! How cool is that?*

You'd think a kid who worshipped all things Hendrix would have recognized the guy's drummer, but I knew Mitch mostly from album jackets and other photos, most of which had depicted him with a towering white man's afro. Apparently he'd opted for a style change shortly before the New York Pop Festival.

I stopped everything and dropped the smooth façade.

"Mr. Mitchell . . . ," I stammered. "Man, I love your music."

He smiled, gave me a cool little nod, and put out his hand for me to shake.

"Thank you," he said.

And that was it. We finished putting together the kit, and the show went on. The entire time I felt like I was having an out-of-body experience. I mean, just two years earlier I'd gotten my first Hendrix album; played it till it warped. Now here I was, at the side of the stage, just a few feet from the man himself, having helped set up the equipment for his drummer.

It was almost like I was part of the show. I was so starstruck that I could have died on the spot and gone to heaven happy.

As the show went on I totally lost track of time; I also lost track of the people with whom I had come to the show, a development that bothered me only at the end of the evening, when I realized I had no way to get home. At that time of night there was no public transport readily available from Randall's Island, and I didn't have the money for cab fare. So I walked out of the Downing Stadium parking lot and put my thumb in the air. The very first driver that went by hit his brakes and pulled over.

"Where to, buddy?"

"Mosholu Parkway . . . in the Bronx."

The guy laughed.

"I'm going to Bedford Park Boulevard. Hop in."

Amazing. Bedford Park Boulevard was about five blocks from my house. What were the odds? I opened the door, slid into the front seat, and let the warm summer breeze fill the car.

"Guess it's your lucky night, huh?" the driver said as he pulled away from the curb.

He didn't know the half of it.

The craziest thing is, just three weeks later (August 6, to be precise) I went to another massive, daylong concert with multiple acts, and again found my way backstage. This event was known as the Festival for Peace, at Shea Stadium. And just like at Randall's Island, they ended up putting me to work, juggling multiple duties. When Johnny Winter took the stage, I stood behind the band and fed sticks to his drummer. I was there, dumbstruck and wide-eyed, when Janis Joplin went strolling down the ramp to the stage, a half-empty bottle of Southern Comfort hooked between her thumb and forefinger (like Hendrix, she would be dead of a drug overdose within a few short weeks). I got to hang out backstage and shoot the breeze with promoter extraordinaire Sid Bernstein, the man who brought the Beatles to America in 1964, for Christ's sake, essentially kicking off the British Invasion and changing rock 'n' roll (and, by extension, my life) forever.

Best of all, I got to meet John Kay—again! This time he didn't even say, "Who is that fuckin' guy?"

It happened when I was backstage. One of the roadies asked if I knew anything about guitars. I didn't want to brag, but . . . yeah, I'd played a little bit. He handed me John Kay's guitar, a fresh pack of strings, and told me to get to work. There was something almost magical about that experience: prepping the instrument of a guy whose work

I really admired; it brought me closer in some way to my dream of one day becoming the man onstage, as opposed to just another wannabe. While I carefully fed the strings, my attention focused entirely on the job, I heard a door open. In walked the man himself: John Kay.

I tried to play it cool. You know, act like a professional. A part of me (okay, a big part) wanted to ask him if he remembered meeting me at Randall's Island, but that felt like such a pathetic fanboy thing to do that I decided to just keep my mouth shut. I figured the guy had probably met a million people since our paths crossed. What made me so special?

Worse, as he watched me stringing the guitar, I got the sense that he was critiquing my work, and that at any moment I'd be revealed as a fraud and a fake. I half expected him to say, "What the fuck does this guy think he's doing?"

But he didn't. Instead, Kay sat down next to me, introduced himself, and quietly picked up the package of guitar strings.

"You want to take over?" I asked nervously.

He shook his head. "No, that's okay. You're doing fine. Why don't you finish up?"

Then you know what he did? John started feeding me strings. He would thread them through the bridge, and I would tie them off. We were partners, me and the founder of Steppenwolf, bound at least for a few short minutes by our love for the guitar, and our respect for how it worked, and the care it deserved.

If you believed in the notion of a karma bank (and who didn't back then?), this represented either a massive deposit or a massive withdrawal. Depended on your point of view, I guess.

NOT EVERY CONCERT EXPERIENCE ENDED SO NEATLY, although a surprising number involved backstage banter with some of the biggest stars of that era. I don't know how I pulled it off, but I did. Repeatedly.

The following summer, for example, I went to a Grateful Dead show at Gaelic Park in the northeast section of the Bronx (Riverdale). Situated on the north side of 240th Street, not far from Manhattan College (which later purchased and significantly upgraded the property), Gaelic Park wasn't exactly the bucolic setting its name might imply, but rather a collection of dusty athletic fields separated from the surrounding streets and elevated trains by a chain-link fence topped with barbed wire. The place was used primarily by Irish neighborhood folks for soccer and hurling, as well as the occasional concert. Usually they were smaller, more intimate affairs involving Irish folk bands, but once in a while, especially in the early seventies, more-ambitious ventures were undertaken.

Like the Grateful Dead.

This particular show occurred on August 26, 1971. It was my first Dead show and I certainly got into the spirit of things, drinking buckets of alcohol and smoking enough pot to qualify, at least for the day, as a Deadhead. No acid, though. As I said, I left that to the pros.

Somehow, yes, I ended up backstage again. As usual, security was lax, and I just wandered around, looking and acting like I belonged; soon enough an opening occurred and there I was, hanging out with Jerry Garcia. (I know—you're probably thinking that I'm stretching credibility at this point, but it all happened. Seriously. I have no reason to make this shit up. For a while there I was the Zelig of the American rock scene, popping up randomly alongside the biggest stars in the business.)

I don't remember the exact details of my meeting with Jerry; instead I recall dreamlike bits and pieces of a trippy conversation. I can hear myself asking Jerry, "How's it going, man?" And I can see him standing there, smiling through that beard.

"Good, man, good. We're taking it to the people tonight."

I think I might have thrown a "Right on, brother" back at him.

Jerry was exactly as advertised: a laid-back hippie who seemed less like a rock star than a guy you'd see strumming his guitar outside a subway station, case open, bumming for quarters. He was a god at the time, but you'd never have known it by watching him. Even onstage he was content to just stand there and jam, his demeanor no different in front of 10,000 fans (or 100,000) than it was when he played in Bay Area coffeehouses. You had to admire that about him. The guy was genuine.

The weirdest thing about that day was not my meeting with Jerry, however, but the way it came to a close. At some point in the evening, after many hours of drinking, I passed out. When I woke it was four o'clock in the morning. I rolled over and looked across the Gaelic Park lawn, which had been utterly crammed with people just a few hours earlier. Now, though, it was almost empty. And by "almost" I mean I was the only person there. Not another soul. Just me, adrift in a sea of empty cans and bottles and paper cups—an assortment of garbage that gave the place a post-hurricane feel.

*Where the fuck did everyone go?*

I still have no idea what happened—why none of my friends roused me from my slumber (maybe they tried), or why the security guards left me there. They had to have known, right? They couldn't possibly have not noticed. Maybe they didn't care. Maybe this was the way things went down at a Grateful Dead concert. Regardless, I was on my own, locked inside the park.

I shambled over to the main gate. Locked. I tried another gate. Also locked. Very quickly I came to the realization that I was either going to spend the rest of the night outdoors, sleeping on the lawn, or I was going to have to climb over the fence. Like a convict breaking out of jail, I scaled the chain-link fence, pausing briefly near the top to catch my breath and to assess the likelihood of shredding my balls when I went over the barbed wire for the last few feet. I glanced back down at the park, at all the garbage and the empty bandstand. I knew what was involved in breaking down a stage after a concert—the noise and the barely controlled mayhem. I had slept through that?

Unbelievable . . .

I decided to go through the barbed wire, rather than over it, so that

I could maintain my balance by hanging on to the chain link. A few careful moments later I was on the ground, walking home, my first and last Grateful Dead concert now officially in the books.

Thanks to the generosity (or at least the tolerance) of my parents, I still lived at home during this time period. (In fact, I didn't move out until after I joined KISS.) We'd stopped fighting by this point about what I was going to do with my life. I'd appeased them somewhat by going back to school, and I think they figured I was probably safer under their roof than bouncing from place to place, bumming off my friends. I wasn't home all that often, anyway, and when I did come home, it would be late. I pretty much used the house as a crash pad. There wasn't much dialogue going on between us. They were getting older and had less energy to deal with the disparities in our lifestyles. I'd throw them money once in a while to help with rent, which made things better, and at least the cops weren't bringing me home at night. It could have been worse, and Mom and Dad knew it. Basically I just tried to keep the peace. Any insanity—or at least most of the insanity—I tried to keep outside the house.

All of my energy went into playing music. I was in multiple bands at any given time, juggling gigs, rehearsals, sometimes playing two different venues in a single night. I did whatever I had to do to make some cash and hone my craft. If that meant throwing on a tux and playing a wedding or bar mitzvah, then that's what I did. If it meant driving up to Kutsher's or one of the other resorts in the Catskill Mountains and playing for families on vacation, then I did that. There was dignity in all of it. Sometimes there was fun to be had, too.

The Catskill gigs represented my first taste of the road life, and I didn't find it unappealing. The Jewish girls up there loved us (and we loved them!), although I'm not sure how their parents would have felt . . . had they known what went on after hours. We'd go up for a few days or a week, serve as the house band, get free room and meals, and a small stipend for our efforts. Not bad at all. It was a like a free vacation—with girls and alcohol and great food. All we had to do was play a couple of sets per night. That could get a little tricky—blending material that wouldn't offend parents with the stuff we really wanted to play. But the same was true when you played weddings. I always managed to sprinkle in an assortment of songs that I liked, a cross section of popular music from Creedence Clearwater Revival, the Beatles, and Stones, along with more album-oriented rock from Led Zeppelin, Cream, Grand Funk Railroad, and Hendrix. Mostly songs you'd hear on the jukebox, punctuated with edgier, harder stuff. Once in a while the resort manager would give me a hard time, but I was always able to talk my way through it. The thing is, there was no way I could get up onstage and not play at least some of the music I really loved. I knew too much about the music scene—about what really mattered—to play nothing but Top 40 covers. Shit, I was at the Fillmore East in 1969 when Zeppelin made its first New York appearance. Incredible though it might seem now, they opened for Iron Butterfly that night, and absolutely blew the headliners off the stage. I can still see half the crowd walking out, disillusioned, midway through Iron Butterfly's set.

No reason I couldn't play "Whole Lotta Love" for the folks at Kutsher's; they'd get over it.

The most professional and polished (and overtly ambitious) of the bands with which I played in those days was undoubtedly Molimo. The name of the band, as I understood it (though I've never verified), was taken from a Portuguese word that could loosely be translated to mean "music of the forest."

I also recall one of the guys in the band saying the name was an African word for an instrument used during sacred tribal initiation ceremonies.

So who knows? Either way . . . totally sixties, right?

I didn't know what to expect the first time I showed up to rehearse with these cats at their loft on Canal Street in lower Manhattan. Conceptually speaking, Molimo was an odd little hippie band that modeled itself after Jefferson Airplane. We had two lead singers—one male (Tom Ellis), one female (Christine Murphy)—who alternated at the microphone. It was totally out of character for me, unlike anything I'd ever done before. And to be honest, it didn't interest me much. But they'd written some good songs, and as a result had landed solid management and a speculative recording deal with RCA Records.

I remember how exciting it was the first time we went into the RCA building in Midtown to put together our demo—walking into the very same studio where Frank Sinatra had recorded. If you care about music, that kind of history is palpable; you can feel it the moment you enter the room. I was twenty years old and trying to become a professional musician. Working with Molimo was as close as I'd ever been. We played a few shows, including one at the Fillmore East, and it seemed then that we were right on the cusp of hitting the big time (until RCA pulled the plug, midway through the recording of our first album).

For me, though, it was a mercenary pursuit. I got involved with Molimo not so much because I fell in love with their music, but because I saw it as an avenue to become more deeply involved with the music business, particularly the recording end of it. I considered it a gig, not a passion; simply put, I did it for the bread, and that's about it. You do what you have to do to make ends meet.

I liked the people in the band, though—a diverse bunch that included not just male and female singers, but a New York City cop who was moonlighting as a keyboard player. He used to comb his hair straight back when he went to work and tuck it up under his cap. When he'd show up to play with Molimo, he'd comb it forward and let it hang down over his collar. I also became friendly with the drummer, Dave Polinsky, and the bass player, Barry Dempsey; in fact, at the same time that we were working in Molimo, we formed a power trio designed to fulfill our hard rock desires and to put some extra money in our pockets. The name of that little group?

The Muff Divers.

I shit you not.

Obviously, with a name like the Muff Divers (and I forget which one of us came up with the name, or why we thought it was appropriate, although you can probably guess), we weren't particularly concerned with commercial success or the likelihood of securing a record contract. The Muff Divers just wanted to play hard, fast rock 'n' roll. Molimo played only original material, so it was limited in scope. I'd been in Top 40 cover bands before, playing songs people recognized, and so had Dave and Barry. So when Molimo wasn't working as much and we all needed extra bread, we went out as the Muff Divers.

Any chance to play was all right by me. The name of the band? The venue? The size of the crowd or even the size of the paycheck? All irrelevant. I tried to treat every performance in every dive club as if I were headlining Madison Square Garden. Arrogance was not part of my makeup. If anything I was insecure. I never considered any gig to be beneath me. If someone wanted to pay me (even if it was just a few bucks), and people were willing to listen (even if their numbers barely reached double digits), then I was more than happy to give them my best effort.

Some nights, naturally, were more memorable than others, though not necessarily because of anything that happened onstage. There were the occasional bar fights, for example. They're unavoidable when you're playing in shitholes, with loud, drunken customers challenging you for the crowd's attention. Usually they ended benignly, with barely a punch being thrown. Once in a while, though, the band was equally loaded, and when that happened it didn't take much to provoke a violent disagreement.

There was the time in Paterson, New Jersey, when I was invited to sit in with Tommy Doyle's band because they were short a guitar player for the night. I expected a typical Jersey bar, filled with guys in T-shirts and jeans, smoking and hanging out with their girlfriends, tossing back bottles of Rolling Rock. Instead I stumbled into a place that looked more like a mob lounge, very laid-back and moody, with guys in suits accompanied by ladies who probably were not their wives. It was most definitely not a rock 'n' roll venue, but I didn't care. I started drinking early and hard, and kept right on pounding through the night; with each successive beer my guitar playing became, if not necessarily sharper, definitely louder.

Much louder.

It's probably fair to say that I failed to exercise the appropriate level of respect or restraint, given the nature of the clientele and ownership. When the owner approached me during a break and complained about the volume, I blew him off. By the end of the night he'd had enough. And I'd had one (or ten) too many. As we broke down the stage and packed away our instruments, I asked Tommy if we'd been paid. He explained that the band had in fact been paid its fee, but that the owner had originally promised a little something extra for me, since I filled in on short notice. That way Tom wouldn't have to pay me out of pocket, and the other guys wouldn't feel shortchanged.

So I found the owner, who was working behind the bar, and asked him (rather impolitely, I'm sure), for my money.

"Fuck off, asshole. You already got paid."

That was probably the least hostile thing either of us said in a profane exchange that lasted roughly five minutes, and ended with the owner reaching over the bar and leveling me with a right hand so solid that at first I thought he'd cracked a beer bottle against the side of my skull. But he hadn't. The guy had simply used his fist to shut up a drunken guitar player, and he'd done it effectively. The next thing I knew, the guys in the band were carrying me across the parking lot and stuffing me into the back of a van. They drove me back to the Bronx, brought me upstairs to my room, and put me to bed.

I woke the next morning feeling like utter shit. My face was swollen and bruised, and my right eye was so red that it looked as though blood was leaking into the socket. Coupled with the natural awfulness of a twelve-pack hangover, these symptoms left me feeling like I was on the brink of death. But it was when my mother saw me that I realized just how bad it must have been.

"Oh, my God!" she screamed, putting both hands over her mouth. "You need to get to a hospital."

When your mother doesn't even ask for an explanation, but simply tells you to get medical help immediately, you know you're in trouble. So I went to see our family doctor, who immediately ordered an X-ray. The diagnosis: a shattered cheekbone.

"The whole thing is crushed," he explained. "You need plastic surgery or you're going to have problems with breathing and eating for the rest of your life."

He paused.

"Not to mention, you'll look like shit."

Our family didn't have a lot of money or fancy insurance, or anything like that, which made the prospect of reconstructive surgery daunting, to say the least. Luckily we had an ally in our family doctor. This guy had been treating me literally since the day I was born—he delivered me. He was an old-time family doctor who wanted quality care for his patients, regardless of their financial state, and sometimes he intervened on their behalf to make sure things worked out.

"Let me make a call," he said. "I'll see what can I do."

He did plenty, arranging for the services of a Park Avenue plastic surgeon named Dr. Lane, with whom he had gone to medical school. This guy was top-notch, one of the best reconstructive facial surgeons in the city. His specialized in putting people back together—people who had been battered in automobile accidents or victimized by violent crime. The doc took my case for practically nothing. I can still vividly recall the consultation, during which he told me not only that I didn't have to worry about the money, but that I was fortunate to be alive.

"You came within a sixteenth of an inch of puncturing your brain when the cheekbone shattered," he explained. "If that happened, you wouldn't be here right now."

Dr. Lane's plan was to wire my cheek back together. It was a complicated, tedious procedure, and one with significant potential for error, which scared the shit out of my family. The night before the surgery, my aunt Ida, who was something of a religious fanatic ("born again" in her mid-forties, and a Holy Roller from that point on), and who was prone to praying on my behalf anyway (which I doubtless needed), encouraged the entire congregation at her church to keep me in their prayers. I don't think my mother slept a wink that night. I'm sure Dad was nervous, too. When they put me under I had no idea how things were going to turn out.

When I woke in the recovery room, Doc Lane was standing over me, smiling.

"You won't believe what happened."

I mumbled something incoherent in response. My head felt almost as bad as the morning after the bar fight.

"I didn't have to wire a thing," he said.

He paused and shook his head. Later, when the anesthesia had worn off, he would tell me in greater detail exactly what had happened, comparing my mutilated cheekbone to the shell of a hard-boiled egg. It had been caved in and cracked in multiple places, but had somehow held together. With a gentle push, the cheekbone popped back into place, without so much as a fragment splintering off.

"That rarely happens," the doc said incredulously. "You're a very fortunate man."

6

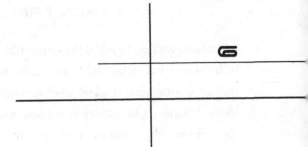

# FLASH AND ABILITY

It's hard to know exactly when it's time to let go of your dreams.

By the fall of 1972 I was twenty-one years old, dead broke, still living at home with my parents, playing in an assortment of bands, hoping that one of them would turn out to be the right vehicle for my guitar playing. I still believed in myself, still thought I could make a living as a professional musician. But there was no plan, no strategy. There was mainly just a lot of gigging and practicing and partying.

Through it all Jeanette remained supportive, if somewhat quizzical. I remember driving around one night in her car (I didn't have the bread to buy my own wheels), talking about the future, trying to explain why I didn't want a day job, why I thought I'd wither and die in the nine-to-five world.

"It's a waste of my time and talent," I told her. "I'm going to be a rock star. Trust me—we'll be rich someday."

Jeanette laughed.

"You're out of your mind."

True enough. You have to be a little bit nuts to be an artist in the first place (we don't look at the world like most people), just as you have to be somewhat detached from reality to think that you can beat the million-to-one odds stacked against anyone who tries to make it in the music business. On both counts I was guilty. I'm also an inherently lazy guy—if something doesn't motivate me in a visceral way, I'm unlikely to embrace it with any sort of discipline or enthusiasm. That's why I was a bad student, and it's why I would have been (and was) a lousy employee. I loved playing the guitar and I knew I was pretty good at it, so that's what I wanted to do with my life.

There were no other options. I had to be patient and wait for the right opportunity to come along. Which it did, in the form of an advertisement that appeared in the *Village Voice* on December 17, 1972.

LEAD GUITARIST WANTED
With Flash and Ability. Album Out
Shortly. No time wasters please.
Paul

I didn't know who "Paul" was. Nor did I know anything about the band he fronted or the supposed record deal they'd secured. This was a free ad, one of hundreds I'd read over the years. Like any New York musician with an ounce of ambition, I scanned the classifieds regularly, looking for new and interesting opportunities, especially with bands that claimed to have record contracts or upcoming tours. There was no shortage of these; from experience, though, I knew most were pure bullshit, and thus easily ignored. For some reason, though, this one was intriguing. I figured, Fuck, I have flash, and I sure as hell have ability. I doubted the part about the band having an album "out soon," but it seemed worth investigating, at the very least.

So I picked up the phone and dialed the number that appeared at the bottom of the *Village Voice* ad. On the phone was the man who had placed the ad, Paul Stanley. (It wasn't until much later that I would discover that his real name was Stanley Eisen. I still find it interesting that I was the only member of KISS who performed under his actual surname.) Paul was professional and businesslike on the phone. He asked me about my credentials and my appearance ("I look a little like Keith Richards," I said, playing up the fact that I was tall, skinny, and had long hair—pretty much the way every guitar player looked in those days); told me a little bit about their project, about how they wanted to be a theatrical band that played loud, hard rock; and then told me they would be conducting auditions in a couple of weeks.

"You're welcome to come down," he said.

I hesitated, partly because I didn't want to seem too eager, but also because I was naturally skeptical. I'd been down this road before, most recently with Molimo. The idea of auditioning for a group of guys who probably didn't even have a record deal, and, for all I knew, couldn't play worth a damn, didn't exactly get my motor running.

"Maybe," I said. "I'll think about it."

I decided to get some feedback from my buddy Chris Cassone, who was also a guitar player (and who would later become a successful sound engineer).

"Hey, Chris, you see that ad in the *Village Voice*?"

"Yeah," he said. "Interesting."

"I know, man. I'm thinking about going down there."

There was a pause.

"Me, too."

This surprised me. Chris was a solid guitar player, but he really didn't have the rock star look. He dressed like a prep school kid and didn't have long hair.

"Don't take this the wrong way, Chris . . . but I'm not sure you have the image they want."

The open audition was scheduled for January 3, 1973, which gave me a few weeks to consider the invitation. If I'd known the truth at the time, I probably would have stayed home that day, which obviously would have been the mistake of a lifetime. What I didn't know, fortunately, was that Paul and his partner in this project, Gene Klein (whom

I would come to know as Gene Simmons), had played together in a band called Wicked Lester, and while they had indeed been offered a contract from Epic Records, that deal had fallen through. So the ad, like so many others I'd come across, was not entirely true. At the very least, it was misleading.

But that's okay. It's become part of KISS mythology and I'm cool with that, just as I'm all right with some people thinking the *Village Voice* advertisement sought a "guitarist with flash and balls." Nope. The term was "flash and ability." Paul and Gene have long maintained that the *Village Voice* refused to print the word "balls," and instead substituted "ability." I don't know if that's true or not—seems unlikely, considering the *Voice* was a liberal publication that had never been shy about allowing profanity on its pages—but it makes for a good story, I guess.

Here's another good story: my mom had to drive me to the audition.

I had come to the conclusion that I had nothing to lose. What was the worst that could happen? I'd get to jam with some guys downtown. If they were talentless hacks and the whole thing turned out to be fraudulent, well, so what? I'd have invested nothing more than a few hours of my time. And maybe, just maybe, it would turn out to be something more than that.

On the afternoon of the audition I dragged my 50-watt Marshall amp (armed with eight ten-inch speakers) out to the curb and stuffed it into the trunk of my parents' Cadillac. There was no requirement for aspirants to show up with their own amp, but I thought it would give me more confidence, and more of an edge; I also presumed my Marshall would be superior to anything these guys had at their loft. It was a great amp, and sounded even better with my single-pickup Gibson Reverse Firebird blowing through its speakers, the same model Clapton used on the Cream farewell tour. I knew how to get great sustain and feedback out of this combo, and I wasn't willing to settle for something less. There had been other times when I had plugged into someone else's amp; the results had almost always been disappointing.

I'll say this about my mom: She was pretty cool about the whole thing. She knew I had talent and probably figured if I was going to make something of myself in life, music would be the likely avenue. And, of course, I was her baby boy, so she worried and fretted about my happiness and safety. When I told her I needed a ride downtown to audition for this new band (couldn't bring the amp on the subway, and I didn't have the money for cab fare), she was more than willing to lend a hand. I don't think she had any inkling that it would turn out the way it did; you never know if any audition will lead to anything, right? Most are dead ends. As she sat behind the wheel of the Caddy, waiting for me to load my gear into the trunk, I'm sure her mind was elsewhere—probably trying to figure out what we would have for dinner that night. It couldn't possibly have occurred to her that I was about to join what would become one of the biggest rock groups in the world.

Hell, it hadn't occurred to me, either.

Interestingly, though, as we pulled up to the curb on Twenty-Third Street, just off Fifth Avenue, where the audition would occur, I felt a strangely intense attack of the jitters. It was almost like I sensed there was something important about this one. There was no reason to feel that, but I did.

I got out of the car and leaned into the window.

"Wait here a second, Mom. I'll be right back."

I jogged off in the direction of a deli just a few doors down the street, as my mother yelled, "Where are you going?!"

I returned a few minutes later, with a sixteen-ounce can of beer stuffed into a brown paper bag. I popped the trunk, withdrew my amp and guitar, and dragged them into the small lobby of the building. There, alone beside the elevator, I popped the can and chugged the contents.

*Okay . . . good to go.*

The loft was basically just a long, dark, narrow room, with dozens of empty egg cartons glued to the walls and ceiling for soundproofing. There were three people already in the band, and all three were there that day: the drummer, Peter Criss; the bass player, Gene Simmons;

and the rhythm guitar player, Paul Stanley, with whom I'd already talked on the phone. It was pretty obvious that Gene was in charge of the audition. He was the most serious member of the trio and seemed not to have even the slightest sense of humor.

My introduction to the guys in KISS (although they weren't called KISS as yet) wasn't particularly smooth. I mean, I wouldn't say it was love at first sight. There had been a steady stream of musicians going in and out of the loft all day. Each was required to fill out a job application before auditioning. Now, I don't think I'd ever filled out a job application in my life—not even for a real job (the one exception being the holiday season a couple of years earlier, when I worked briefly for Uncle Sam as a letter carrier). And I wasn't about to do it for this gig. Being a musician wasn't a job to me—it was a way of life. If they wanted to know more about me, they could ask.

I took a seat, read a few lines of the application, and then crumpled it up and tossed it on the floor.

I'm sure that didn't go over very well with the boys, just as I'm sure they weren't thrilled with my attitude. Yeah, I did in fact look a little bit like Keith Richards, as advertised. I had the shag haircut, the bony frame with veins popping out on my forearms. I wore the requisite T-shirt and jeans, nothing too wild or psychedelic. Just straight-up rock 'n' roll.

With one little quirk.

My sneakers didn't match.

One was red, the other orange. A lot has been made of this over the years—was Ace too spaced out to know what he was doing? Too nervous to realize he'd picked mismatched shoes out of the closet? Was it a fashion statement?

Here's the truth: I was in a hurry and grabbed two sneakers, slipped them on, and rushed out the door. By the time I realized what I'd done, we were on our way downtown. I wasn't worried, though. I thought I looked kind of cool.

Gene and the boys, I would later discover, had a different response. They thought I was at best a fuckup; at worst, inconsiderate. It didn't help matters that I wasn't entirely respectful of the audition process.

Protocol dictates silence while waiting your turn, but as the guy ahead of me was finishing up (his name was Bob Kulick, and he would come to be associated with KISS in a number of different ways over the years, though never as a live performer), I pulled out my guitar and started warming up with some scales in the far corner of the room; my actions were definitely a distraction. As they conducted a post-audition interview with Bob, I continued to play, trying to stay loose.

When Gene saw what I was doing he walked right over and got in my face.

"You know, that's pretty fucking rude. Why don't you put your guitar away and sit down and wait your turn."

"Oh . . . sorry, man."

I can look back on all this now and laugh. Maybe the guys can laugh, too. At the time, though, I'm sure they weren't real appreciative of my behavior, and probably didn't anticipate I'd be the person who would eventually end up in the band. But it all comes down to one thing in the end: can you play the fucking guitar or not?

I could fuckin' play and I had the image!

The audition itself went smoothly—well, not counting the part where Gene threatened to kick my ass if it turned out I was wasting their time. My reaction to that, unspoken (as I still wanted the job), was *Who is this fuckin' asshole? Doesn't he know I could break him in half?*

In terms of playing, I hadn't known what to expect. Sometimes at an audition you'll jam to something familiar. But these guys put me to the test.

"We're going to play one of our songs," Paul explained. "It's called 'Deuce.' See if you can keep up."

Honestly? I think they were trying to get rid of me as quickly as possible. It's not easy to hear someone else's material for the first time and try to jump right in on lead guitar. In fact, it's hard as hell.

But that's what we did. They told me what key they'd be playing in, and then they gave me a demonstration. After a few minutes, they paused and invited me to jam along.

"I'll cue you when it's time for the solo," Paul said.

I nodded. At the appointed time I ripped a blistering solo, tried to impress them with every cool lick I had in my repertoire. I wasn't even sure it was what they were looking for, but it felt right. I liked the energy in the room, I liked the fact that they were playing loud and hard. And I really liked the song itself—a lot. I remember thinking, If this is the kind of stuff these guys are writing, then they might just be onto something.

We played for about twenty minutes, maybe a half hour, at the end of which they thanked me for my time and sent me on my way, offering little in the way of an assessment.

"Nice job," Paul said, shaking my hand. "Thanks for coming. We'll be in touch."

Gene and Peter also shook my hand and smiled in agreement. And as I walked toward the door, I could hear Peter talking to Paul and Gene.

"Yeah, very cool," he said with a laugh. "I love Chinese food."

I wasn't quite sure what he meant at the time, since I was so excited about what had just happened, but afterward I remembered that sometimes people thought I was of Asian descent. The illusive Cherokee strain in my blood confused people at times. I guess that's what happened with Peter. Really, though, all that mattered to me was that these guys seemed to know what they were doing. They were professional and seemed focused and on the same page as me.

I don't want to overstate matters. I felt like I nailed the audition and I felt like these guys had potential, but I didn't have expectations for changing the world or anything. It wasn't that dramatic. It would be one thing if I walked in and they had makeup on and a record deal in hand. But it was just three guys sitting in a loft with egg cartons on the walls. It was very businesslike and low-key.

Nevertheless, I wanted in.

FOR THE NEXT FEW DAYS I floated along, indulging in the occasional daydream about joining the new band and maybe hitting the big time. I'd left the audition feeling confident that I would get the gig; they were still going to listen to a few more people (close to thirty guitar players ultimately tried out for the job), but I had the sense that things would work out in my favor. And I was excited about it. The songs we played were catchy, and Paul, Gene, and Peter were all solid musicians. Granted, I'd barely gotten to know these guys, but I could tell they were serious. In all the years I'd been playing music, I'd never been in a band where everyone seemed not only committed to the cause, but equipped with the necessary chops.

Also, they'd made it clear up front that they were willing to do anything necessary in order to fulfill their dreams. So was I. They wanted to be a theatrical rock group, and I was totally on board with that. Gene used to say, "KISS not only gives you something for your ears, but something for your eyes as well." I believed in that. I'd been heavily influenced by Hendrix setting his guitar on fire . . . by Pete Townshend smashing his guitar. I liked smoke bombs and fireworks and special effects.

I liked the *show*. And I understood how visual effects could supplement the music and make the concert experience more memorable. As different as we were personally, as divergent as our backgrounds might have been, we shared a collective vision and ambition. We just had different ways of dealing with things. You have to understand, I was a happy-go-lucky guy, and I was just going with the flow; I thought maybe it would work out . . . maybe not.

As the days went by, "maybe not" seemed the more likely scenario. Then the guys showed up to watch me play in a club. And finally, in mid-January, about two weeks after my initial audition, I received a phone call from Paul. He wanted to know if I could come down to the loft and hang out with the guys again. I said, "Sure, why not?" When I arrived, Peter's wife, Lydia, was there, as was Gene's girlfriend. I suppose they wanted another set of eyes—female eyes—to determine whether the new guy looked like a good fit. We talked for a little while, jammed a bit, and then they offered me the job. By this time I'd learned that the band actually had no recording contract, which probably should have made me skeptical. But it really didn't. Bands and musicians inflated their résumés all the time; I knew from personal experience that record deals were every bit as fragile as the records themselves.

The important thing was that I liked the material and I had a good feeling about it. I liked the attitude of everyone in the band. Whether I would get along with them personally was hard to say, and didn't really factor into the equation. All I cared about was that they were ambitious. They wanted to make it professionally. I'd been playing with other people, been in other bands, and it always seemed like everyone had too much noise in their lives. They held day jobs and did gigs on the weekends. They had wives and kids. They had car payments and rent. Some even had mortgages. Not me. I had my guitar and nothing else. Music was my life, and it was nice to get together with three other guys who seemed just as single-minded.

We started rehearsing almost immediately at the Twenty-Third Street loft—kind of a pain in the ass for me, since I still didn't have a car or enough money for daily cab fare. Obviously I wasn't going to ask my mother to drive me to rehearsal every day, so I had to find alternative means of transportation. Sometimes I took the subway to Manhattan; more often, though, I turned to friends for help, most notably a cat named Eddie Solan. Eddie would drive to the Bronx from his house in Yonkers, and then we'd go downtown together in his Volkswagen Bug. Eddie wasn't a musician but he deserves a lot of credit for what KISS accomplished in the early days. Not only was he a loyal friend and good sound mixer, he was also a master carpenter and electronics wizard who built the PA system for our first shows. By day Eddie worked at an electronics supply store; by night he was an unofficial member of KISS—the band's very first roadie (and so much more). Eddie was really into mixing and sound, and I don't think his efforts and contributions during the early days of the band have ever been sufficiently acknowledged.

We rehearsed four, five, six days a week—probably overkill, considering we had less than a dozen songs. We'd play them repeatedly, for hours on end, beating the dead horse until there was no flesh left on its bones. This wasn't easy for me. While I loved playing guitar, my approach to the craft was less workmanlike than some of the other guys in the band. I took the artist's approach: *When inspiration strikes, I'll be ready*. Peter was kind of the same way. Paul and Gene? Uh-uh. They were workaholics, committed to practicing until their fingers bled, and then turning their attention straight to the business end of things. Admirable, I admit, but it wasn't the way I lived my life, and in the beginning I found it curious.

Not to mention exhausting.

But I got used to it pretty quickly. We spent a lot of time in close quarters in those first few months, rehearsing, planning our shows, talking about image and the direction we wanted the band to take. Considering all the problems and personality conflicts we'd have down the road, it's worth noting how well we all got along in the beginning. I wouldn't say we were best friends, because that just wouldn't be true. We were very different people. As a result, our relationships were at first (and then much later) more businesslike than anything else. Everything was very diplomatic, with each band member putting in his two cents' worth on all subjects, regardless of how important or trivial. Paul and Gene did most of the songwriting in the beginning, but once I got the hang of it, I started writing as well. And so did Peter, although to a lesser extent.

We all became friends, but once we started working together on the road, Paul and Gene quickly became aware of the fact that Peter and I were a little different from them. We liked to party. Hard. Everybody "partied," but in different ways, and to varying degrees. Gene, for example, doesn't drink (and Paul hardly drinks at all). But Gene, especially, was a total whore. Peter and I were the more traditional (and hard-core) partyers in the group, favoring alcohol and drugs, with women merely part of the mix. Like me, Peter had been a member of a gang when he was younger, and his personality had been partially shaped by that experience. We gravitated toward each other as the band went forward.

But I don't want to imply that the four of us didn't get along. We did, especially in the formative months and years. You can't spend that much time together, working toward a common goal, without fashioning some type of bond. Just as you can't help but get on each other's nerves after a while. By any reasonable standard, we were destitute. A few of us had part-time jobs—Paul and I drove cabs, Gene worked at a magazine—but there was never much money. It didn't seem to matter. We all believed that soon enough we'd be supporting ourselves solely as musicians. We had good songs, solid musicianship, and confidence that there was a market for theatrical rock. We wanted to take it further than any of the acts that inspired and influenced us, like the Who, Hendrix, the Move, Alice Cooper, and the New York Dolls.

The Dolls were a gender-bending, pre-punk group fronted by David Johansen and Johnny Thunders. They wore high heels and makeup and generally favored androgynous clothing. They influenced a lot of other musicians on the New York scene, and they had an effect on KISS, both musically and stylistically.

So did Alice, probably even to a greater degree, because Alice's sound was more polished and commercial, and his show revolved around theatrics. Alice Cooper in the 1970s brought blood and guts to the stage, combining rock and performance art in a way that had never been attempted. He wasn't just a singer; he was a character in his own band, and that character did crazy, repulsive things in the name of art. Alice, like the Dolls, wore androgynous fashion, only with a sadomasochistic flavor. He utilized guillotines and snakes and buckets of blood in his shows. And people loved it.

Well, not all of the people, obviously. Conservative groups (and more than a few parents) thought Alice was doing the devil's work, corrupting kids and peddling sex and violence. They hated him, a response that predictably helped fuel sales of record albums and concert tickets.

Alice knew exactly what he was doing. He made melodic but hard commercial rock, and he sold it with a grisly flourish (as well as a wink and a nod, I might add, though not everyone noticed), promising to make every night Halloween. It was nothing short of brilliant.

He's now one of the most recognizable icons in rock 'n' roll. (Little did I know Alice and I would become good friends later on down the road.)

We knew from the beginning that we wanted to follow his lead. We wanted to wear makeup and have outlandish costumes, and play hard rock. Beyond that, we weren't so sure. We also weren't sure about what we wanted to call ourselves. Choosing the right name was important—it had to be a good fit, convey the right image and attitude. And we all had to be comfortable with it. Looking back now I realize that one of the things that made KISS unique was the fact that we were such a democratic organization. That may seem hard to believe now, with only Gene and Paul left from the original lineup, and Gene having so carefully cultivated an image of calm control. But we were four equal partners almost from the moment the lineup was complete.

Names were tossed around for several weeks, with most being discarded in a matter of minutes. At one point, probably out of exasperation, someone suggested that we call the band, simply and graphically, FUCK! That one, too, suffered a quick demise. We wanted to be radical; we wanted to really push the envelope in a way no other band had done. FUCK! would have done the trick. It also would have made it impossible to get a record deal, or radio airplay, or any of the other things we wanted to achieve. So that wasn't going to work. FUCK! was a dead end, in the same way that Muff Divers would have been a dead end. You want to be taken seriously as a band? Well, then, your name can't be a punch line. And it can't be so profane that no one will want to say it out loud (unless they're really pissed off).

Eventually we began talking about other bands we had been in, mainly as a source of inspiration. One name can cause a spark, and suddenly you're tossing out ideas, until finally you settle on something that just feels right. I'd been through the process multiple times with other bands. It was simple brainstorming, and it usually worked. Peter had once been in a band called Lips, and at some point the conversation went in that general direction, until finally Paul suggested "KISS." The collective response was, "You know, that's not bad."

It was that simple, that organic.

It was the same way with the now famous (or infamous) KISS logo. As soon as we settled on the name, I went home and started messing around with various stylistic renderings of the band name. While it's true that I wasn't much of a student when it came to traditional courses, I did have artistic ability. In fact, I used to double up in art at DeWitt Clinton. I got really close to the head of the art department, Doc Goldberg. He encouraged my interest in sketching and design; he'd even write passes for me when I came in late. Doc was used to dealing with students who had trouble fitting in. Most of the kids in his department were uncomfortable in a public school setting, but that didn't mean they lacked talent. They were just . . . different. I was one of the best artists at DeWitt Clinton. I even designed a very cool psychedelic cover for the biannual school magazine, the *Magpie*. My idea was to sketch the words "Youth Revolts" on the cover, but the faculty advisor on the project felt that was too inflammatory.

"How about 'Youth Dissents'?" she suggested. "That might be better."

I'm not sure I even understood the meaning of the word *dissent*, but I did as I was told and the cover still looked very cool.

After moving on to Roosevelt High, I was prompted by my art teacher to enter one of my paintings in an art competition involving all the high school students in the five boroughs of New York City. That's more than one hundred thousand kids! I was good enough to have won an Art Achievement Award naming me one of the top one hundred high school artists in the city and my painting was displayed in the Museum of Modern Art in Manhattan. Not bad for a street punk from the Bronx.

Like Paul, I probably should have gone to the High School of Art and Design in Manhattan. I definitely would have had a better academic career, that's for sure. But I didn't want it bad enough. I loved art, but I loved music even more, and constantly dreamt about where it could take me. Like I said, I lacked focus and discipline.

Being excited about my new band, I roughed out a sketch of the original KISS logo in no time at all. It wasn't a whole lot different than the logo as it appears today. My original concept featured the twin S's in jagged detail, like lightning bolts, and a small dot in the shape of a diamond over the letter *I*. I then transferred the logo to a button using a felt-tip pen and presented it to the group. I later dropped the diamond over the *I* and that was that. Designing one of the most recognizable rock logos in history wasn't really that difficult. Everyone loved it. Paul was a trained artist, so when things got really serious he polished my design, making everything nice and neat. (Thanks, Paul!)

And that's how "Kiss" became "KISS."

Incidentally, there was never any secret meaning to the logo or the name. I've been accused of trying to mimic the SS of the Nazi storm troopers. Fucking ludicrous. I wasn't that subversive or nihilistic. I thought lightning bolts would look cool, and I had already decided that my character in the band would be called the Spaceman, and that my costume would be adorned with lightning bolts. So it all went together.

As for the notion that KISS was some sort of satanic metal band, with the name an acronym for Knights in Satan's Service? Complete and utter bullshit. All that satanic crap came out of left field; more precisely, it came out of the southern Bible Belt, where so many of our fans were reared. I remember on some of our early tours, there were religious fanatics outside the shows burning our records, saying we were devil worshippers. Give me a fuckin' break! I was brought up a Lutheran, Peter was a Catholic, and Gene and Paul were Jews. None of us had ever been involved in any sort of satanic activity.

Period.

The truth is, not only were we not a satanic metal band, but we weren't really a metal band at all. We were just a melodic hard rock band. Some of our songs were pop, some were heavy rock, bordering on metal, but I never thought of us as a metal band per se. As for the protesters, well, I didn't pay that much attention to them, but I kind of believed in the old adage "Any publicity is good publicity."

Really, though, if KISS stood for anything, it was a far more common acronym: Keep It Simple, Stupid. (That saying would end up having a much more profound meaning to me later on in my life.)

Just play the music, play it well, play it loud.

And look good doing it.

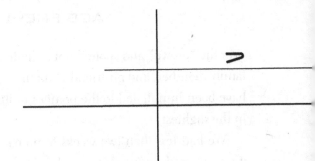

7

# KISS COMES TO LIFE

**January 30, 1973**

By the time we hit the stage for our first performance, at a Queens nightclub called Popcorn, interest in KISS hadn't exactly built to a thundering crescendo. There might have been more people in the band and crew than in the audience. You try to put experiences like that out of your mind, but it isn't always easy. My memory suffers sometimes, thanks to all the drinking and drugging, but the brain has a funny way of cataloging events as it damn well pleases. You forget some of the good stuff, and you remember some of the pain. A lot of it, actually.

Of course, even the stuff that hurts can be kind of funny. And to me, in those days, just about everything had its humorous side. So I could stand up there alongside Paul and Gene, the three of us jockeying for space on the stage, unsure how to move or where to position ourselves, and thus sometimes crashing into one another or wrapping our legs around each other until we looked like some multiheaded, hard rock serpent. And I could laugh at the absurdity of it all, even as I looked out over the "crowd" and spotted not a single unfamiliar face. A few of our family members and girlfriends, and that's about it. A lesser band might have been humiliated to the point of quitting, but we weren't deterred in the slightest.

We had less than two weeks to prepare for that gig, and I suppose if anyone had captured it on video, and I saw it today, I'd be less than thrilled with our performance. I'm not even sure how we managed to put together a full set in such a short amount of time, but I know that we did. KISS played nothing but original songs that night—a dozen or more tunes that Paul and Gene had already written, and that I'd tried to absorb as quickly as possible. I faked a lot of it, using my natural musicianship to cover gaps, hoping no one would notice. Then again, since the place was practically empty, it wasn't like there was a lot to lose.

For all my disagreements with Gene over the years, I have to give him credit for being a tireless worker and self-promoter. I never had all that much interest in the financial side of the business; Gene was obsessed with it. From the first time I met him, he seemed like a guy who put as much value on the marketing and promotional end of KISS as he did on the music we produced. Don't get me wrong. Gene was a decent songwriter and bass player, and I respected him on that level. But it was clear to me that he considered the music to be only one piece of the puzzle. I was like that, too, but to a much lesser degree. I saw Alice Cooper wrap himself in boa constrictors and fake executions onstage, and I thought, *Wow . . . cool.*

Gene saw the same thing and thought, *How can we expand on that, and how do we put together a business model to ensure its success?*

I always had a lot of friends when I was growing up. For better or worse (and my parents would probably say worse), I spent a lot of time away from the house, hanging out with my buddies. I liked being one of the guys. I still do, in fact, although I'm much more careful about the people I let into my life these days. Even when KISS blew up, I tried to keep it real, mainly by hanging out with my old friends, doing the things I always enjoyed doing: fishing, shooting pool, drinking beer . . . and of course getting into a little trouble.

"Guys, don't call me Ace," I'd say. "Call me Paul, okay? Ace is the guy in KISS."

That was the absolute truth. While some of my friends had called me Ace, the nickname remained just that: a nickname, to be used in certain situations and by a select group of people. I was always "Paul" to my family, and to most of my friends. When I joined KISS we decided that two Pauls was one too many.

"No problem," I said. "Just call me Ace."

So, to the guys in the band, I was never Paul Frehley. I was Ace. When I went home, though, I became Paul again. It was a reality check. The people who knew me only after I became famous used to put me on a pedestal, and let me tell you, that kind of treatment can really mess with your head. It made me very uncomfortable.

Peter and I both had lots of friends. Paul and Gene were different. Especially Gene. It was the weirdest thing. When I first got into KISS, and I found out that Gene didn't have any friends, I didn't know what to think of the guy. Should I feel sorry for him? Should I keep him at arm's length? Can he be trusted? I'd never met anyone like that. Gene was only a couple of years older than me, but he seemed . . . I don't know. I guess I could be diplomatic and say he was wise beyond his years, or some bullshit like that, but mainly I just felt like he had a stick up his ass. He was like a fifty-year-old accountant in the body of a twenty-three-year-old kid. One of my best friends was our sound engineer; another of my buddies was a KISS roadie. My friends used to come to our shows regularly. Peter's wife and friends showed up all the time, and Paul's friends showed up occasionally. But Gene? He was such a loner. His entire focus was on the business end of KISS, creating something big and successful, whatever that might mean. And God bless him, he did that. He made it happen (although not by himself, which I think Gene sometimes tends to forget; we were all riding the same rocket, after all). But there were times when I wanted to say, and did say, "Gene . . . come on, man, lighten the fuck up. Have a few beers."

He never did. Not once. To my knowledge the guy has never gotten loose in his life. I'm probably the last person on earth who should be advocating alcohol use—it nearly killed me—but Gene is one of those guys who might have benefited from having a drink once in a while. Just maybe?

To his credit, though, Gene was the most responsible member of the band and was always thinking ahead and brainstorming. I don't recall anyone getting all that upset about the Popcorn debacle. For one thing, it was easy to rationalize the minuscule turnout. We'd been in existence only a few weeks and had advertised the show simply by passing out leaflets on street corners in New York. Not exactly sophisticated marketing. I don't think anyone knew that a band called KISS was going to be playing at a club called Popcorn that night. And if they did, well, good luck finding us. By the time we arrived Popcorn had been shuttered and sold, and reopened with a new name: Coventry. So you had an unknown band, still in its infancy, playing a brand-new club.

No wonder the place was empty.

It stayed that way for three nights and three shows. We approached it with the professionalism of a dress rehearsal, which is really what it was. A dry run, so to speak, in terms of both musicianship and theatricality. Each of us had a specific character in mind by this time, but we hadn't figured out how to bring the characters to life.

Gene was leaning toward horror because that was his shtick. He was obsessed with comic books and horror movies. I was leaning toward the spaceman because I was fascinated with space travel and science fiction and technology in general. Paul? I don't know. He basically just became Paul—a glamorous singer with sex appeal. And Peter, well, he had a thing for cats. What can I tell you? It seemed to work for him. Funny thing is, he was probably the guy in the band whose makeup was the least consistent with his actual personality. I'd be sitting next to Peter in the dressing room sometimes, watching him put on that little button nose, and the cute whiskers and studded collar, and I'd think, *Man, you look so tame. If people only knew.*

I'll admit it—I really was something of a space cadet. But Peter?

He'd grown up in the streets (like me), and that fact, combined with his drug use, could occasionally make him a tough guy to get along with.

Simply put, he wasn't always a pussycat! But neither was I, for that matter.

Peter became my best friend in the band and is a really sweet and sensitive guy and I miss hanging out with him.

We all did the best we could to become the characters we had chosen, but resources were limited. For the most part (Gene being a notable exception, as he had the most consistent and well-paying day job), we were all broke. We couldn't afford stylists or costume designers, so we assumed those roles ourselves. If you look at photos of KISS from the early days (I'm talking about the first few months), you'll notice that I'm wearing satin pants and a black shirt with wings across the chest. Gene is wearing a T-shirt emblazoned with skull and crossbones. My mother and I worked on those together. I designed the wings and the skull and crossbones, even cut out the fabric. Then Mom, who was a talented seamstress, sewed everything together. I can remember asking my mother for help. She didn't offer an opinion of any kind, just nodded and said, "Whatever you need, Paul." Mom wasn't easily shocked, especially by this point. I'd been a thorn in her side for a number of years by this time. She'd already endured the school expulsions, the arrests, the drinking, the music . . . too many annoyances and inconveniences to catalog, really. I was a weird kid, and had been since my early teens, when I started creating elaborate psychedelic paintings, illuminating them with a black light hung from my bedroom ceiling. Mom had seen it all. By the time I was in my twenties, my behavior didn't faze her in the least. She loved me, obviously—I see that now more than ever. But I also think she'd given up any hope of changing me; so, better to just climb on board and hope the ride wouldn't end tragically.

The facial makeup we wore in those early shows was sloppy and imprecise. Gene looked a bit like an angry mime, with whiteface and bat wings; Paul dabbed a little blush on his cheeks; I smeared silver paint all over my face. If anyone had seen us at Popcorn/Coventry, with our high heels and makeup, they'd have assumed we were trying to mimic the New York Dolls . . . on acid! By this time, though, the Dolls' feminine look had fallen out of favor. We were after something else. Something more original and shocking.

More than a month would pass before we'd get another opportunity to play a live gig. Our manager (although I don't believe he ever officially held that title) was a man named Lew Linet, who had worked with Paul and Gene when they were playing with Wicked Lester. For whatever reason, Lew didn't have a lot of faith in what we were doing. He thought the music was too loud and too heavy, the characters offensive and stupid. I'm not sure what he wanted us to be—something a little more in the Top 40 tradition, probably. You can't blame the guy. To any objective set of eyes, we must have seemed like we were out of our minds. Nevertheless, Lew was handling our career, so it was his responsibility to find us some work, which he did, at a club called the Daisy on Long Island.

In Amityville, to be precise, in early March. This was a few years before *The Amityville Horror* was released, but our weekend in town was about as strange as anything I'd ever experienced. I remember doing our makeup before the show, and getting the idea for the first time that maybe I'd look better with stars around my eyes. You have to imagine the scene: four guys sitting around together in a makeshift dressing room, using handheld mirrors, applying makeup and primping our hair. Then we hit the stage and were transformed. It was like our first show at Coventry/Popcorn, only wilder. The place was owned by a man named Sid Benjamin, and it was obvious that Sid had no idea what kind of act he had booked into his club. There were maybe fifty to seventy-five people in the place, and when KISS began playing, the response wasn't exactly what we hoped for. We hit them with everything we had, playing as loudly as possible, even running into the audience and trying to get people to clap their hands and get up and dance.

At one point late in the show, after sweating right through my costume and downing a few beers, I looked over at Peter, who had a mirrored drum kit, and I could see my face reflected in the Mylar, all distorted and elongated, as if in a fun-house mirror. I started cracking up, even as I kept playing, and Gene kept singing, and the audience responded with awestruck silence. Peter started laughing, too. The crowd must have thought we were insane.

So did the club's owner. Poor Sid wasn't even sure he wanted us back the next night, but we returned, and the audience swelled to twice what it had been the previous show. Obviously word had gotten out. This time there were fewer people sitting on their hands, a lot more people drinking and getting into the show. In many ways I'd say that was the night KISS became KISS.

And you know why? Because we had conviction. We looked utterly ridiculous, and yet we wanted to be taken seriously. Here we were, in makeup, costumes, and platform heels, but we weren't acting like clowns. Whether there were two people in the audience or two hundred, we didn't take the performance lightly. From the very beginning there was intensity and seriousness about making something of ourselves, about being fully committed to KISS, whatever that might mean. Much more than any group I'd been with in the past, KISS carried itself with an air of confidence and professionalism. Failure wasn't an option, and I think that came through to the audience. We weren't just getting up there and going through the motions like some shitty Top 40 cover band. We might have looked like rejects from a science-fiction or horror movie, but we were deadly serious about what we were doing.

The songs themselves were simple and straightforward rock 'n' roll. Songs about girls and parties and cars and music—universal themes—delivered at breakneck pace and eardrum-shattering volume. An exception was a song called "Life in the Woods," which was written by Paul in what must have been a contemplative, softhearted phase. It's a song about love and nature, almost sappy in its sincerity. It didn't fit neatly into the hard-edged image we were cultivating, and that our fans came to love, so the song never made it onto a KISS album, for obvious reasons, but I have to say, just for the record, that I really liked that song and enjoyed playing it in concert. It was a nice departure.

Nothing ever seems to happen quickly enough when you're starving for success. But the truth is, KISS was on the fast track almost from the day the band was formed. When I look back on it now I can hardly believe the way things evolved, how we went from playing dive clubs in front of almost no one to headlining major venues in less than a year; how we released our first three albums in a span of thirteen months! That would be absolutely unimaginable today. Hell, it was unimaginable even then. But we did it, and it all began with a demo produced over the course of a few short days in the spring of 1973.

As with so many things that happened in the early days of KISS, the demo appeared to be mainly the result of luck and timing. But that wasn't exactly the case. The truth is, very little about KISS was left to chance. We rehearsed constantly. Hours were devoted to grassroots marketing and public relations. Again, I'll give credit where credit is due in this case. Paul and Gene were totally obsessed with creating a KISS brand and finding creative ways to attract attention to the band—no small task considering we were completely unknown. Whenever we had a gig coming up, Gene would utilize the resources and supplies available at his magazine job to create flyers and mailing lists, and to spread the word about our performance.

We were not a big-time band, but we acted like we were. It's humbling to pack your own equipment and drive from one little club to another in a rented panel truck, not knowing whether anyone will show up to see you play. But we plowed ahead, confident that eventually people would figure out that we were doing something unique and interesting. Some of my fondest memories of my time in KISS are from those earliest shows, when it was just the four of us, along with maybe Eddie Solan and a friend or two acting as roadies. We'd unpack our own equipment, drag it into the club, set it up, go through a quick sound check, and then retreat to whatever space was available to put on our makeup and transform ourselves into KISS. Afterward we'd tear everything down and go home.

In the name of accuracy, I should acknowledge that while I carried my share of the load before concerts, I rarely carried equipment afterward. I liked to drink while I was playing, and after eight to ten beers I was in no shape to haul speakers or amps. I dropped a few things in the beginning, and then everyone agreed that it was best if I just fell asleep in the back of the truck. But it wasn't a problem then; I didn't let it affect the show. Not until much later did the drinking escalate to the point where my judgment was compromised and I got into all sorts of trouble. You can get away with a lot when you're twenty-three years old; I actually believed then that a handful of beers during a show accentuated my ability on the guitar.

And maybe it did. It felt like it, anyway, which was all that really mattered.

When I found out that we were going to be putting together a demo, I tried not to get too worked up. I'd been down the recording road once before, with Molimo, and that hadn't turned out so well. But then I found out where we were going to be recording, and who would be at the controls, and suddenly I couldn't help but get excited.

Paul and Gene, it turned out, had done some studio work in the past for which they'd apparently not been appropriately compensated. They also had a relationship with a producer named Ron Johnsen, dating back to their Wicked Lester days. Ron was affiliated with the famed Electric Lady Studios in Greenwich Village, and as a way of evening the studio's debt with Paul and Gene, he offered KISS a small block of recording time. They could have fought for the cash they were owed instead, but they wisely opted to take the deal. When I found out, I was thrilled. Electric Lady had been around only a few years but had already earned status as a legendary studio. The place was originally built by Jimi Hendrix and had quickly attracted the attention of many of the top recording artists of the early seventies, including the Rolling Stones, Led Zeppelin, and Bad Company. The production genius behind albums recorded by those artists at Electric Lady was Eddie Kramer. He was a giant in the business, and I saw no reason to believe he'd want to work with an unproven band, especially one as unusual as KISS.

Apparently, though, I was wrong.

Eddie had been dragged to one of our shows by Ron Johnsen and had been impressed with our energy and ambition; he even kind of liked the makeup and costumes. So when we went into Electric Lady to work on our demo, Eddie Kramer was there, standing right beside Johnsen. The two of them worked together, with Eddie eventually taking over. For a kid like me, who had grown up idolizing Hendrix, this was a surreal moment. To be in that studio, in the same spot where Hendrix had stood, with Eddie Kramer turning the knobs . . . well, how could this be happening?

But it was happening. We laid down the instrumental tracks on the first day, the vocals on the second, and mixed everything on the third. Within three days we had a five-song demo: "Deuce," "Strutter," "Watchin' You," "Black Diamond," and "Cold Gin."

The last of these, "Cold Gin," represented my first writing contribution to the band. It was a song about loneliness and poverty—hard times in general—and the comfort that can be found in a bottle, a concept I'd come to know well in the future, but that I understood only in the abstract at the time:

*It's time to leave and get another quart*
*Around the corner at the liquor store*
*The cheapest stuff is all I need*
*To get me back on my feet again*

"Cold Gin" is a good song. It became a KISS concert staple and it holds up well today; it's withstood the test of time. But I have to admit—I'm not even sure what I was trying to say, or why I wrote a song about gin (let alone *cold* gin). I didn't drink gin; didn't drink liquor of any kind very often. I was a beer man then, and not even a connoisseur. Gimme a can of whatever you had in the fridge, and I was happy. I wanted to write a drinking song, and "Cold Gin" sounded like a great title. So I went with it.

Working with Eddie Kramer was a trip, in the best sense of the word. Right from the start (and we would go on to work together on several projects), Eddie and I got along great. We had a terrific working relationship and, later, a friendship as well. Eddie wasn't just a brilliant producer and engineer; he was gifted when it came to managing talent. Not in a business sense, but in the sense that he understood how to get the best out of a musician in the studio. He tolerated, maybe even appreciated, quirks and eccentricities, and I had a shitload of both. What I liked about Eddie was that he seemed to respect my ability as a guitar player. I wasn't the most secure guy. I needed a pat on the back once in a while. Eddie used to offer praise and criticism in roughly equal amounts. At least where I was concerned, he was a generous guy. When I was around him, I wanted to play well, and I wanted to give my best effort. I needed the encouragement, and I got it from Eddie.

In fairness, we all did, and it was Eddie's encouragement and skill that helped make that demo one of the best recordings KISS ever did. I think everyone in the band would agree that even though it was only five songs, the demo is a stronger record than the first "official" KISS record. It was cleaner, harder, better. It came straight from the heart . . . from the gut. We were all proud of it and felt like it would be the perfect calling card when it came time to land a deal with a major label. And that's exactly what it was.

As much as we all wanted to succeed, we couldn't make it on our own. There was no way for KISS to become the juggernaut it did without some serious muscle behind it. After we finished recording the demo, nothing really changed. Not right away, anyway. We just kept rehearsing and working odd jobs to help pay the bills. A series of shows in New York attracted some people within the industry—both artists and management types—which made it fairly clear that word of KISS was getting around. In July we rented out a ballroom at a sleazy little place called the Hotel Diplomat, and more than five hundred people showed up to watch us play. Our makeup had become more refined by this time, and our special effects had finally begun to creep beyond goofy stunts that were better known as staples of the Harlem Globetrotters (you know, tossing buckets of confetti into the crowd). Mainly, though, the music was good. The music was *always* good, and we delivered it with our usual intensity and volume.

On August 10 we played the Diplomat once again, on a bill that included the bands Street Punk and Luger. But it was totally our show. We paid for the hall, and we did our own advertising and promotion. As usual, we put on a dynamite show, totally overwhelming the audience. One of the things we had going for us was our physical presence. With the help of gigantic platform shoes, we were all approaching seven feet tall. Add the costumes and makeup, and put us all in a small, sweaty club, and you have a seriously intense, claustrophobic atmosphere. I honestly think some of the people who showed up for those early shows were literally scared of us.

One man who wasn't scared, in any sense of the word, was Bill Aucoin. Bill was one of the most interesting people I've ever met, a real eclectic guy who, on the surface at least, probably seemed like exactly the wrong person to manage the career of KISS. For one thing, he'd never been a rock 'n' roll manager. For another, he didn't exactly look like the hippest guy in the room. But Bill wanted the job and that's why he came to the Hotel Diplomat that night—to see us in person, and to pitch his services.

Bill was a former television producer whose credits included a show called *Flipside*, which was actually about the record business. Gene always figured that KISS was a media venture as much as it was a rock band, so he was intrigued by Bill's television experience. That's why Bill was one of the hundreds of industry executives who regularly received information about KISS. Gene saturated the marketplace, targeting anyone who might possibly be of use to the band, in almost any capacity. And remember, in those days it took a ton of effort to communicate this type of information. You didn't just send out an e-mail blast. You wrote letters and made flyers and brochures (sometimes including fake reviews of your concerts), and you made hundreds of copies, and then you put them all in the mail. Multiple lines in the water, so to speak, waiting and hoping for a strike.

We never would have guessed that Bill would turn out to be the big fish, or at least the right fish, but he was. By this time he owned a company that produced television commercials, usually related to the music industry. Bill had been worn down by our persistence. I guess he figured that any band with that much ambition was at least worth investigating. So he showed up at the Diplomat . . . and we blew him away. And very quickly our roles were reversed. Bill came backstage after the show and said that he wanted to manage our band. Suddenly we weren't chasing him anymore; he was chasing us. He showed up backstage again a few days later, after another show, this time making an even stronger pitch.

"Give me two weeks," he said, "and I'll get you a record deal."

I was skeptical. I think we all were. But Bill seemed so genuine, and so enthusiastic, that we were willing to give him a shot. Anyway, what did we have to lose? There was no contract, no risk. Just a handshake agreement with a guy who promised to turn KISS into a household name. All he wanted in return was a small and exclusive window of opportunity.

So we gave it to him.

We also gave him a copy of our demo, in case he wanted to introduce the music of KISS to people in the industry. In fact, Bill did have someone in mind. Someone very specific. Bill was a shrewd guy, far more savvy than he appeared. Think about it. Who in their right mind would guarantee that he could line up a recording contract for an unknown band? In a span of two weeks? Unless, of course, they had a close, personal relationship with someone in the industry. Someone who had power and influence.

Someone who could make miracles happen.

Someone like Neil Bogart.

8

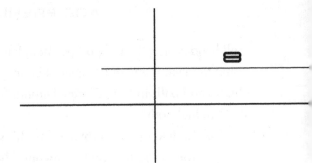

# HERE'S LOOKING AT YOU, KISS

Two weeks came and went, without any indication that a record deal was in the works. Bill was so much smarter (and shrewder) than I realized, smarter than any of us realized. Impatient as we were for our big break, we all sort of presumed that Bill merely talked a good game. Two weeks was a ridiculous deadline, of course, but it was Bill who had made the offer, so we figured we might as well hold him to it.

One day we all went down to his office in midtown Manhattan, the idea being not necessarily that we'd dump him, but merely to ask for an update. But so much had been happening. In fact, as I'd learn much later, Bill had put the KISS machinery in motion well before he even met us that night at the Diplomat. What we perceived as an outrageous promise ("Give me two weeks!") was actually just Bill being the master showman that he was. Like any great gambler (and KISS represented the biggest gamble of Bill's career, by a wide margin), he'd done his homework and manipulated the odds in his favor. Managing a rock 'n' roll band is at best a risky proposition; bankrolling that band and promising to make it one of the biggest bands in the world requires gigantic brains and balls in roughly equal amounts.

Bill had both.

He also had the proverbial ace up his sleeve.

"Let me introduce you to someone," he said that day in his office.

The "someone" was Neil Bogart, the president of Buddah Records, and one of the more powerful (and interesting) men in the recording industry. Neil and Bill enjoyed a friendship; they also had worked together—Buddah had been one of Bill's biggest clients when he was producing music commercials. Before he'd even met with us, Bill had discussed the possibility of taking the band to Neil, who was in the process of leaving Buddah and starting his own record label. It was all very clandestine, insider shit, and I had no idea that any of it was taking place. Frankly I didn't care. I just wanted to be told that we had a real record deal; if Bill Aucoin was the guy who could make that happen, then he was fine by me. I doubt that even Gene, who prided himself on being a shrewd businessman, had any idea what was really happening behind the scenes.

Neil Bogart was a marketing genius whose early career (he was a record company VP by the time he was in his mid-twenties) included the rise (if not the creation) of what came to be known as bubblegum music. He was the man behind such hits as "96 Tears" by Question Mark and the Mysterians, "Yummy, Yummy, Yummy" by the 1910 Fruitgum Company, and "Green Tambourine" by the Lemon Pipers. Not exactly my cup of tea when I was learning how to play guitar (bubblegum was disposable crap, as far as I was concerned, as it was to any self-respecting musician who loved the Stones and the Who and Hendrix). But there was no denying Neil's talent. The guy had demonstrated an uncanny ability to find and promote acts that otherwise might have gone completely unnoticed; bands that were . . . *different*.

KISS certainly fell into that category. Neil was the kind of guy who could stick a finger in the air and figure out which way the wind was blowing. He was always a step ahead of everyone else in the business.

We needed someone like that. In retrospect, it's clear that he and Bill Aucoin were the perfect team for KISS. Their vision and ambition were equal to ours, and without them in our corner, I doubt KISS ever would have become the blockbuster that it did. We owe a lot to those two men, and to at least one woman: Joyce Biawitz, who was both Bill's business partner in Rock Steady Management and Neil's future wife.

When those three came on board, everything changed for KISS.

The main thing I remember about Neil in that first meeting was his enthusiasm. The guy was incredibly energetic and passionate. He told us he loved our demo and that he wanted to make KISS one of the first bands signed to his new label. Our album, he promised, would be the first to appear on Emerald City Records. I guess Neil was a big fan of classic movies; for some reason he decided to change the name of the label before we were even signed, but he still went with an old-time Hollywood theme. The new label would be called Casablanca Records, and it went on to become one of the most successful record companies of the 1970s. For better or worse, Neil was the man behind some of the biggest acts of the disco era, including Donna Summer and the Village People. Whatever else anyone might have thought of him, you couldn't say he didn't know how to sell records.

It's funny, though. As much as Neil claimed to like our music, I'm not sure he completely understood what we were all about when we first met. He had a lot of big ideas about turning KISS into a multimedia supergroup. There was a lot of sales lingo thrown around in that first meeting, talk of cross-platform promotion and multilevel marketing, shit that didn't appeal to me in the least, but that was undeniably important to the band's success. I just wanted someone to tell me that we had a deal, and then tell me what we had to do in order to reach the greatest number of fans. And I'd do it.

You want me to wear makeup? Fine.

You want me to wear platform heels and spandex? No problem.

You want me to shoot rockets out of my guitar? Cool. I'll do that, too.

Whatever it takes.

We all had that attitude, and we were excited to be working with people who seemed to share our vision and willingness to sacrifice, to put everything on the line.

Only later would we find out that Neil didn't fully understand what he was dealing with. He'd been told that we were a theatrical rock group, but he'd never seen us play live. So I don't think he had a clear idea of what that meant. KISS, after all, was like nothing that had come before it. We made Alice Cooper seem tame; we made the Dolls look like a bunch of schoolgirls.

To get that point across, and to secure the contract with Casablanca, KISS played what amounted to a private audition at the LeTang dance studio in Manhattan. The place was located right across the street from Bell Sound Studios, where KISS would record its first album. LeTang was tiny, really nothing more than a rehearsal space, but we treated it like it was a regular gig, with flash pots and smoke bombs, and enough noise to compromise the hearing of anyone in the room. We ran into the "audience," which consisted mainly of Neil and Bill and some of the people who worked for them, along with some journalists. We forced people to stand up and clap their hands.

Basically, over the course of a half-dozen songs and roughly thirty minutes (including solos), we fuckin' killed it. I remember looking at Neil and thinking he looked almost shell-shocked, like he didn't know whether to applaud or get up and leave.

Clearly, though, Neil was impressed, because not long after that we had a deal with Emerald City (soon to be Casablanca) Records, and a distribution arrangement with Warner Bros. Neil had a lot of faith in KISS; there was a bit of the old carnival barker in him, and so he could appreciate what we were trying to do and see the potential for reaching a massive audience. But even Neil wondered whether we were a little too far out on the fringe for our own good. He loved the music and the brashness of our performance. But the makeup?

"I'm not sure it's necessary," he said.

This came up in early discussions, and again when we were shooting the cover art for the *KISS* album. I can remember Neil calling us up on the phone on the eve of our first album being released and saying, "Boys, are you sure you want to wear the makeup?"

Yeah, we were sure. By this point the costumes had evolved from denim to leather and were on their way to spandex. Sneakers had been replaced by platform shoes. Each of us had refined the hair and facial makeup of his particular character. We'd been gigging throughout the city and its environs as KISS, a band like nothing you'd ever seen before. The characters were an accepted (and highly anticipated) part of the show. There was no turning back. If you wanted KISS, you got the entire package, makeup and all.

It was, admittedly, a completely unproven formula at the time, so I'm not surprised that Neil might have had some minor misgivings. But we stuck to our guns. Once we said we were going to do something, we did it. We hadn't attracted the attention of major record company executives by playing it safe, and we weren't about to start doing that now. Neil agreed. Both he and Bill (and Joyce) put everything they had into KISS, and I'm not just talking about their time and energy. These guys, especially Bill, reached deep into their own pockets to keep the band afloat in those first few months (and even years). KISS was Casablanca's first signee, so in many ways the success of the label would rise or fall on our backs. KISS was also the sole client of Rock Steady Management. Bill couldn't afford to have us fail. If we failed, Rock Steady would crumble. So he did everything he could to prevent that from happening, including draining his life savings.

One of the first things Bill did was convince the guys in the band that we should establish an equal partnership. To an outsider, or to someone familiar only with the regular business world, this probably doesn't sound like such a novel concept. In the music business, however, it's highly unusual. Bands are not democracies. Oh, sure, they start out that way sometimes—four kids hanging out in their parents' garages, playing music and dreaming of stardom, splitting everything (the money, the chicks, the cars) equally. But when the dream edges toward reality, practical considerations tend to get in the way. The truth is, very few bands are composed of equal parts. More often than not, one or two people do most of the heavy lifting: the writing, the singing, the marketing. The guy at the front of the stage tends to get more attention and thus more of the money. The same is true of the person who does the majority of the writing. Publishing revenue can really skew the income of any band, leaving one or two primary members (think Keith Richards and Mick Jagger, or John Lennon and Paul McCartney) with bigger bank accounts, bigger egos, bigger fan bases, and groupies with bigger breasts. When that happens . . . *adios, amigos*. The four guys in the garage become warring factions, and the band invariably splits up. Bill Aucoin had seen that happen too many times in the past, and he envisioned it happening with KISS before we even released our first record. So Bill had this unique idea:

"Why not form a partnership?" he suggested. "With everything split equally."

It seemed like a noble approach to problems (greed and ego) that weren't really an issue at the time. Well, I don't mean to imply that we were a completely unselfish group of guys. We all had egos; we all liked the spotlight and craved stardom and success. I don't deny that, and I'm sure Gene, Peter, and Paul would acknowledge as much. Hell, Gene is one of the most arrogant and egotistical people I've ever met. Those characteristics served him well when we were building KISS from the ground up, and I suppose they serve him well today, although I've heard his cocksure, abrasive attitude has gotten him into trouble on more than one occasion. But in 1973, when we were just getting started, we were a little like the Three (Four) Musketeers:

*One for all and all for one!*

I liked that about KISS. We were sort of a family. A strange, dysfunctional family comprising disjointed and unrelated parts, but a family nonetheless. As primary songwriters Gene and Paul certainly could have argued for a greater share of the pie; to their credit, they did not. Bill convinced them, and all of us, that we should be equally invested in the band's future. If everything worked out the way Bill and Neil planned, then money would come raining down on all of us, and everyone would be happy. There would be no petty bickering about percentages and splits. Everything KISS earned, including merchandising, concert revenue, and record sales, would be divided equally among the four founding members.

What could possibly go wrong?

Eventually quite a lot went wrong, as so often happens when the checks get big enough. There was a time there in the late seventies when the money ran like water. I couldn't spend it fast enough: cars, houses, boats. And drugs, of course. Lots of drugs. But it always seemed like there was plenty of money, so I didn't worry about it. Instead of royalty checks being cut to each individual member of the band, all proceeds were funneled back into the corporation, into a single, huge, ever-boiling pot. Only later did we discover that the arrangement was a bit of a scam, and we ended up suing our business managers and accountants, and parting ways with Bill.

Whatever Bill received for his work with KISS, though, it probably wasn't enough. In a very real sense, he was part of the band, his expertise and ingenuity every bit as important to our success as anything we contributed as musicians. A strong sentiment, perhaps, but I believe it. Bill was remarkable.

For example, before we even formalized an agreement with Rock Steady Management—before we had anything in writing—Bill agreed to pay us out of pocket so that we could concentrate on writing and rehearsing and preparing to record our first album. While the "salary" wasn't much by today's standards—seventy-five dollars per week for each band member—it was a life-changing gesture for us. You have to understand: I was dead broke, driving a cab a couple of times a week, making deliveries for a liquor store, so that I could afford to eat. When you don't have a lot, seventy-five dollars is pretty good money. Paul was able to quit his job at a deli, where he'd been forced to wear his hair tucked up under a wig so that no one would freak out while he was making sandwiches. Gene was the only person in the band who continued to work, probably because he was the only one of us who had anything resembling a legitimate job. I think Gene enjoyed walking into the offices at Condé Nast. And if KISS fell apart, he had something to fall back on. I didn't look at cab driving as a career. It was something to be endured; it was a means to an end, nothing more. As soon as I got my first check from Bill, I put my hack's license in a dresser drawer.

I still have it, in fact. But it hasn't hung on a visor in nearly four decades.

On October 10, 1973, KISS entered Bell Sound Studios in New York to record its first album. I would have preferred to work with Eddie Kramer again, but the recording industry, like so many others, is ruled largely by politics and personal relationships. Kenny Kerner and Richie Wise, a production team that had worked under Neil at Buddah, ended up getting the assignment to produce our first record. You couldn't really argue that they were the wrong people for the job, or that they weren't qualified. Kenny, as I understand it, had been a strong advocate for KISS from the first time he heard our demo. He and Richie were former musicians (they had played together in a band called Dust, along with Marky Ramone) who had worked on the production end of things for a number of bands, most notably Badfinger. They were technically sound and I think they understood exactly what KISS was trying to accomplish with its first album.

The actual recording of the album went smoothly, as we had pretty much all the parts already worked out before we went into the studio. There wasn't a lot of writing or improvising to be done. That happens sometimes with albums. You go into the studio with a blueprint, and then you tinker and expand and see how everything works out. With *KISS*, our first album, we used exactly the opposite approach. We had been rehearsing the songs over and over again. We'd been playing them live at every gig. The goal with *KISS* was simply to get the songs on record—to replicate, as closely as possible, the sound of our live performances.

To make that happen we worked quickly and efficiently. I think we did the entire album in about three weeks—laying down basic tracks first, and then adding vocals and solos afterward. I was simply the lead guitar player at the time, not doing a lot of vocals or even background singing. I remember stressing out a little about the solos; I was less relaxed than I had been when we went into the studio to record our demo. There was a lot more at stake this time, and I felt the pressure.

There's a big difference between session guys and performers. I was always a performer, thriving on the audience response and never quite repeating any solo in exactly the same way. Session guys pride themselves on precision and repetition. They are very different skill sets. It's one thing when you're playing live and you have an idea of what the guitar solo is, and you can just sort of freelance a bit. The audience doesn't hear the mistakes, doesn't notice that maybe you've made some minor adjustments. Performing live is all about spontaneity and energy; the audience and musician feed off one another. It doesn't really matter whether each note is perfect, or whether the song is performed exactly as written. In fact, no two renditions should sound exactly the same.

I was comfortable in that concert setting. The studio? Totally foreign to me. The demo was challenging enough, but at least that's all it was: a *demo*. By definition it was imperfect and temporary. This time it was serious. I walked into Bell Sound on that first day with my heart racing. There's something about entering the studio and realizing that when you sit down to play, every note will go down in history. It's intimidating to the point of distraction. Or at least it was for me. Throughout the recording of *KISS* I was anxious. I wanted to do the best signature guitar solos I could do, and I'm not sure I succeeded. Playing live is all about . . . *entertaining*. You don't have to be exact. You have to have the attitude and the style, and you have to be able to put it across to the audience. In the studio it's about being precise and focused, and that was very challenging for me in the beginning (and by "beginning" I mean the entire first album). As the process went on, album after album, I realized you had to approach studio recording differently than you would a live performance, and you had to prepare differently.

Also, I was spaced out a lot of the time, either because I'd been drinking or because I was so nervous about fucking up that I couldn't concentrate. I took my guitar work very seriously, but I often wondered whether I was good enough. It didn't help matters that I received very little positive feedback from the other guys in the band. I always felt like they wanted me to do better, like they expected more. It wasn't something that was verbalized; it's just something I felt. I never got the sense that they appreciated me as much as other people did.

As for the first album, I didn't know what to expect. I remember thinking that it seemed like we were working hard and fast, and everyone was excited about producing a good record. But you don't really know when you're in the moment. If you're not sitting at the sound board, it's hard to tell exactly what's going on, or to know whether it's good. We were all so young and inexperienced, and we were green as studio musicians, but we gave it our best effort, and I think the songs hold up really well even after all these years. Several of them—"Deuce," "Strutter," "Cold Gin," and "Black Diamond"—have become KISS classics. I'd love to redo some of those songs today using state-of-the-art equipment.

In the eyes of Bill Aucoin, nothing was deemed too outrageous. I remember sitting in Bill's office one day, talking again about what it meant to be a theatrical rock group. It was a sweepingly descriptive term, one open to all sorts of crazy interpretations. Each of us in the band had his own opinion about what it meant to be "theatrical," so there was no line we couldn't (or wouldn't) cross. I remember Gene once telling me he would go out onstage dressed in a tutu if people would pay money to see it! Things would change over the next few years, especially for me, as the music began to take a backseat to the show. In the beginning, though, before we went out on tour in support of *KISS*, we were all equally invested in putting on the greatest rock 'n' roll show the world had ever seen.

Bill had some interesting ideas about what that entailed, so it shouldn't have come as a surprise when we showed up at rehearsal one day and found Bill waiting there with a magician.

That's right—a magician.

"How far are you guys willing to go?" Bill asked.

And of course the answer was, "Where no man has gone before!"

The magician spent the next few hours demonstrating some tricks of the trade, including how to use flash paper and breathe fire. I can vividly recall watching as the guy took a swig of kerosene and held it in his mouth. Then he held up a small torch a short distance from his face and sprayed the kerosene at full force.

"Holy shit!" Gene shouted. "I want to do that!"

The sight of Gene Simmons, in his demon makeup, spitting blood and breathing fire, soon became signature images of KISS, and both were born that day in Bill Aucoin's office. Usually the gimmick, like all others in a KISS live show, went off without a hitch. But there were risks and occasional mistakes. Holding a mouthful of kerosene is not a great idea; one swallow and you're in big trouble. That's why we made sure that a hefty dose of ipecac syrup was nearby when we performed. Ipecac is a highly effective emetic—in other words, it induces vomiting—and on more than one occasion Gene had to rush from the stage after accidentally gulping a bit of kerosene. He'd take a quick hit of ipecac, throw up, and return to the stage to finish the show.

It was, I suppose, an occupational hazard, just as it was for me with my smoking guitar, which occasionally malfunctioned and gave me burns on my thighs and hands; or Peter's levitating drum kit, which sometimes began to sway in the breeze, leaving us all with a lump in the throat. The crazy, outlandish things we did in the name of rock 'n' roll!

Gene became a real student of the craft, practicing with the magician for hours on end in anticipation of breathing fire for the first time in front of a live audience. The opportunity came on December 31,

1973, during a New Year's Eve show at the Academy of Music. That show was intended to be the official unveiling of KISS in advance of our debut album. The Academy of Music was the biggest venue we'd played, with seating for more than three thousand people. Judging by advertisements for the show, KISS was an afterthought; or no thought at all. Blue Öyster Cult was the headliner, with Iggy Pop and a band called Teenage Lust on the undercard.

KISS?

Nowhere to be found.

Not that we gave a flying fuck. We took the stage and made it our own, playing a ferocious half-hour set. Near the end, during the song "Firehouse," Gene spewed kerosene onto a handheld flame, lighting up the stage and prompting the audience to go berserk. It wasn't a KISS crowd, obviously, because there was no such thing. Not yet. It was just a good, solid rock crowd. I'm sure some of them were baffled by what they were seeing, but I'm also sure not one of them was bored! I realized early on that people either loved us or hated us; luckily, it turned out that most people fell into the former camp.

You can practice an effect all you want in private; you can exercise immense caution and think you've got it down pat. But when you get onstage in front of an audience, your adrenaline is pumping and maybe you're not being as careful as you should. Hence all hell can break loose. Accidents will happen. It's Murphy's law, right?

The next thing I saw was Sean Delaney, Bill's lover and confidant, who became an important member of the KISS creative team, running out onto the stage and wrapping a towel around Gene's head.

His hair had caught fire!

And I remember the oddest sensation as I watched them wrestling, Sean frantically whacking Gene about the head and shoulders, snuffing out the flames, and I could hear the crowd roaring.

*Pretty fuckin' cool . . .*

Believe it or not, none of it seemed that weird to me. Things happen. Nothing was going to stop us. By this time we were in full costume, with our makeup completely developed. We were no longer Paul, Gene, Ace, and Peter.

We were KISS.

After the show, while Teenage Lust performed, I went to the dressing room and removed my makeup. Then I went up into the balcony (no one recognized me, of course, since I was no longer in character) and watched Iggy Pop's set. I was struck not only by how cool he seemed, but by how odd it was that we had opened for him. For the first time I had the sense that we were on our way. New Year's Eve in New York . . . at the Academy of Music . . . with Iggy Pop and Blue Öyster Cult.

It was a big deal, and I knew it. I could feel it: *This is it. This is the beginning of something special.*

9

# ON THE ROAD

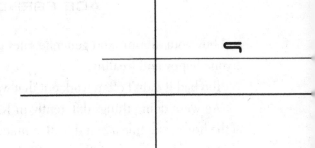

We didn't become superstars overnight. People forget that sometimes. Three albums came and went—generating only modest sales and nearly bankrupting Casablanca Records, Bill Aucoin, and Neil Bogart along the way—before KISS became the juggernaut folks recognize today. I can still remember a moment in late February 1974, not long after our first album was released, that was simultaneously one of the happiest and weirdest of my life.

The music business was different back then. For better or worse, it lacked the cohesiveness and marketing power it has today. Rather than magically appearing in stores across the country, with prepackaged publicity campaigns, records were often released slowly and cautiously. Audiences were allowed to build as an album gradually worked its way from the coasts to the heartland, from major cities to smaller markets. Singles accompanied the release of an album, and if the proper wheels were greased (payola was alive and well in those days, whether anyone wants to admit it or not) you'd get enough airplay to create some buzz. And, obviously, you went out on the road for months on end, trying to build an audience for your music, an audience that would then go out and buy your albums and generate sales of merchandise and make everyone happy and wealthy.

Too bad it didn't often work out that way.

We were doing things differently in KISS, putting the cart in front of the horse, creating a brand, with a unique marketing concept, before we'd even developed a following. So I guess it shouldn't have been a huge surprise that the first record didn't exactly take the world by storm. Hardly anyone knew who the hell we were, or why we were wearing this ridiculous makeup. Was the band a joke? A gimmick?

No, man. We were dead fucking serious. But it took some time to convince everyone else.

On that February day I walked into (the now-defunct) Alexander's department store on Fordham Road in the Bronx, right across the street from Fordham University. Alexander's stood near one of the busiest intersections in the borough. There was always a crowd hanging out nearby, and the traffic in and out of the place seemed never to slow. I'd been shopping at Alexander's since I was a little kid—bought a big chunk of my album collection there. So you can imagine how I felt walking through the store, my heart racing as I headed to the music section. You can imagine what it must have been like for a guy who had bought his first Hendrix record—and his first Led Zeppelin record, his first Who record—in this very spot to suddenly be thumbing through the stacks of vinyl, looking for a record of his very own.

And there it was, staring out at me from a wall of new releases: *KISS*.

I picked it up, held it for a moment, flipped it from back to front. I smiled and laughed a little as I looked at my silver-painted face, gazing stoically from the upper right-hand corner.

Then I walked to the cash register, pulled out a ten-dollar bill, and paid for the record without saying a word.

Why, you might reasonably wonder, did I have to buy my own record? Well, because Casablanca had not yet sent me a copy. Or maybe our manager hadn't given me a copy. I don't even remember. I just know that when the album came out, I went to Alexander's to see it for myself, and to buy my own copy. That's how slowly things worked sometimes; that's how little clout we had in those days.

I didn't really feel offended by the oversight. Mainly I was just thrilled to be walking out of the store with my own album. I wanted to take it out of the bag and shout to everyone, "Hey, look at this: I made a record!" But I didn't. There was some comfort in the anonymity, too. No one knew who I was, so even if I had shown them the album cover, they wouldn't have recognized me as the person in the upper right-hand corner. That would be one of the strangest aspects of the KISS phenomenon: for a number of years when we went out in public, we were seen primarily, if not exclusively, in character.

Life as a rock star at the highest level is weird beyond words. It's great in a lot of ways, obviously, but it's disorienting, too. You very quickly begin to realize that you are part of something much bigger than yourself. Everything you do is designed to help keep the machine moving, the record sales flowing. This was especially true with KISS, since so much of our popularity was based not merely on music, but on image. After a while the makeup became almost like a prison. We couldn't appear anywhere out of character. If we pulled into a town and we had a radio interview scheduled, we had to get up a couple of hours early to put on our makeup before going to the radio station. Think about that. Full costumes and makeup for a radio appearance, where no one would even see us. I wasn't Ace Frehley when I represented KISS. I was the Spaceman. That's just the way it worked.

Again, that's not a complaint, just an observation. For a long time, the benefits of being in KISS far outweighed the liabilities. Weird as it was to put on makeup for every public appearance, it did have the fringe benefit of allowing each of us to maintain some semblance of a private life away from the spotlight. For a little while, anyway.

Not that I cared much about my privacy in those days. Like the rest of the guys in the band, I craved attention. You don't join a band and put on makeup and crazy costumes if you want people to ignore you, right? So I walked out of Alexander's and immediately began calling up my friends, and Jeanette, and telling them about the record. I played it in my bedroom at home, an experience so strange—listening to my very own record for the very first time, on the same turntable that spun Clapton and the Stones—that I can hardly put it into words. I sat on the edge of my bed, listening to KISS fill the room . . . listening to Gene sing the words to "Cold Gin" . . . listening to my guitar solos . . . and I started to laugh out loud.

*This can't be real.*

But it was real, a fact made even clearer a few weeks later when I was driving around with the radio blasting, changing stations, absent-mindedly trying to find something I liked, when I heard "Nothin' to Lose," the first single off *KISS*, pulsating through the speakers. I was so distracted that I nearly drove my car off the road (not the first time that would happen, incidentally), but after regaining my composure I turned the volume up as far as it would go and rolled down the windows (even though it was still winter).

Those are the moments you live for, the moments you dream about when you're a gangly teenager teaching yourself chords in your bedroom, wondering if you'll ever be any good, or if you're just wasting your time. I suppose I might have been a little different from most kids; like I said, I honestly believed I was going to be in a famous band someday, and from the moment I met Gene, Paul, and Peter, I thought KISS would be the vehicle to make it happen. Still, there's nothing quite like holding your own first record album in your hands, tearing off the shrink-wrap, and getting a whiff of freshly pressed vinyl; if there's anything better, it's hearing one of your songs on the radio for the very first time.

It's hard to imagine any scenario in which you're closer to a group of people than you are when you're out on the road, touring with a band. That's not necessarily a good thing or a bad thing; it's just an observation. KISS built its reputation through live performances. In the beginning, especially, we were road warriors in the truest sense of the term, living out of suitcases in semi-shitty hotels, traveling by bus (or, if we were lucky, flying coach), sleeping a few hours a night, eating at IHOP or Denny's, and fucking almost anything that moved. One town blended into the next, as we crisscrossed North America, from Asbury Park to Atlanta to Anchorage . . . and back again. More than one hundred separate shows the first year alone. We toured constantly, and when we weren't touring we were back in the studio working on the second album. We lived together, ate together, slept together. We were four very different and unique personalities, but somehow we made it work, because we were working toward a common goal.

You can tolerate a lot when you're in your early twenties. Your body recovers quickly from abuse inflicted by the road life. Too much to drink the night before? No big deal. You wake up, puke, down a few cups of coffee, and get on with the day. Guys in the band getting on your nerves? Ah, fuck it! Just a phase. You'll get over it. While the road definitely loses its appeal with age, there's something legitimately romantic and exciting about living that nomadic life when you're young. As we became increasingly rich and famous, the quality of the accoutrements improved: hotter chicks, more drugs, five-star hotels, and private jets. But we had no complaints about life even on the lower rung of the rock star ladder.

Groupies were there from the beginning, although it wasn't as big a deal to me as it was to some of the other guys in the band. I never had problems attracting women. I started having girlfriends when I was twelve years old; sex was no great mystery to me by the time I went out on the road with KISS. Don't get me wrong—I could whore with the best of them, especially when Jeanette and I were in one of our many periods of estrangement. But I didn't chase pussy like I'd never seen it before. I've heard stories about these guys who become rock stars and all of a sudden they're getting laid all the time, and they basically lose their minds. I mean, I had already been with at least fifty women by the time I put on the KISS makeup for the very first time. If you've been with only one or two women (and had to beg for whatever you got off them), it must be intoxicating to suddenly have groupies falling all over you. You go from getting laid once or twice a year to getting laid a hundred times by a hundred different women. It can be a little disorienting.

I sort of got the feeling that Gene fell into this category. I can't say for sure because I don't know a lot about his sexual history prior to KISS, but I do know that once we got out on the road, Gene reacted like a starving man at a smorgasbord. I believe Gene is a sex addict, in much the same way that I'm an alcoholic. We all have our issues and vices, and I saw Gene's behavior affect him and the band sometimes in a negative way. Maybe not to the extent that my drinking impacted the band, but certainly there were consequences.

Gene has had a lot of unkind things to say about me over the years. Some of the criticism is legitimate. In sobriety you embrace accountability, and I can't deny that my drinking and drug use eventually became highly disruptive and problematic. But some of the personal jabs have been harder to take, partly because we were all friends at one time, and we did do something remarkable, but also because Gene wasn't exactly the easiest guy to get along with, either. Fastidious, if not downright anal in his professional life, Gene was an utter mess in his personal life. I guess having a love for money doesn't have anything to do with cleanliness. I should know—for the first several tours Gene and I were roommates. Strange, considering we had so little in common. A more logical pairing would have been Paul and Gene in one room, me and Peter in the other. At first I thought it had something to do with the fact that Peter and I were the guys who liked to party, and by splitting us up the risk of catastrophic behavior was minimized. But that wasn't the case at all. Paul knew Gene well enough by this point to understand that he was a lousy roommate. As I quickly discovered, Gene was an epic slob. I remember the first time we were sitting in our hotel room after a show, and I looked over at Gene, and saw him spitting on the floor, over and over.

"What the fuck are you doing, man?"

Gene cleared his throat, dragged up a thick wad of phlegm, and spat it onto the carpet.

"Throat's killing me," he said in a raspy voice.

On one hand I felt bad for him. Gene had a problem. Whenever he did the fire breathing, which was just about every night, for hours afterward he'd be spitting and coughing up shit. The kerosene really agitated his system, which was understandable. What wasn't understandable was his insistence on spitting all over the floor. I was afraid to walk to the bathroom in the middle of the night for fear of stepping in a pile of mucus.

"Jesus, Gene, can't you at least use a garbage can or something?"

"*Hwwwwwwwwwk.*"

Another gob of phlegm, another puddle on the floor. It was disgusting, although not as unnerving as the crabs.

See, Gene in those days seemed to live in a state of perpetual infestation. He would fuck almost anything (and I think he's admitted as much). Short, tall; plump, svelte; attractive . . . merely tolerable. We all opened our beds to companionship on a regular basis, but somehow Gene was the one who would end up with bugs in his bush. I got creeped out just thinking about it; when you're rooming with a guy, and you know he has pubic lice . . . well, it's a little disturbing. Every time I scratched my balls I'd wonder whether the little bloodsuckers had crept into my bed as well, leaving me infected simply because of proximity.

Sometimes it turned out that I had been. It wasn't just the fact that I shared a room with Gene that left me vulnerable. In those days we did everything on the fly. Stages were set up and torn down in record time. We packed lightly and traveled fast. As a consequence, our costumes were often thrown together in a single pile and packed into one suitcase, sometimes without even being washed. You can imagine how that worked out—the suitcase filled with hot, sweaty leather, crabs jumping gleefully from the Demon to the Starchild to the Cat and the Spaceman. Must have been like a giant petri dish. And sure enough, within a few days we'd all be walking around, tugging at our crotches, scratching incessantly.

Gene would just laugh.

"Occupational hazard, boys. You'll be fine."

So you see, even when we weren't sharing women (which we did from time to time), we were still sharing the experience and the aftereffects. The thing is, when you're young and crazy, it isn't that big a deal. You go to the drugstore, apply some ointment or medicated shampoo, and you move on. Almost nothing bothered us back then. Compared to the modern-day consequences of unprotected, anonymous sex, pubic lice was a relatively minor inconvenience. You didn't have to worry about sexually transmitted diseases—well, not anything that could kill you, anyway. I remember when AIDS hit the scene in the 1980s; it was scary. Prior to that you worried about crabs, or maybe syphilis or gonorrhea if you were really unlucky. Those things were easily dealt with. Every month or two you'd go see the doc and get a shot of penicillin. Not necessarily because you'd contracted anything, but just as a precautionary measure. Given my behavior over the years I was incredibly lucky. Never had anything more debilitating than a urinary tract infection. It could have been so much worse.

The funny thing is, Gene was actually somewhat bashful when it came to his sexual escapades. He was, by nature, a private man. Peter and I occasionally shared women. Paul and I, too! Sometimes the three of us would share women. Later on, when there were more women than we could handle, we'd pass the chicks on to our bodyguards and the road crew. There was a pecking order (or fucking order), mind you. Bodyguards and roadies got leftovers or extras; it was never the other way around. Gene rarely joined the festivities. No orgies for Gene. Shit, he wouldn't even shower with any of the other guys in the band. The three of us, we'd take off our makeup in the dressing room, jump in the shower room together, then get dressed in front of each other and go back to the hotel. It was like being on a baseball team or something, and this was our locker room. Not to Gene, though. He'd go off by himself, or wait until we were done. Maybe he never played team sports when he was younger?

What can I tell you? Gene is eccentric. Always has been. He had a lot of idiosyncrasies. That's okay. To each his own. I just thought it was a little strange.

Our first tour began in Canada, in the dead of winter, and the main thing I recall is being unbelievably cold the entire time. I didn't mind, though. Here I was, almost twenty-three years old, and I'd never even been on an airplane before, so the whole experience was new and exciting. Our first show was in Edmonton, Alberta; there was about two feet of snow on the ground, and yet still people came out to see us. I'm not even sure how they had any idea who we were. Maybe they were confused. Sure seemed that way sometimes. We'd hit the stage at 100 miles an hour, blowing the roof off the place, and people would just stand there for the first twenty minutes, their mouths hanging open in stunned disbelief. I couldn't even tell if they liked the music or hated it, or if they'd come just because they'd heard about this strange new band that wore makeup and costumes, and they just wanted to see what it was all about.

The special effects on those first few tours were naturally limited by technology and resources, but we did the best we could with what we had. On one of our first trips through Canada I decided to go out and get some smoke bombs and fireworks and try to incorporate them into the show. The physics of a Les Paul (my Gibson guitar of choice at the time—and I'm still a Gibson guy after all these years) presented some obstacles to what I wanted to accomplish. It had a back plate that was virtually airtight, meaning everything went to the channel where the wires met the pickups. I wanted smoke to come out of my guitar—real smoke, not dry-ice smoke—but I realized that if I put a smoke bomb in that back chamber and lit a fuse, all the smoke would have to come out of the pickups, because that was the only canal through which it could travel. So in the middle of a show, right before one of my solos, I picked up a cigarette lighter and lit the fuse. It looked all right and the crowd seemed to get into it, but I wanted more smoke. Unfortunately, I soon discovered that while the smoke didn't necessarily affect my playing, it did affect the equipment, screwing up tone and volume controls. So that whole concept went out the window for a while, until I could get together with an engineer and come up with a more practical design.

The most important thing was that we played with conviction, regardless of whether we were headlining or opening for another act, and we came across as being a serious band—a powerful, exciting visual band. People got caught up in that. Usually by the end of the show, or even halfway through, as the special effects (the flash pots, the fog and the fire, and the smoke bombs) kicked in, people would get completely wrapped up in the show and we'd win the audience over. Even the folks who started off being skeptical would invariably be applauding and calling for encores, asking for more. They might not have known what they'd just seen, but they sure as hell wanted to see more of it.

Critics were less easily impressed. We got ripped in the *New York Times*, ripped in *Rolling Stone*, ripped in *CREEM*. Serious rock journalists seemed incapable of looking past the makeup and costumes and objectively reviewing our performances or recordings. Or maybe they just hated everything about us. I don't know. But the negative reviews served mainly to fuel curiosity and controversy. Some critics were less spiteful, offering grudging respect for our musicianship and writing, and especially for the energy we brought to our shows. Mainly, though, it was word of mouth that proved most beneficial to KISS. We built a fan base the old-fashioned way, by getting out and playing night after night, in town after town, encouraging legions of fans to join what would come to be known as the KISS Army.

The most interesting moments occurred when KISS tried to enter the realm of stodgy, mainstream entertainment. Bill Aucoin and Neil Bogart weren't about to leave any opportunity for publicity unexploited, so while KISS might have been seen by some as a hard rock band (bordering on metal) whose members were into weird satanic imagery or sadomasochistic fetishism (neither true, of course), our management craved exposure to a more diverse audience. In short, they wanted KISS to be seen and heard by everyone, from teenage stoners in New Jersey to housewives in the Midwest.

So we taped three songs during a performance on Dick Clark's *In Concert*, which was one of the few places on network television (cable was little more than a blip on the radar at the time) where a band could be seen and heard. We taped the show in late February—performing "Firehouse," "Black Diamond," and "Nothin' to Lose"—and it aired at the end of March. Dick was terrific, as smart and gracious as I'd expected him to be. I'd grown up watching *American Bandstand* and always thought Dick was not just an astute businessman but a real music fan as well. He treated us professionally, without a hint of condescension or bemusement. In return we performed live and with our customary fury. This wasn't a small thing—most bands who appeared on television shows in the seventies opted for the safety of recorded music and lip-synching. Not KISS. Same thing when we went on NBC's *The Midnight Special*. KISS was a live band, a spectacle. There was no point in faking it.

KISS just trying to be KISS—with each of us staying in character, regardless of the circumstances or venue—could lead to moments of unintended hilarity and genuine "What the fuck!?" cluelessness. Like the time we appeared on *The Mike Douglas Show*, in April 1974. Now, I'll say for the record that I always kind of liked Mike Douglas. Like Dick Clark, he was a Philadelphia guy seemingly too polite and well-mannered for the town that made him famous. A bit of a square, too, but that was okay. I'd grown up watching *American Bandstand* on weekends and *The Mike Douglas Show* on weekday afternoons. It was a plain-vanilla TV talk show, weirdly comforting in its blandness. You could always count on Mike to smile his way through a show, regardless of the guests, and to perform a song or two in his own little lounge act sort of way. He seemed like a legitimately nice guy, and I don't think it was just an act.

Still, it was a bizarre decision for KISS to use *The Mike Douglas Show* as the forum for its first live interview on national television. But, as always, there was a method to the madness, and it sprang mainly from the dementedly fertile mind of Neil Bogart. Neil heard about a promotional contest, hatched by a pair of Florida disc jockeys, to use our band's name as a hook for a kissing contest promoted by their radio station. This was the sort of nonsense that could help a band in its infancy; too much of it, though, could destroy a band's reputation. KISS always walked the fine line between parody and promotion. It was easy to lose your soul if you did too much of this sort of thing, and God knows there was no shortage of people who wanted to exploit the fanaticism of KISS fans.

In this case the idiocy began with what appeared to be a fairly benign kissing contest. But Neil took the concept nationwide, and even suggested that KISS do a cover of the old Bobby Rydell song "Kissin' Time" as a way to help promote the contest.

If ever there was a moment when the guys in the band were united in their opinion of Neil, this was it. We owed the guy just about everything, sure, but a cover version of "Kissin' Time," the sugary little teenybopper tune from the late 1950s?

It was spectacularly inappropriate. Completely fucking nuts. And we all knew it. KISS covering "Kissin' Time" made no sense at all. It made a mockery of everything we were trying to do. We were supposed to be loud, edgy, dangerous. Why in the name of Christ would we try to be a bubblegum band?

"Because it's brilliant," Neil argued. "People will love it."

There was a twisted logic to the promotion, and I suppose, in the end, it had precisely the impact Neil wanted, which was to get people talking about KISS and to create more opportunities for exposure. It was never about the music with Neil. It was about the show. It was about making money and expanding the brand. But at what cost? We all wanted fame and adulation, but in the weeks that we rewrote and recorded "Kissin' Time," none of us felt very good about what we were doing. This was the first time I felt like our deal with the devil—choosing style over substance—had unintended and seriously unpleasant consequences. And I think all the guys—even Gene, who never met a promotional opportunity he couldn't wrap his tongue around—felt the same way. But Neil was the boss. He owned Casablanca Records. He could pull the plug any time he wanted. He could cut our touring and recording budgets. He was the ringmaster, and we were part of the circus.

The show must go on, right?

"Kissin' Time" was recorded as a single and added to the first album when it was reissued a few months after initial release. We all hated the song—much more than we hated the contest promotion, actually. The contest was stupid but harmless; the song damaged our reputation.

Anyway, it was the contest that brought us to Philadelphia and *The Mike Douglas Show,* where we'd perform live (we did "Firehouse," not "Kissin' Time"), but only after Gene had been invited to chat with Mike and his panel (which included comedians Totie Fields and Robert Klein) for a few minutes, just prior to introducing the winners of the national kissing contest. Serving as the unofficial face of KISS, Gene sauntered out onto the stage in character while the rest of us watched on closed-circuit television backstage.

"We have a new rock group for you, Totie," Mike had said, just before holding up a copy of *KISS*. "But before we see them perform, I want you to meet one of the members of this act close-up."

As the boys and I howled with laughter backstage, and the crowd reacted with disbelief, Gene took a seat between Mike and Totie.

"Mind if I spread my wings?" he asked, unfurling his spindly frame (made even longer thanks to eight-inch platform shoes) and exposing the batlike torso of his costume.

Mike played along good-naturedly, but when Gene described himself as "evil incarnate," Totie Fields cast him a look that at first seemed to betray disgust or revulsion, but was quickly revealed to be merely annoyance. Hey, Gene was just doing his shtick. He was being the Demon, or whatever the fuck he thought he was. If it had been me, and I was supposed to stay in character, I would have walked out there and cackled stupidly and said, "Hey, Mike, I'm the Spaceman! Nice to meet you." None of it was real or to be taken seriously. It was supposed to be fun, and I thought Gene did a great job with it. But as the interview went on, and the repartee grew sharper, I couldn't help but be thankful that I hadn't been asked to do the job.

"Wouldn't it be funny if under this he was just a nice Jewish boy?" an exasperated Totie said at one point.

The crowd roared as Gene smiled coyly.

"You should only know," he said with a chuckle. It was intended as an inside joke. Gene, of course, was 100 percent Jewish, having been born in Israel under the name Chaim Witz. I doubt Totie Fields knew anything about Gene's background, but she didn't miss a beat. Totie, after all, was a professional comedian, and Gene was no match for her when it came to trading one-liners.

"I do," she shot back. "You can't hide the hook!"

Gene furled his brow and snarled halfheartedly. He was smart enough to know when he'd been beaten. The interview then turned to the subject of the national kissing contest and the "winners" were brought out onstage. Gene stood and wrapped them both in his bat wings, and a few minutes later we all came out and performed "Firehouse."

The whole thing came off fairly well, I thought, and we got good reviews for the show. Believe it or not, some people didn't know how seriously to take Gene. It was brilliant that way, even if it wasn't necessarily intentional. It allowed KISS to maintain the element of danger that was such an important part of our early persona . . . and our early success.

It wasn't all an act.

Although not exactly "evil incarnate," we were threatening. Our fan base was composed largely of adolescent boys and young men, and what parent wants their kids listening to hard rock by a band that looks like it just stepped off the set of a horror movie? We looked dangerous, and at times we behaved recklessly and hedonistically. We didn't try to hide any of that. Well, most of the time, anyway.

In August 1974 we paused in the middle of a tour and relocated to Los Angeles to work on the second KISS album, *Hotter than Hell*. As with the first record, it was an intense experience: three weeks of ten-hour days at Village Recorders, again with Richie Wise and Kenny Kerner producing. We were all tired and starting to feel some pressure from Casablanca, as the first record hadn't exactly been a big hit. Yeah, it had sold around 75,000 copies, but that hadn't even been enough to cover the band's expenses. We hoped to do better with *Hotter than Hell*, but everything was happening so fast that it was becoming hard to tell whether we were even on the right track.

Using songs leftover from the demo and material we'd written on the road, we assembled the record at breakneck speed. My contributions were much more significant than on the first record. I cowrote "Comin' Home" with Paul, and also wrote "Parasite" and "Strange Ways," a song that remains one of my favorites, even though KISS never performed it in concert. I wish now that I'd had the balls to sing "Strange Ways" on that record. It's an emotionally demanding song, heavy and rhythmic, with a great guitar solo at its center. It was all mine and I should have claimed it as such for the record. But I had no confidence in my own vocal ability, especially around Paul and Gene and Peter, who thrived in the spotlight and had a way of pushing through a song—any song—regardless of any vocal limitations. Great singers are talented, sure, but they also have passion. And they're usually arrogant as well. You can't get up there and sing if you don't believe in yourself.

I knew I was a good guitar player.

I had no idea whether I could sing at all. So for the longest time I didn't even try.

"Parasite" I offered to Gene, because it seemed to suit him and he liked it. Rather than give "Strange Ways" to Paul or Gene, though, I offered it to Peter. As the drummer he was the least visible member of KISS (elevating drum riser notwithstanding!), so his ego was perpetually bruised anyway. I thought having a vocal track on the record would make him feel less threatened. Besides, I liked Peter's voice and thought it was right for the song.

Although basically we recorded the album live, the *Hotter than Hell* sessions lacked the spontaneity and thrill that we experienced while making *KISS*. That's not surprising. There's nothing quite like the first record, when everything is new and exciting. Making *Hotter than Hell* felt more like a job . . . a responsibility. It didn't help matters any that we were fish out of water: four New Yorkers in L.A., sequestered on the West Coast for the better part of a month. We'd already been on the road for months and wanted nothing more than to get back home. But Neil wanted us closer to the Casablanca offices so he could keep an eye on things.

In my case the plan backfired. I can look back now and say that my drinking began to escalate during the making of *Hotter than Hell*, partly as a response to the pressure, and partly because I didn't want to be in L.A. Those are just excuses and I offer them not because I want sympathy, but simply as point of illumination. Drinking was my crutch. It had been since I was a teen, and it remained that way through my time in KISS, only with more profound consequences.

On the night before we were supposed to do a photo shoot for *Hotter than Hell*, I got into one of my first serious car accidents. Now, I have a reputation for being one of the world's worst drivers, but that's not entirely well deserved. I'm actually a pretty good driver; I'm just a really bad drunk driver. I've totaled a lot of cars over the years, but I've never had so much as a fender bender while sober. Trouble is, from roughly the mid-1970s to the mid-2000s, whenever I got behind the wheel of a car, the odds were pretty good that I'd been drinking.

This was one of those times.

We were staying at the Ramada Inn on Sunset Boulevard, basically just hanging out and partying whenever we weren't at the studio. I've tried over the years to remember exactly why I left the hotel that particular night and climbed into the front seat of my rented Chevy. But that's the thing about being a forty-year drinker: it takes its toll on your memory, leaving some recollections strikingly vivid, and others filled with holes. I know I was pissed off about something (probably something stupid) because I remember feeling angry as I cruised through the Hollywood Hills, accelerating through turns like I was a Formula One driver. I found this one particular street in the hills challenging, so like an idiot I kept circling around these twists and turns over and over again, trying to navigate the course a little faster each time. Must have made it around the loop at least five or six times! The next thing I knew, my car was spinning out of control and a telephone pole was coming up fast, rising to meet the windshield. The car spun sideways at the last minute, just enough to avoid a head-on collision, but the impact was still severe enough that I was catapulted forward into the windshield.

As the dust settled on the shoulder of the highway, I started to laugh, a natural by-product of being drunk and relieved to be alive. At first I was pretty sure I hadn't even been seriously hurt at all—until I felt something warm trickling down my face. I put a hand to my cheek and wiped away the blood, but the flow continued. I glanced at the rearview mirror, only to discover that it had been shattered, probably after getting rammed by my head.

The car wasn't completely totaled, but neither was it functional. Luckily the accident had occurred not far from the Ramada, so I got out of the car and began to walk. I can only imagine what I must have looked like, lurching along the side of the road, long hair matted, and blood running down my face. I still don't have any idea what happened to the car. I just left it there. Presumably the cops came by, traced the registration, and contacted someone in the band. I don't remember any legal ramifications, but there was blowback for sure.

When I arrived at the hotel I went straight to our road manager's room. He was a big guy named Junior, adept at everything from managing schedules to fighting with shady promoters. Not much scared Junior, but when he threw open the door and saw me standing there, his eyes widened.

"Jesus, Ace! What the fuck happened to you?"

"Doesn't matter," I said. "But I think we need to go to the hospital."

Encrusted in blood and dirt, with a substantial gash on my forehead that was beginning to swell up, I probably looked like I was more seriously injured than I really was. I felt like shit, though. Anyway, they cleaned me up at the ER, gave me some stitches, painkillers, and antibiotics, and sent me on my way.

With one stern order: no makeup allowed.

"If anything gets in that cut, it's liable to get infected," the doc explained. "Trust me—you don't want that."

No, I didn't want that at all. As luck would have it, though, I was supposed to be wearing my makeup the next day for a photo shoot to supplement the new album. I did as instructed and showed up with makeup on only one side of my face, which is why all the photos from that session only show my profile!

As we were shooting, the other guys in the band alternately expressed their concern for my health and shook their heads in disbelief, as if to say, "Fuckin' Ace, man. What's next?"

# 10

# ALIVE!

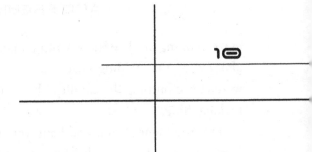

One of my biggest mistakes with KISS was a failure to pay attention to details. That was my nature back then (still is, to a degree). I wasn't that interested in the business side of the business; I was into the creative and fun side, which proved to be problematic when things stopped being fun. In the early days I used to say to myself, "You have the greatest job in the world. You get to do what you love to do, and you're getting paid to do it."

Then one day I woke up, looked in the mirror, bleary-eyed and hungover, and thought, *Man, I'm not digging this at all.*

Maybe if I'd been a bit more attentive and clearheaded as we steamrolled through those first few years, and gotten more positive feedback from everyone on my accomplishments, I'd have been in a position to offer more input and possibly help create a scenario in which I wouldn't have felt compelled to leave. Hindsight, man. It's a bummer. A waste of time, too.

So much shit went down behind the scenes during the first few tours and during the recording of our first three albums. It's almost a miracle the band survived at all. We were working our asses off, touring like crazy, refining our live show, writing material and cranking out record after record, maintaining a pace that today would be unimaginable. We weren't just burning the candle at both ends; we were incinerating the fucking thing.

I'm sure Gene, Peter, and Paul were somewhat aware of the challenges we were facing at that time, but I was basically clueless. When I heard that Neil Bogart wanted us to get back in the studio just a few months after we released *Hotter than Hell,* I was surprised. I knew enough about the record industry to know that it made little sense for us to make a third record so quickly. Unless, of course, things were going very well . . . or very badly.

Even weirder was the news that Neil planned to produce our next album himself. Hey, I liked Neil a lot. We used to hang out a bit and party and I still believe he was one of the most creative people the music industry has ever known. KISS can never repay him for what he did and for the gambles he took on our behalf. Let's be honest, though: Neil was not a hard rock producer. He was a record company executive whose creative instincts about our music were not as reliable as his marketing savvy. My first choice for producer, as always, would have been Eddie Kramer. My second choice would have been to stick with Kenny Kerner and Richie Wise. But Casablanca was Neil's baby; he got to call the shots. And he wanted to sit at the control board.

I didn't understand Neil's motivation, and frankly I didn't care. But I didn't think it made any sense, and neither did anyone else. After the "Kissin' Time" debacle we were skeptical when it came to Neil's artistic input (Paul seemed the most bothered by the idea). What I didn't fully understand at the time was that Neil was fighting for his career, and for KISS's career as well. Our first couple of albums had sold reasonably well—75,000 copies for *KISS* and about 100,000 for *Hotter than Hell.* Not bad considering we weren't getting much radio airplay and hadn't produced anything close to a hit single. Apparently, though, we still weren't making any money for Casablanca and, more importantly, for our distributor, Warner Bros. Our promotional and touring budget in those days was significantly higher than could be justified by our record sales. It didn't feel to me like we were living extravagantly. Our "salary" was still less than one hundred dollars per week and we continued to book rooms at the lesser hotel chains, doubling up at every stop. Fast food and cheap beer got us through the days and nights. Sure, it was mostly fun, but believe me—it wasn't glamorous.

What I considered frugality, though, Warner Bros. considered wasteful. When Warner declined to give *Hotter than Hell* the promotional push Neil felt it deserved, he basically said to them, "Go fuck yourselves."

Then he told us to get back in the studio.

As was the case with the first two albums, *Dressed to Kill* was assembled quickly. Even though we had to write much of the material while we were recording, and even though Neil wasn't the ideal producer, the whole process was more enjoyable than it had been on *Hotter than Hell.* Knowing that we had hated our time in L.A., Neil agreed to come to New York and record the album at Electric Lady Studios. So we were home, which greatly improved our mood. One thing I didn't understand was why, during the recording process, Neil would smoke pot almost constantly without any objections from Gene or Paul, who were so antidrug. They just looked the other way. Go figure?

There was other crap going on, too. Neil had begun dating Joyce Biawitz, which obviously left Joyce looking like she had a conflict of interest. She and Bill Aucoin were our comanagers, and while managers and record company executives often enjoy cordial relationships, they're not supposed to be having sex with each other. They do, of course. Happens all the time. But it looks very bad and makes everyone uncomfortable. Bill and Joyce were supposed to be looking out for the best interests of their clients, the biggest of which was KISS. And sometimes what KISS wanted was not exactly what Casablanca wanted. That's just the way it works. Talent managers and record company executives are supposed to spar once in a while. And they make strange bedfellows, to say the least. Joyce is a terrific gal and a good manager, but when she started dating Neil, it put everyone in a difficult position. Ultimately, Neil and Joyce married, and Bill became sole manager of KISS, which was the only practical solution. I missed her for some time after that, since she always had a kind word to interject just at the right time and always encouraged me to do my best.

Hanging over all of this was the nagging sense that maybe Casablanca wasn't the right place for us. Primarily out of loyalty to Neil, we'd turned down offers from other labels that wanted to buy out our contract. But the stakes were getting high. We all needed a breakthrough.

*Dressed to Kill* wasn't it.

It's a good album, I think, though not nearly as strong as either of the first two records. Having Neil in the studio with us was kind of a trip—like having your boss looking over your shoulder while you work—but it became obvious fairly early in the process that while Neil had a lot of opinions about how the band should sound, and what types of songs we should record, he lacked the expertise to bring those ideas to life. Paul and Neil butted heads most of all. As a result, many of the technical and creative decisions on *Dressed to Kill* were made by the band members (along with Dave Wittman, the engineer) and we were listed as coproducers with Neil.

Two things really distinguished *Dressed to Kill*. The first was the clever album cover, which featured the four us standing on the corner of Eighth Avenue and Twenty-Third Street, wearing suits and ties . . . and full makeup. We'd done something similar for a *CREEM* photo shoot and liked the concept so much that we went with it for the album. *Here we are, world: just regular guys going to work!*

The second was a song called "Rock and Roll All Nite," written by Gene and Paul with the specific intention of creating a KISS anthem—something fans would wait all night to hear when they went to a live show, and then stand and scream their lungs out to when it was finally played. An anthem is a signature song, the ultimate sing-along. Neil felt like KISS needed something like that and basically instructed Gene and Paul to come up with one. It's an ass-backwards approach to the craft of songwriting, of course. Songs become popular for all kinds of reasons, but the most obvious one is because they're good. You try to write well and perform with honesty, and then you hope your fans respond. There's something very cynical about the idea of creating something designed specifically to provoke a certain reaction.

But that was the way Neil worked, and in this case he was absolutely right. The first time we rehearsed "Rock and Roll All Nite" in the studio I knew it was a good song. When we actually laid down the track, I had a feeling it would be something special. To simulate the effect of thousands of concertgoers chanting along with the chorus, we invited our friends into the studio. It was wild—Neil and Joyce were there, leaning into a microphone. Bill Aucoin, Peter's wife, Lydia, and other people on our team all shouting along with the guys in the band:

"I WANNA ROCK AND ROLL ALL NIGHT! AND PARTY EVERY DAY!"

I think we all knew we had something unique with that song, and in fact it did do fairly well as a single. But it wasn't until we started playing "Rock and Roll All Nite" live (with a blistering guitar solo thrown in for good measure) that it really became the anthem we had hoped for. Fans loved it, and it quickly became one of our signature songs and a reliable showstopping encore for live performances.

Unfortunately, we often weren't given an opportunity to do an encore. As our popularity increased and word of our live shows spread, an interesting thing began to happen. You see, we were still almost exclusively an opening act through our first two tours, but as time went on we began to notice that a growing percentage of the crowd represented KISS fans. It's a tricky thing when you go out on the road as a supporting act. You want to put on a great show; you also want to get the audience all pumped up for the headliner. Those two goals aren't necessarily complementary. If you suck, the crowd will get pissed and boo you off the stage. If you're too good, though, the headliner will get pissed and fire you from the tour, or at least refuse to hire you again. In the beginning a lot of people simply didn't know what to make of KISS, and we won them over anyway. As time went on we found that even though we were the opening act, the audience would sing along to our songs and sometimes get so worked up that they'd want an encore. We always delivered—unless the headliner forbade it, which happened on more than one occasion. It's understandable, really. I mean, KISS was a tough act to follow.

*Dressed to Kill* was released on March 19, 1975; by the time it hit stores KISS had become a live phenomenon. We weren't just a fringe band or a gimmick anymore. We were a band everyone wanted to see, a traveling circus that earned new fans with every stop along the way. Two days after the record was released we played the Beacon Theatre in New York. This was among the highlights of my time in KISS. More so than the other guys, I'd grown up in the New York club scene. The Beacon was a New York landmark, a former movie theater that had recently been converted into a concert hall; in the coming years it would be one of the most popular live music venues in the city. And KISS was at the forefront.

The very first time we played there, we also were the headlining act. What a trip, man! Just a few weeks earlier we'd been in California, opening up for a band called Jo Jo Gunne. By the time we got to New York, the roles had been reversed, and Jo Jo Gunne was opening for KISS. We sold out the Beacon; in fact, we sold out so quickly that a second show was added. More than six thousand tickets were sold, an incredible number for a band that still had not yet had a hit single or album.

I remember feeling an incredible rush of pride and adrenaline when we took the stage at the Beacon, with the crowd outside chanting our name. This was what we had been working so hard to achieve, and the satisfaction was immeasurable. I had a ton of friends in the audience that night. Jeanette was there. So were my parents. I remember the look on my mother's face when I saw her after the show. It was almost as though she couldn't imagine that her son was the same person she'd been watching. It was a mixture of pride and disbelief. Same thing with my father. Dad didn't say much, but I could tell he was proud. Or maybe just relieved that I hadn't turned out to be the complete fuckup he suspected I'd be.

I'm not one to worry about what journalists have to say about my music. Critics can be a snotty and self-important bunch of assholes. I discovered early in KISS that they're completely out of touch with the general public. We made music for the masses; it was popular entertainment, and we were damn good at it. The very things fans loved about KISS—the simplicity, volume, energy, and especially the theatricality—were the things that made so many journalists hate us. And the more highfalutin the publication, the more likely they were to take a crap on our records and performances.

So imagine our surprise the morning after we appeared at the Beacon Theatre, when a review published in the *New York Times* was not only fair, but downright flattering.

*"The whole audience was standing on the seats for the last 45 minutes, an event even in these days of rock emotionalism. . . . It may be overly simple and unpretentious rock, not so much sung as shouted, but Kiss* [*sic*] *communicates a sense of fun and commitment to the music."*

Yeah, I could live with that.

The months that followed the release of *Dressed to Kill* were in some ways among the weirdest of my time in KISS. Not in terms of bad behavior or disputes within the band or anything like that, but simply because we found ourselves treading water, commercially speaking. It made no sense. Here we were, playing bigger venues and drawing bigger crowds. Fans were starting to show up in KISS costumes and makeup. They sang along throughout the show. We had moved something like 200,000 copies of *Dressed to Kill* (again, without the benefit of a Top 10 single). Our live show was so popular that suddenly we were viewed as a threat to many of the bands we had once supported.

At the same time, we kept hearing horror stories from management about our dire financial situation. After splitting with Warner Bros., Casablanca was in big trouble. Neil was financing projects out of his own pocket. KISS was selling a decent number of records, but apparently still not enough to cover the cost of touring. I kept wondering where the money was, only to be told by Bill Aucoin that everything was a bit of a mystery, since Casablanca had been withholding our royalty statements. Bill began running up his credit cards to help keep the band afloat.

I tried to ignore most of this and stay focused on the things I found important: playing and performing. But I couldn't help but wonder what we had to do in order to make KISS a financial success. How could we tap into the enthusiasm (which was rapidly becoming fanaticism) that we saw every night from the stage?

The answer, in retrospect, seems obvious: do a live album. But you have to remember that in 1975 live albums weren't exactly cash cows. A number of bands had tried and failed, so record labels were understandably reluctant to support them. Live albums generally were reserved for supergroups—bands with fan bases so large that you could expect to sell at least a moderate number of albums and therefore not lose money. The prevailing wisdom within the record industry at this time was that live albums were basically a waste of time and effort, especially if the band in question hadn't already accumulated a bunch of hit singles. Live albums for the most part were really nothing more than "greatest hits" packages rearranged and served warm to a ready audience. KISS had no hit singles, no gold records.

Why in the hell would anyone want to buy a live KISS album? More importantly, why would any record label support the idea?

For some reason, though, we thought we could buck the trend. I don't remember who came up with the idea, and I don't think anyone has ever taken credit for it. Everyone involved with KISS understood that we were primarily a live band—a two-hour thrill ride for concert-goers. Our first three records were all solid, but none of them had captured the KISS experience. Maybe the only way to do that was to put out a live album.

The idea was kicked around for months. One night somebody pulled out a copy of *Uriah Heep Live*, a two-record set released in 1973, and that gave us some ideas about concept and packaging. The idea simmered for a while, until Bill got involved and took it to Neil. For the longest time I couldn't believe that Casablanca gave a green light to the project, but I now realize it was basically a decision born of desperation. Part of Bill's argument centered on the fact that a live album would be cheaper to produce than a fourth studio album; even if it failed, there would be less of an investment to recoup. Neil was already floundering. I guess he just figured, *What have we got to lose?*

When I heard that Casablanca had opted to go forward with the live project I was intrigued, and when they told me Eddie Kramer would be in charge, I got really excited. We hadn't worked with Eddie since the demo days, and we all had a ton of respect for him. Even with three albums on our résumé I knew we'd yet to record anything that sounded as strong as the demo we'd put together with Eddie. The guy was a fucking genius. If anyone could do justice to KISS—if anyone could produce a live album by a road-weary theatrical hard rock band and turn it into something unique—it was Eddie. I knew in my gut that he was the right man for the job.

There were a number of different approaches you could take when assembling a live record. The simplest, and probably most cost-effective, was to set up equipment at a single show and try to capture the songs and experience of one night on the road. Eddie had different ideas. Since it's almost impossible to be perfect on any given night, he decided to record five different concerts and cull the best material. When *Alive!* was released in September 1975, hardly anyone knew that this was the strategy we'd employed. Most people presumed the album was an exact re-creation of a single KISS concert performed on May 16, at Cobo Hall in Detroit. This was not the case at all. The recording and remixing of *Alive!* has been the subject of endless speculation and gossip over the years, so I'll try to set the record straight here.

Eddie came out on the road with us and made it clear from the start that he would do whatever he had to do in order to capture the KISS experience on vinyl. No way that was gonna happen in one day. He set up mobile equipment in Detroit, as well as Davenport, Iowa; Cleveland; and Wildwood, New Jersey. Eddie was totally into the whole process, probably more committed to it than we were. It was actually kind of strange. We'd forget that he was there, or what sort of impact his presence might have on the show. I don't think any of us had a clue that a live record would prove to be the turning point in our careers. I sure as hell didn't. Before each of those shows I'd be hanging out in the dressing room, going through the usual routine—applying makeup, warming up, throwing back a few beers—when Eddie would walk in and give us a little pep talk, as well as specific instructions.

"Remember, we're recording tonight, boys. Maybe you could do me a favor and try to move around a little less. Not jump quite so high."

I'd just laugh. KISS was KISS. Asking us to hold back onstage was like asking a dog not to bark. It was in our DNA.

You had to feel a little bit for Eddie. He had his work cut out for him. The things that mattered most to him as a producer—precise playing, clear, pitch-perfect singing—were secondary to us. Not that we didn't want to hit the right notes. I took great pride in my solos and always felt a bit of frustration or sadness after a show if I fucked something up. But the reality of playing live in a theatrical rock band is that mistakes are not uncommon. A live concert is a different animal than a studio performance. When the audience is screaming and you're running all over the stage, sweating and exhausted, your heart racing, things go by in a moment that would be unforgivable in a studio setting. The audience rarely even recognizes the clunkers—they're too caught up in the show. If we were onstage and somebody made a mistake, we'd just plow through it. There was no other option. In the end, all that mattered was that the audience went home happy.

With a KISS concert, the mission was accomplished on a nightly basis. That's what we wanted to project with *Alive!*—the sense of fun and excitement and energy that was such a big part of the KISS experience. Eddie wanted that, too; he also wanted to make a record that sounded great. In order for that to happen, he explained, some minor adjustments would have to be made.

"What do you mean?" I asked him.

"Well, it might be easier if you just listened."

Eddie proceeded to play some of the tracks off the tapes he'd recorded from our concerts, and I have to admit—they were problematic. Oh, sure, they were loud and spirited and generally well played, and the crowd was into it. But there were many mistakes. Not just by the band, either. A lot can go wrong when you're recording a concert, technically speaking. The mix can be off, recording equipment can fail, instruments can be out of tune. Getting it right on the first try, to a degree that would please people who've paid ten bucks for the album—mostly hard-core fans who already know how the songs are supposed to sound—is no small task.

"Don't worry," Eddie assured us. "We'll fix everything in the studio."

*The studio?*

So that's what we did. We all went into Electric Lady, and for the better part of three weeks we tinkered and tweaked . . . and sometimes completely overdubbed songs. None of us got off the hook completely. There were times when Eddie was unhappy with Paul's singing or Gene's singing. While he was generally pleased with my solos, I didn't nail every note as well as I might have. Sometimes Peter's tempo was off just a bit on the drums. As the studio sessions went on we became increasingly flexible in terms of what we considered to be acceptable doctoring. We all agreed that Eddie had a strong ear and a great production sense. We trusted that he could bring *Alive!* to life in a way that would please our fans without compromising our integrity.

Eddie wanted a record that seemed like a live album, that reminded people of how it felt to be at a KISS concert . . . without having to indulge the imperfections of a live performance. Does that mean it was a fake? I don't think so. The end justifies the means in this case. And anyway, Eddie didn't do anything that producers of live records hadn't been doing for years, in one form or another. He just did it better. I remember the first time I walked into the studio and saw these long loops set up, running between mike stands and tape machines, to add canned applause in the mixing process. This is done all the time with live records, although most people don't realize it. You add applause at the end of a song or the beginning of a new track not simply to heighten excitement or to give the record a more concertlike feel, but also for the sake of continuity. It sweetens the sound.

Same thing with the vocals. We rerecorded a bunch of tracks not with the idea of replacing whole songs but rather so that Eddie could grab bits and pieces and make it seem like we nailed the harmonies in concert. This all seems pretty harmless today, in the age of prefab, cookie-cutter pop stars with shitty voices made listenable only through the magic of Auto-Tune. To be perfectly candid, I didn't even think much of it back then. We were just trying to make the record a better product. And let's be clear about something: it wasn't just Eddie's idea; it was a collaborative effort. KISS was never known as one of the greatest live musical bands. We were a *show*. In fact, that's what started to bother me after a while—the inescapable notion that with KISS, the music was secondary. Even by this point the majority of reviews focused less on our songs than on the special effects and makeup. That's just the way it was and we all accepted it (me less than the others, as it turned out). But Eddie was absolutely right. There was no escaping the fact that the original concert recordings needed . . . *enhancement*. I suppose if we had been a major platinum-selling band prior to the recording of *Alive!* we might have been slightly more cautious about screwing around with the actual live tracks. At this point, however, we were all starving for a breakthrough.

I looked at the live album as a roll of the dice. What was the worst that could happen? People would ignore it? Or our fans would buy it and we'd have another modestly successful record? The one thing I couldn't envision was that *Alive!* would become one of the biggest-selling live albums in history, or that it would utterly change my life. But that's exactly what happened.

*Alive!* was released on September 10, 1975. Our fourth album in eighteen months. Christ, that's amazing. I remember feeling overworked and tired, but when I look back on it now, the pace seems almost suicidal. Four albums, including a double-live album—in a year and a half. That's a ridiculous amount of KISS music out in the public realm in a very short span of time. No one would do that today. No one would even consider it. Even the most devoted fans of the best bands would overdose.

Not KISS fans. They devoured *Alive!* in numbers we couldn't have imagined. It went gold, then it went platinum (one million copies sold) . . . double platinum. "Rock and Roll All Nite" (with a new guitar solo) became our first Top 20 single. The album hit the *Billboard* charts quickly and stayed there for two years.

Two fucking years!

Last time I checked, *Alive!* had sold more than four million copies worldwide; it continues to sell well even today. The album's impact was apparent not just to us, but to the whole record industry. A year later Peter Frampton became a superstar with the double-live record *Frampton Comes Alive!* And with the release of the live album *At Budokan* Cheap Trick became one of the biggest-selling bands in the world.

I'd like to think we had something to do with their success.

No one questioned whether the album was really live or whether we sounded that good in person. People simply ate it up. Nearly a decade would pass (and I'd be on a prolonged hiatus from the band) before Eddie started talking about the making of *Alive!* and the amount of studio work that went into it. Some fans were angry; many didn't care. If someone asks me today whether *Alive!* truly is a "live album," I'll usually answer with a question and a shrug:

"Does it really matter?"

It's a terrific album, true to the KISS spirit in every way. Nothing gives me greater pride than to hear some young guitarist say he learned how to play by listening to *Alive!* or a veteran guitarist (like my buddies Mike McCready of Pearl Jam and Slash of Velvet Revolver and Guns N' Roses) tell me how inspired he was by the solos on *Alive!* In many ways that's more rewarding than all the gold records in the world. *Alive!* is an iconic album, one that reflects as clearly as possible what it was like to be at a KISS concert in 1975.

Isn't that what counts?

11

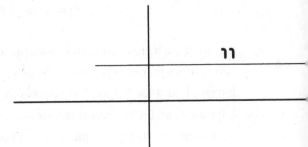

# THE KISS HITS THE FAN

Is it possible to circle a date on the calendar—a specific day or time—when you realize everything has changed? I'm not sure. In the year following the release of *Alive!* my life was turned inside out, to the point where I barely recognized myself or the life I was living. It happened gradually, and then all at once. I don't know how else to explain it. You wake up one morning and find that you've traded a bedroom in your parents' house for an apartment in Manhattan or a mansion in the Connecticut woods. You're no longer taking cabs or relying on your girlfriend for transportation. Instead you're driving a Porsche (and three other cars are sitting in the driveway,). No more Ramadas or Holiday Inns. Five-star hotels all the way. No more Denny's (not that there's anything wrong with Denny's, by the way), no more IHOP.

But the biggest change, for me—the most glaring reminder that KISS was no longer just four guys from New York with big dreams and weird ideas about how to make them come true—was when we actually went out to play at night. Not only were we headlining almost every show, but we were playing some of the biggest arenas in the country, and soon we were touring in Europe and Asia. More often than not, the venue was sold out. The money is nice, of course, especially when you haven't had a lot before. The money buys freedom, if not necessarily happiness, and it is a barometer of success. But if you're a serious musician there's nothing like playing in a packed arena, in front of twenty thousand screaming fans. That was my fantasy when I was a kid, and suddenly it wasn't a fantasy anymore.

In the mid- to late 1970s KISS was as hot a ticket as there was in rock 'n' roll. I remember playing three nights at Madison Square Garden, with my family in the audience, and thinking, *How the fuck did this happen?* Here I am, the black sheep of the family, and by the time I'm in my mid-twenties, I'm the golden kid. I can do no wrong. It really warmed my heart to see the reaction of my parents and in-laws and other family members when they would come to a KISS concert in New York. I'd call them up, give them the full treatment: limo ride, backstage VIP passes, meet-and-greet with celebrities. The whole nine yards. And it was wonderful to be able to do that for them. To be honest, though, I'm not sure how much everyone really understood the whole rock scene. The only thing they knew was that I was famous and there was a lot of money being made, which must have meant that I was successful. Everyone seemed proud of that, but it probably baffled them a bit. I mean, shit . . . it baffled me, too.

How do you prepare for something like that? You don't. You *can't*. Eighteen months earlier I'd been happily pocketing seventy dollars a week from Bill Aucoin. And making it last! Now we were breaking attendance records everywhere we went. We'd gone from freak show to household name seemingly overnight. All hell broke loose. Everywhere we went, it was KISS mania. We'd built a fan base prior to *Alive!*, but now everything was amplified tenfold.

In Cadillac, Michigan, the entire town celebrated its love affair with the band, hosting what amounted to a weeklong KISS festival. Bill Aucoin thought it would be great publicity to play along with the town, so we flew into Cadillac on October 9, 1975, and took part in the Cadillac High School homecoming parade; we even played a live show (a tamer, more family-friendly version of our usual performance). We turned it into a big media event. I had a lot of fun doing that because it was kind of tongue-in-cheek and irreverent. We put makeup on the mayor and some of the other local officials. Everyone got into the spirit of things. I thought it was a terrific event, because it represented thinking outside the box; it deviated from the norm, which I always enjoyed. I like the unexpected. I don't like to know what I'm going to be doing a year from now, or five years from now. I like spontaneity; that's what keeps my creative juices flowing. That said, I can't stress strongly enough how little involvement I had in the promotion, marketing, and merchandising of the KISS brand. I just went along for the ride.

A lot of the time it was fun, of course. It's fun until . . . well, until it's not fun anymore. I felt invincible for the longest time—I think we all did. There was a rhythm to each show, and it began in the dressing room, while we were putting on our makeup. Like four chicks in a beauty parlor we'd sit in front of the mirrors and dab at our faces and gossip, never really looking at each other but carrying on an endless four-way discussion. The dressing room was completely off-limits to anyone but our innermost circle. Not even wives or girlfriends were permitted in the dressing room. Just band members, our road manager, and the wardrobe girls who helped us with our costumes. Later on we hired a hairdresser to apply wigs to those band members who needed a little help. We'd sit in our chairs, in full costumes, being transformed into our various characters, and we'd chat about what had happened during the day (or the previous night) or whatever little changes we had planned for the show. If someone had screwed up the previous night, or in sound check, this was the place where we'd talk about it. Sometimes the conversation could be blunt:

*"Watch the tempo!" "Don't fuck up again!" "Ace, don't forget the fuckin' solo!"*

More often, though, the mood was light. Gene often showed us Polaroid snapshots of the girls he'd been with the night before, and that brought out mixed reactions from all of us. Sometimes to the point of hysterical laughter. We'd pump ourselves up, talk about putting on a great show, and joke about how much fun we were going to have afterward. Even then, for me, the party had already begun. I started drinking before the show and kept at it while we played. Afterward we'd usually jump in a limo and head back to the hotel, where we'd shower and change and become acquainted with the more attractive members of the burgeoning KISS Army. If we needed to be somewhere right after the show, we'd use the shower facilities at the arena. Usually, anyway. Once in a while there would be a party at the venue, which allowed us to fulfill the wishes of fans who were more interested in having sex with the *characters* in KISS than in having sex with the men behind the makeup.

*"Pleeeeeeease, I want to fuck the Spaceman!"*

I sometimes accommodated. Different strokes, right?

More often, though, we retreated to the hotel and the privacy of a hospitality suite, where an assortment of beautiful gals would be waiting. We used to call it the "Chicken Coop," for obvious reasons.

To any normal person living a regular life, this probably sounds completely bizarre. But it was normal for us. The hedonistic, aberrant behavior becomes a way of life when you're at the top of the rock 'n' roll ladder. If you want to have sex five times a day, with five different women? All you have to do is open the door. That wasn't normally my cup of tea, but Gene loved every minute. It becomes a game, a way to pass the time (or, in Gene's case, maybe an addiction?). You take advantage of it for any number of reasons, the most obvious being boredom and availability. Same thing with drugs. I have an addictive personality. I'm an alcoholic. I don't want to minimize the damage that drinking can do, but for the longest time that's all I was: a drinker.

When the money began pouring in, that all changed.

There was a time when cocaine absolutely scared the shit out of me. Not in the way that it scares me now, which is basically the way any drug, including alcohol, scares me—a good, healthy "if I start using again I will die" kind of fear. I'm talking about a gut-level fear. The kind you have when you're a little kid; a fear of the unknown. Even though I started drinking at a young age and experimented with sniffing glue and became a casual user of marijuana, all by the time I got into high school, there was something about cocaine or any hard drug that scared me. As a kid I considered cocaine and heroin to be on the same level, and to be capable of approximately the same degree of devastation. I didn't want to touch hard drugs, and in those days cocaine fell into that category. It wasn't a chic drug; it wasn't cool or hip. In my eyes, it was no different than heroin, which was the dangerous drug . . . the *loser's* drug.

I never did get into heroin. In fact, aside from the one or two times when I suspect someone laced my coke with it, I never even tried heroin. But cocaine?

Oh yeah. Big-time.

Our next album, *Destroyer,* represented a departure for KISS, and not merely because of the cocaine and Courvoisier on the mixing console. The producer on *Destroyer* was Bob Ezrin, a studio wizard best known for his work with Alice Cooper, and a guy so widely acknowledged as being a production genius that everyone was basically willing to look the other way when it became apparent that he had a few vices of his own.

That was one of the things that bothered me most about Paul and Gene—they were very selective in their moral indignation. Bob was a brilliant producer, so they gave him a free pass, much the same way they did with Neil Bogart during the production of *Dressed to Kill.* I think the word *hypocritical* might be apropos at this point.

I remember the very first time I tried coke. It was during the recording of the *Destroyer* album, in December 1975. Watching Bob and others partake of the glittery crystalline powder during the recording and mixing process intrigued me and brought out my curiosity. I figured that if a genius like Bob did it, and he was very successful at what he did, then maybe it was the missing link I had been looking for in my life. I asked Peter if he could hook me up with some since I knew he had a connection. He scored some coke for me and it changed my life from that day forward.

The first time I ripped a few lines of blow I felt like I'd discovered something almost as good as sex. My whole body came to life. It was a terrific buzz on its own, and in the beginning it gave me focus and clarity, but you know what I liked the most about coke?

It made me a better drinker.

I was already damned prodigious, but cocaine put me in a different league. It allowed me to drink longer and harder without passing out. I could party way into the wee hours, into the next morning and afternoon, maybe right on into the next night if I felt like it. If I had my blow I could keep on going—like the Energizer Bunny. Hour after depraved hour. What I discovered—what any connoisseur of cocaine discovers—is the remarkable ability of the human body to withstand abuse. Cocaine is a stimulant, alcohol a depressant. Used smartly (notice I didn't say "intelligently"), the two chemicals balance each other out. It's almost like a speedball, the alcohol (or, in the case of a speedball, the heroin) depressing the central nervous system and the cocaine jolting it back to life. Of course, I'd never done a speedball, never would have considered it. Mix heroin and cocaine? No fuckin' way. Too dangerous. People I knew had died from that concoction. You'd have to be out of your mind. But cocaine and alcohol? Oh yeah. All night long, baby.

Once I started doing cocaine, there was no stopping me. It really was that clear a line of demarcation, and it began with *Destroyer*. For a while it didn't even have an adverse impact on my playing. Cocaine can actually make you sharper. For me, in smaller doses, it was like guzzling coffee. I had tried speed a few times and didn't like it—made me too jumpy. But coke worked beautifully, especially in combination with alcohol. I'd get comfortably numb, as they say.

Coke went hand in hand with sex, too, which was another terrific selling point. You could have more sex on cocaine. You could have better sex on cocaine. In the beginning, at least, I thought it was a wonder drug, the perfect enhancement for the rock star life.

As with every drug, though, you can build up a tolerance to cocaine, and after a while it doesn't work quite as well. You have to do more blow to get the desired effect. You're always chasing the memory of that first buzz from the first line, but you never seem to get it again. Then you need more alcohol to come down. Pretty soon the highs aren't as high and the lows are crushingly painful. There's a cycle to it. You end up taking tranquilizers or sleeping pills to fall asleep. I always called it a triad. If you're going to do alcohol and coke in large quantities, you have to have downers at your disposal, because the alcohol ain't enough. If you're going to stay up for two or three days doing coke (which I did on several occasions), you need tranquilizers or sleeping pills. Then, after a while, you start taking pain pills to manage the crushing morning-after pain—hangovers like nothing you can imagine. It's crazy stuff. My hangovers were terrible, like the worst migraine in the world. I'd wake up and vomit so hard I'd see stars. I was doing champagne for a while, and those were terrible hangovers. A champagne-cocaine hangover is unbelievable. Any drug-alcohol hangover is worse than an alcohol hangover by itself. Your whole body aches, because the cocaine intensifies the headache and makes you feel more edgy once it wears off. Your nerves are frazzled.

So what do you do? Quit drinking? Lay off the blow?

Course not. You start taking painkillers and tranquilizers. Every morning begins with Percocet and every night ends with Valium. Then night blurs into day, and pretty soon you're taking both of them by the fistful, and slowly you begin to lose your edge, as well as your mind. One day you wake up and realize you've crossed a line, and you say to yourself, "Man I am strung out. And not only am I strung out, I don't even know me anymore."

That's pretty scary.

It happens more quickly for some people than for others. The disease progresses differently in each person. For some people it takes only a year or two to become a full-blown addict. For others it takes much longer. I was leading a life totally detached from reality. I went from having little money or worldly possessions to having staggering wealth and fame. And I hadn't the vaguest fucking clue as to how to handle any of it.

Like I said, I'd had a couple of bad experiences with drugs in high school, so for the longest time I was content to stick with what worked for me, which was mainly booze. Cocaine was extremely expensive in 1975. We're not talking about cheap cocaine; we're not talking about crack. You didn't get into cocaine unless you had the resources to do it right.

After *Alive!* I had the resources, and pretty soon I had the contacts, which led me down the rabbit hole in fairly short order. For example, one of my coke dealers was this guy named Geoff who supposedly had been a mercenary in South America. I don't know whether that was in fact true, but the guy certainly had an intense and dangerous vibe about him. He also had some of the best blow in the city. I'd gotten to know Geoff through Peter, and before long he became my primary source of cocaine. Whatever else the guy might have been, he was no slouch in the drug trade. His shit was uniquely pure and powerful. Not cheap, either. As a result, Geoff had a very elite clientele, with lots of celebrities, as well as the usual assortment of doctors, lawyers, and Wall Street types. I remember stopping by his place on Eighth Street one day and passing one of the Stones on the way out. Not that it was a big deal that they used blow. In the late seventies, it was hard to find anyone with money or fame who *didn't* do coke. People did blow the way people today drink beer. It seemed almost normal.

I used to hear stories about Geoff and how his clientele was expanding beyond the point where he could safely or reasonably accommodate everyone. He was selling shit uncut, the story went, and to get uncut blow from South America was considered a real score. Word got out and the traffic in and out of Geoff's apartment building became uncomfortably busy. It was the weirdest thing. He was clearly running a business, but he didn't treat it that way, probably because he was too busy getting fucked up himself. Sometimes he'd deliver, and other times I had to call him up, set up an appointment, and go down to his place in the East Village. Most of the time I'd exchange cash for blow, and instead of just running out of there, I'd hang out and do a few lines with Geoff and whoever else was hanging around. He wasn't exactly a friend of mine. Like a lot of people I got to know in those days, he was just a guy I did drugs with.

One day I missed an appointment to cop some blow. I forget why or what happened. It really doesn't matter. The point of the story is that on the day I was supposed to meet Geoff, he and his girlfriend were killed. Shot in the head—execution-style, the cops said—right in their own apartment. I remember seeing the story on the news and feeling a mixture of sadness and relief. It shouldn't have come as a surprise that Geoff was killed. If his background story was accurate, it's easy to envision a scenario in which he had managed to offend his distributors in South America, or had maybe edged into territory previously controlled by the mob in New York. He was playing with fire. And as one of his best clients, and one of his party partners, so was I. If something hadn't come up, I could have been there the day Geoff was killed.

I guess a guardian angel was looking over my shoulder on that day. It wasn't the first time, and it wouldn't be the last.

When we set out to make *Destroyer*, Bob Ezrin had been brought in specifically because he understood the challenges associated with taking a big, live theatrical act and translating its sound to the studio. So far, KISS hadn't done that. We were a popular live band that reached a tipping point on the strength of a live album. The next logical step was to capitalize on that newfound popularity by recording a terrific studio album, which meant making some changes in the way things had been done.

Around the time we hooked up with Bob, he was among the hottest producers in the business, having worked with Dr. John, Alice Cooper, and Lou Reed. Going strictly by his reputation and résumé, I was looking forward to working with Bob, and while I think *Destroyer* is an interesting and even innovative KISS record, the recording process isn't something I recall with great affection. Part of that is due to the fact that sometimes I was intimidated by Bob, especially when I couldn't come up with a guitar-solo idea fast enough to suit his needs.

You have to understand where Bob was coming from. I had heard that when he worked with Alice Cooper's band he had brought in a session guitar player to do a lot of the solos, and I got the feeling that there was a chance he was going to follow the same plan with KISS if I didn't produce quickly enough. The pressure was on—and with a hangover as a frequent distraction, I hit a brick wall occasionally.

But part of it was also due to the fact that Bob wasn't very patient with me; I got the feeling that Paul and Gene might have told Bob about my drinking problem, and he may have put me in the same category as the guys in Alice's band. The difference is that I had the chops; those just needed to be finessed.

Bob was an interesting guy with a great mind for music and production, but at times he had the demanding, volatile demeanor of a football coach or drill instructor. I guess you'd say he was a high-strung artistic type, which didn't always mesh well with my laid-back personality.

Bob used to bring a whistle to the studio, and while cutting basic tracks he really intimidated Peter by putting a small box over a microphone and hitting it with a drumstick, as if Peter couldn't keep proper time! I really felt for Peter during those sessions. It was at times a very demoralizing experience for all of us, and no matter what any of us said, Bob's word was the law.

Early on, in preproduction, we'd sit in a little room, almost like a classroom, and Bob would stand in front of us at a blackboard, lecturing about the recording process. It was like he was conducting a class—he was the teacher and we were his students. The funny thing is, Bob wasn't a whole lot older than any of us. He was only in his late twenties when we recorded *Destroyer*, so it wasn't like he was the grown-up and we were the children. But it sort of felt that way. Bob carried himself with an air of maturity and importance. He believed in himself, which is probably half the battle if you want to be a record producer. And we wanted to believe in him.

But there's something I learned later on in my career about the duties of a good producer. His job is not only to help a band make a great record, but also to bring out the best in his musicians by creating an encouraging, comfortable atmosphere in the studio, so that everyone feels good about themselves. That was a quality Bob sadly lacked.

Remember, we struggled with the fact that people were still calling us a carnival act. I struggled with it, anyway, and I'm sure the other guys did, too, even if they don't want to admit it. It bothered me to read reviews in which more attention was paid to the special effects than the music we played. Obviously I have no right to complain about any of that. We set out to create the greatest theatrical band in the history of rock, and that's what we did. I invented a character. I wore makeup. I figured out how to shoot rockets out of my guitar and have smoke billow out of the pickups. I bought into the whole thing and reaped the benefits. But there was always a bit of dissonance, a nagging sense that I had sold out to a degree I never quite envisioned. And that really gnawed at me. I wanted to be respected by my peers, and I wanted to be taken more seriously as a musician.

A step in that process was to make a studio album that even our harshest critics could not dismiss. *Destroyer* was supposed to be that album, and it damn near succeeded. For me, though, I knew I hadn't come close to doing my best work. I had a wealth of musical ideas yet to be discovered, and with the right producer, maybe they'd be brought out.

Bob Ezrin was brilliant, no question about it, but his style did not suit my personality. I've never been great at creating under pressure, so when Bob would tell me to do something in a particular way, and give me a small window of time in which to do it, I didn't always deliver.

You have to realize—I always strive for spontaneity. To this day, my best solos are not planned. I hit the record button and I just wail. If I'm in a good frame of mind, and there are good vibes in the room, I can do some amazing guitar work. On the other side of the coin, if there's tension, or I'm not coming up with stuff as quickly as people would like me to, I shut down. That happened to me on a couple of songs during the recording of *Destroyer*, which is one of the reasons I wasn't present for some of the sessions. I got the feeling I wasn't contributing enough, and Bob was always threatening to bring in a studio guy. Sometimes I have it, sometimes I don't. And when I was hungover or stressed, I didn't have it.

It's long been a suggested that studio guitar players were brought in to help out on *Destroyer*, filing in for me on the days when I simply wasn't there. Well, the truth is that it happened a few times. I can't deny it. Most of the guitar work on *Destroyer* is mine, but not all of it. I was hitting the clubs a lot at night in those days, living the life of a rock star. Sometimes that lifestyle wasn't particularly conducive to making a record. I was starting to get out of control, but I probably would have been a lot more cognizant, and I would have showed up more and been on time, if I had gotten more encouragement from Gene, Paul, and Bob. But it wasn't my record. In fact, of all the KISS records to that point, *Destroyer* felt the least like my record. It belonged more to Paul and Gene, and to Bob.

Interesting, really, since *Destroyer's* signature song belonged to Peter Criss.

"Beth" was such an odd song for KISS at the time, and the circumstances behind its writing and recording, and subsequent ascent up the singles charts, only add to its legend. All were completely improbable. Like me, Peter was always a bit hesitant about presenting material to the band, primarily because he figured he'd be shot down anyway. In the case of "Beth" his reluctance was understandable. First of all, it was a ballad, and KISS did not do ballads. Second, it was a bittersweet love song, filled with tenderness and regret. KISS didn't do tenderness, either. KISS did sex. KISS did volume. On the surface, at least, everything about the song seemed . . . wrong.

But Peter had guts. He'd originally coauthored the tune with another bandmate a few years earlier, prior to KISS. The song had originally been titled "Beck," which was short for Rebecca (the wife of a different bandmate). The first time Peter played the song for the guys in KISS, the reaction was mixed. Paul didn't like it. I was ambivalent, but Peter and I were such close friends that I usually felt compelled to support his suggestions. Gene actually thought it was interesting—enough of a departure that it might help serve *Destroyer*'s mission, which was to move the band in a slightly different direction. Bob Ezrin agreed, but only if he could put his stamp on the song (just as he would put his mark on the whole album). Bob was not the kind of producer who believed in letting musicians sit around the studio and *create.* He was an active participant in all phases of production. In the case of Peter's ballad, that meant rewriting and reworking.

Whatever you might think of Bob, he deserves significant credit for "Beth." It was his idea to change the title (to something that sounded less androgynous); it was his idea to sweeten the sound of the song with orchestration—strings and piano. Bob was a classically trained musician, and he was blessed with a unique ear. Both of these things impressed the hell out of everyone in the band, since we didn't even know how to read music; we were all self-taught and therefore in the same wobbly boat. To a degree, Bob intimidated all of us in the studio; we felt inferior to him. When you're around a guy like that, especially if he has a bit of a swagger, you tend to think he knows his shit. And while we would have second thoughts down the road, it's hard to criticize much of what Bob did on *Destroyer.* "Beth" was a good song that he transformed into something extraordinary.

The story behind the record's success is part of KISS lore, how it originally was tossed onto the backside of the first single, "Detroit Rock

City." As sometimes happens, though, a few radio stations began playing the flip side of the record, and people started calling in, saying how much they liked it, and how they couldn't believe "Beth" was a KISS song. Eventually the single was reissued, with "Beth" on the A side, and it became our biggest hit single. The song has grown on me over the years. It's obviously not indicative of the sound of KISS, but that's one of the reasons I like it. "Beth" was a crossover song, and the whole point of a crossover song (artistic ambition aside) is to expand your audience—to bring people into record stores who might otherwise never consider picking up a KISS album. It was a bridge—in much the same way that "I Was Made for Loving You" would make KISS accessible to fans of disco a few years later. The difference, of course, is that the years have been kind to "Beth." The song holds up very well.

"I Was Made for Loving You"?

Not so much, in my humble opinion.

Yeah, it became a hit single and I could appreciate the polish behind it, but I never liked the song and frankly hated playing it live—hammering that chucka-chucka-chucka chord for five minutes straight was not only monotonous, but often gave me a cramp in my wrist. "Beth" was different. I didn't see it as a compromise. I saw it as a good song that deserved to be a hit. I was happy for Peter. And it was good for the live show, too—gave it some variety and changed the pace. Instead of nothing but one machine-gun song after another, it provided a nice break for both the audience and the band members. In the same way that my guitar solos would give everyone a breather, "Beth" served as an interlude. Peter would move to center stage and sit on a drum stool, while the crowd would softly sing along, and girls would quietly snuggle up next to their boyfriends, the rest of us would head backstage and fix our makeup, grab a cold one, snort a few lines of blow (okay, I was the only one doing the blow, but you get the point), and generally recharge the batteries. Then we'd hit the stage again and finish up with a kick-ass grand finale. I have nothing bad to say about "Beth." It was a solid ballad, and a perfect complement to the hard-driving rock that made up 95 percent of our live show.

I had little to do with the writing or production of *Destroyer*, but if I take a step back and try to judge it objectively, I'd have to say it's one of KISS's best studio efforts. Some of our hard-core fans didn't agree, although their resentment probably has less to do with the quality of the material than the simple fact that we had tried to do something different. That's another risk when you go from being a cult band to a worldwide phenomenon: the folks who supported you back in the day suddenly get proprietary. Fans who had been flocking to our shows since our demo days resented the legions of newcomers who hadn't heard of KISS, or at least hadn't cared about KISS, until "Beth" began receiving heavy airplay. And they resented us for expanding the brand in a way that seemed untrue to our roots.

But there was so much more to *Destroyer* than "Beth." Parts of it are legitimately great, while other parts—some of the sonic weirdness and studio effects—don't work quite as well as they were intended. As a guitar player this is hard for me to admit, but the solo on "Detroit Rock City" is one of the single best moments in any KISS song. And I had nothing to do with creating it. I always loved that song, and I would be the first to credit Bob Ezrin for writing the guitar solo. He came up with the melody, and I learned how to play it, and Paul figured out the harmony. It's a classic guitar solo, as good as anything you'll find on a KISS record. I wish I'd thought of it, but I didn't. It was all Bob's.

*Destroyer* also contained "Shout It Out Loud," another anthem that became a KISS concert staple. Overall it's a really strong, diverse album that gave us more credibility in the music community and a little more respect from our peers, which was the whole point of hiring Bob as producer. If you listen to that record now, it's clear that we were trying to make a statement: *We're not just a teeny-bopper band; we're not just a gimmick.* It was the right album at the right time, and it helped elevate our status in the industry, selling more than three million copies and cementing our reputation as one of the top bands in the world.

Hard to find much fault with any of that.

But I did.

I had a love-hate relationship with KISS. The bigger we got, the more money that rolled in, the more records we sold . . . the more I found myself questioning my commitment to the band. Paradoxical, sure, since I did like the money and I was pretty good at spending it. But with the success of *Alive!* and *Destroyer*, KISS became more than just a band; we were a corporate entity, the merchandising arm of which generated more revenue than I ever dreamed possible ($100 million a year at its peak in the late seventies). And a distressing amount of it came from the sales of products directed at the younger members of our audience.

There were KISS lunch boxes, KISS action figures, KISS makeup kits, KISS dolls. You name it, we sold it.

I remember feeling that we were getting too commercialized for our own good, and that some of the toys probably turned off the serious rockers who might have been our fans. At the same time that we were trying to branch out with an album like *Destroyer*, we were aggressively peddling merchandise to ten-year-old kids. That bothered me. I thought it was ironic that KISS went from being a supposedly dangerous heavy metal band that promoted satanism to a family-friendly band whose followers included legions of children.

We'd be in the dressing room before shows, and instead of talking about the chicks we were going to bang afterward, we'd be talking about limiting profanity onstage because of the large number of kids in the audience. The pendulum started swinging in the opposite direction. I thought it was absurd that anyone honestly believed we were a satanic band, but I also thought it was ridiculous that little kids were coming to our shows. I'd find myself replaying concerts in my head, cringing because I realized the audience included a lot of younger fans, and I'd dropped an F-bomb or strutted in a sexually suggestive manner. It became a very difficult balancing act.

It was so odd that we even had to think about it, but that's the way we were marketed. We became almost a parody of what we started out to be. I had friends in the business who said, "Man, you guys had this incredible idea, but you went too far with it. You've become so commercialized that you're almost a joke."

Each of us reacted to these sorts of comments in his own way. Gene was the best at letting them roll off his back. If people accused KISS of being a sellout, Gene would laugh and say, "That's right, we sell out every night." In public, at least, he attributed every ounce of criticism, every negative review, to jealousy. Maybe he really felt that way. I don't know. Gene has never been shy about hiding his lust for fame and adulation and money. KISS brought him all of those things. Brought them to all of us.

But they never meant that much to me.

I think we all kind of felt locked into our characters, like we couldn't break loose. The Spaceman was my deal with the devil. When you're generating hundreds of millions of dollars, your work tends to have an impact on other people. Walking away is complicated and messy. The thing is, for me it was never about the money. It was always about the music. I really believed in theatrical rock; from the moment I saw Pete Townshend smash that first guitar, I knew it was the right way to go. But Townshend never put on makeup. Even Alice Cooper stopped well short of what we were doing in KISS. We pushed the envelope so much that in the beginning it seemed crazy.

Then it was accepted.

And finally it was expected.

At that point we were fucked, creatively speaking. It's like a Broadway show: you have to give the crowd exactly what they paid for, note for note, or everyone goes home disappointed. I'm not being hyperbolic, either. By the time we hit our peak in the late 1970s, a KISS concert really wasn't much different from a Broadway show, in the sense that every move was carefully choreographed, every word of banter scripted. Our concerts were so technologically complex—with pyrotechnics, levitations, platforms—that you couldn't deviate from the plan. I didn't like that restraint. The thing I liked best about performing live was the freedom and spontaneity. In previous bands (and even in the very early days of KISS), we always messed with the set list, switched songs around, changed places on the stage. Once we had reached a certain level of technical sophistication and popularity, we couldn't do that anymore.

It was the same thing every night: lighting cues, sound cues, special effects cues. I started feeling uncreative and unfulfilled. I started feeling like I was a caricature. More than once, when KISS was at the height of its popularity, I found myself sitting in my dressing room, staring into a mirror, and shaking my head at the sight of the Spaceman.

*"I don't think I can do this anymore."*

More often, though, these revelations—these moments of clarity—occurred in the morning, when I'd be trying to shake off a hangover while getting ready for a personal appearance at a record store or television station. I wasn't having fun anymore.

KISS was no longer a dream job. It was merely a job.

# 12

# GOING SOLO

**May 1978**

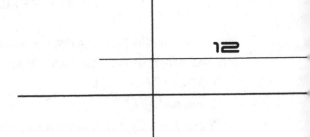

*So we're on this giant roller coaster at Magic Mountain, just me and my friend Don Wasley, the vice president of marketing for Casablanca Records, and his daughter. I've been a coaster fanatic my whole life, from the time I was a kid in New York, riding the old wooden coaster at Coney Island. I love the speed, the excitement, the carefully controlled sense of chaos and impending doom. Roller coasters are safe and fun, but they feel just a little bit dangerous. I seek them out on the road in the same way that some people look for museums or art galleries or great restaurants.*

*The brand-new Colossus at Magic Mountain, a towering double-tracker with two stomach-churning drops in excess of one hundred vertical feet, is on the must-ride list for any coaster nut, and I certainly qualify. So we're standing in line, chatting casually as the crowd snakes its way along, all of us willing to wait nearly an hour for the chance to spend two or three minutes on the Colossus. By the time we finally get to the point where you enter the roller coaster, the Southern California sky has turned gray and a light sprinkle has begun to fall.*

*"Oh, man," I say to Don.*

*"Yeah, bad luck."*

*Protocol usually dictates that rides are shut down almost immediately in the event of bad weather, but the Colossus is new and easily the star attraction at Magic Mountain. A bunch of college kids are operating the ride and everyone in line is bitching about having wasted an hour without getting their roller-coaster rocks off.*

*"Come on, one more trip!" someone shouts.*

*"Yeah, it's not that bad."*

*The college kids relent and open the gate, and pretty soon we're chugging up the first hill, the clackety-clack of the tracks filing the air. My heart begins to race, as it always does on the first ascent. But then, just as we reach the peak, something happens.*

*The weather worsens.*

*Suddenly the rain starts coming down more heavily and we're roaring down the first drop, the rain splashing against our faces. People are screaming, but I'm not sure they understand what's going on. As we hit the first turn I can tell we're going faster than normal. Usually you can feel the brakes on a coaster, but here there is a palpable sense of acceleration at a point when we should be slowing down.*

*Oh shit . . .*

*Especially on these great old woodies, you can often feel the brakes at work and even hear the squeaking sound. Now, however, there is next to nothing, just the sound of people screaming and then a faint disturbing noise of metal on metal . . . the sound of brakes failing. You don't need a PhD in physics to understand what's happening: the rain has seeped into the brake system and rendered it virtually useless! I realize now, as we approach one of the last turns of the ride, that we're reaching a very dangerous speed, a speed that feels like the coaster might even jump off the track! Finally, as the coaster straightens out into the last stretch of the ride, I let out a sigh of relief, thinking we've just barely escaped a major catastro-*

*phe! Unfortunately, the feeling is short-lived, because as soon as we enter the straightaway where we're supposed to slow down and exit, it becomes apparent that we aren't exiting anything, and my worst fears are suddenly realized: We won't be getting off this coaster from hell—and hell is where we all might end up if things don't change quickly! Don and his daughter are laughing out loud; they seem completely unaware of how serious the situation really is. But it's apparent to me that we're in big trouble.*

*Everyone else gets the point soon enough, as the coaster roars right through the exit station! There's fear now on the faces of the riders, but it's also on the faces of the college kids operating the ride—coupled with a helpless look of bewilderment. The brakes have been rendered almost inoperable from the rain, and a hopeless feeling suddenly consumes everyone. We again begin climbing the hundred-foot peak listening to the clanking of the giant chain drive pulling us upward, closer and closer to the summit. Our situation seems grave. What horror awaits us after the first drop?*

*I think, Maybe it's time to start praying . . . ?*

*And I'm not alone. Now people are really getting scared. Everyone is aware of our predicament, especially since the skies have really opened. A driving rain beats against the coaster. This no longer seems like a benign thrill. I ask myself, Is this a dream? It can't really be happening! Have I entered the Twilight Zone?!*

*We're falling again now, faster than ever, careening through turns, seemingly out of control, no brakes, no hope of stopping, and moving at a speed far exceeding the safety limits of the ride. Seemingly in some sort of crazy death spiral. Some riders on the coaster are screaming their fuckin' brains out, while others are completely silent, with a blank look of fear mixed with panic and confusion. We're all wondering whether we're going to jump the track and end up mangled somewhere far below.*

*Soon, though, by the grace of God, we're approaching the final turn again, just before the track straightens out and funnels into the exit station. The brakes aren't squeaking anymore—they've probably been literally sheared off by the friction produced by the runaway ride. The attendants are standing there together, five or six of them, arguing about what to do. I twist in my seat and try to get their attention.*

*"Shut it down!"*

*"What?!"*

*"Turn off the fucking motor, you idiots!!"*

*Again we start ascending to the top of the giant tower to an almost certain horrific ending. Suddenly everything stops. No more clanking sound from the chain drive. No more screams from the riders. A weird calm overtakes everyone. Apparently the operators have finally done what they should have done in the first place: cut the power to the giant motor running the chain drive. The coaster stops dead in its tracks. We're stuck—on the first giant hill. A little scary, but preferable to the alternative. The horror show is over! After a while security guards ascend the catwalk, accompanied by sighs of relief and cheers of happiness from all concerned.*

*Slowly and carefully, one at a time, the guards escort us down the narrow catwalk to safety. Don is holding his daughter, who is visibly shaken. She's not the only one. I've never been on a runaway roller coaster before, and it occurs to me for a moment that it's the perfect metaphor for the way I feel in general right now: like my life is completely out of control. As if being in KISS is a lot like riding a roller coaster that just won't stop. And there is nothing I can do about it.*

*Is this a lesson from someone trying to reach me and make me realize my predicament? A messenger in the form of a giant machine? Maybe so, but I won't realize it or act upon it until much later.*

The pace never slowed. We released two more studio albums in a span of seven months: *Rock and Roll Over* in November 1976, and *Love Gun* in June 1977. In less than three and a half years KISS had funneled an incredible amount of music into the marketplace: six studio albums and one double live record. We never stopped touring, either. Sometimes the road was a blast, sometimes it was a drag. And once in a while it was nearly fatal.

Just a few weeks after the release of *Rock and Roll Over* (on December 12, 1976, to be precise), at the start of a show at the Lakeland (Florida) Civic Center, I was electrocuted and nearly killed. Here's how it happened:

We were supposed to enter the stage by walking down a set of stairs. Every entrance involving stairs was a challenge for us, given the platform shoes we wore. Usually we'd hold tightly to a railing to make sure we didn't slip or fall. Well, on this particular night my guitar wasn't appropriately grounded, so when I touched the metal railing on the staircase I got hit with a big dose of electricity. I didn't even get to the stage before it happened. I was just about to start going down and I touched the railing at the top of the staircase and got thrown backward onto the platform above the amps. I don't think the other guys in the band even realized what had happened—maybe they just thought I'd slipped or something. They continued to march toward the stage and began playing. Meanwhile, I was flat on my back, stunned nearly to the point of unconsciousness.

Some guys from our road crew quickly picked me up and carried me down the back staircase, while the band kept playing. I was out of it for a while. I had burns on my fingertips—that's how much voltage there was. Eventually the guys realized I wasn't coming out, and they stopped the show and came back behind the amps to check on me. I hadn't even gone back to the dressing room yet—I was just sitting there, disoriented, trying to get my bearings. As my head cleared I could hear the audience chanting:

*"We want Ace! We want Ace!"*

That got my adrenaline going, and after about five more minutes or so I went back out and played the entire concert. I had a nasty headache and my fingers were a little numb, but what the hell? The show must go on, right? We all performed at less than peak physical condition at one time or another. There were a few occasions when I could hardly walk because of knee pain and one of the docs would come backstage and shoot me up with needles and I'd go out and play. Paul was sick plenty of times and they'd shoot him up with something to get him through the show. When you've got twenty thousand seats sold, you do whatever you can to get out on the stage. That's just the way it works.

If there was one good thing to come out of that night, it was the fact that it provided the impetus for one of my favorite KISS songs, and the first on which I had the balls to sing lead. The guys had urged me to write about my near-death experience, and while electricity runs through the song and did indeed provide the initial spark of inspiration, the end result is a tune that's less about getting fried onstage than it is about getting laid afterward.

A good KISS song, in other words.

*Shock me, make me feel better, oh yeah*
*Come on and shock me, put on your black leather*
*Baby, I'm down to the bare wire*
*Shock me, we can come together*

Thanks to the return of Eddie Kramer, my favorite producer and engineer, *Rock and Roll Over* was a more enjoyable experience than *Destroyer* had been. It's a good record, more true to the original KISS mission than *Destroyer* had been, and helped placate some of the fans who were angered by the studio gimmicks of Bob Ezrin on *Destroyer*. *Rock and Roll Over* was an unqualified success, shipping platinum and producing another hit single sung by Peter, "Hard Luck Woman," as well as "Calling Dr. Love," which would become something of a KISS classic.

Eddie wanted a return to the rawer sound of earlier KISS albums, so we recorded the album live at the old Nanuet Star Theatre in Rockland County, about twenty miles north of New York City, and then mixed it at the Record Plant. The acoustics at the Star were incredible, and Eddie had us use every inch of the place, setting up instruments in different places to get different types of sounds. At one point he even had Peter playing drums in the bathroom! There was also another really nice feature about recording in Nanuet. I had recently married Jeanette and we'd settled in Tarrytown, New York, which was just across the Hudson River. All I had to do was roll out of bed and shoot west across the Tappan Zee Bridge and I was there in ten minutes.

I think my guitar playing on *Rock and Roll Over* is solid, and I know that I felt more connected to the album while we were recording. That's probably due to Eddie as much as anything else. But the truth is that while I like the record a lot, it was the first KISS album on which I did not contribute a single composition. I didn't feel good about that. I thought of myself as a writer as well as a guitar player, and I had no one but myself to blame. Yeah, it's true that in any band with four strong personalities and big egos, there's a certain amount of time spent marking your territory. Everybody wants to write and sing; everyone wants the spotlight. I was no different. But if you're not bringing material to the table, you can't really complain, can you?

So I sat down and wrote "Shock Me." Everyone loved it and agreed that it belonged on the next album, *Love Gun*. My initial thought, as usual, was to turn it over to Gene or Paul and let them handle the vocals. To my surprise, they resisted.

"You should sing this one yourself," Paul said. "It's way overdue."

And that's how I wound up flat on my back on the floor of a studio at the Record Plant, trying to relax, with the lights turned down low and Eddie Kramer at the board, encouraging me to sing from the gut.

Which is exactly what I did.

I like *Love Gun* a lot; I'm proud of the whole album. There are a few things on it, though, that really make me smile. Like some of my leads . . . and the vocal on "Shock Me." It never actually occurred to me until that album that I was a viable singer. What I learned is that you don't have to be a trained vocalist to be a rock singer, any more than you have to be a classically trained musician to play guitar. Just believe in what you're doing and the audience will go along for the ride.

Looking back on it now, there a lot of things about the KISS marketing machine that make me laugh, and a few that make me cringe. Every time I thought we'd reached a new high (or low), the bar was moved ever so slightly. The cardboard "love gun" that was included in every copy of *Love Gun*, for example. To the relief of parents of teenagers all over the world, this gimmick was merely a toy gun, and not the giant dildo some may have expected. We also included a page of KISS tattoos that were actual duplicates of tattoos we had on our arms. That was a good one. Cheap and effective.

More expensive, and more ambitious by miles, was the first KISS comic book, produced by Marvel Comics in 1977. We got to meet the great Stan Lee, creator of Spider-Man and the Incredible Hulk. I thought Stan was cool, but Gene was the real fanboy, trailing Stan around and asking him questions about everything he'd written over the last thirty years. Gene was and is a comic book fanatic. He told me once that when he first arrived in the United States from Israel, the first thing he learned to read was a comic book. I guess he never stopped, which at least partially explains how he came up with his character for KISS. I was a little bit of a fan, but I could take them or leave them. I was intrigued by the superhero aspect of comic books, but it was the artwork that really grabbed my attention.

Predictably, the KISS comic book wasn't allowed to simply sneak into the marketplace. Like everything else we did, its birth was accompanied by a wild publicity stunt. We all gathered at the printing plant in Buffalo, New York, where the comic would be produced, and together we each donated a vial of blood, which we then poured into a vat of red ink, which was mixed in with the actual ink that would be used to print the comic books. I'm not sure exactly what this was supposed to signify, but as a marketing stunt it worked beautifully. Fans thought it was awesome, critics thought it was ridiculous, and conservative and religious groups were repulsed, claiming that the stunt provided further evidence that KISS was doing the devil's work, and that possibly we were vampires!

To which we could only reply . . . "Ahhhh, bullshit."

---

The marketing silliness reached a peak of sorts with *KISS Meets the Phantom of the Park,* a 1978 made-for-television movie with a plot so ridiculous that I start laughing just thinking about it. We played superhero versions of ourselves, locked in a battle with a demented scientist bent on taking over a popular amusement park by creating four androids that looked just like us.

How could anyone make this shit up?

It wasn't the greatest movie, but that never bothered me because I wasn't under the impression that anyone expected it to be anything other than a ridiculous farce—including the people who wrote, directed, and produced it. If you look at it now, the movie seems kind of campy and cool. The problem is, it wasn't meant to be that way. I watch it now and get a kick out of it, but I know Gene is embarrassed about it. Then again, Gene takes everything so fucking seriously, which is ironic since he was the one who always claimed to be happy that KISS was selling out arenas and moving millions of records, without regard for artistic integrity. How the hell do you make a movie called *KISS Meets the Phantom of the Park* and expect people not to laugh? I also heard that when he saw *This Is Spinal Tap* he didn't think it was very funny. To each his own. I personally thought it was hysterical.

There were a lot of bad ideas surrounding that TV movie project, the main one being: who in their right mind thought the four guys in KISS could act? I suppose you could argue that all rock stars are actors, and obviously more than a few of them have made successful transitions to the big screen. In KISS we were already wearing makeup and portraying characters whenever we went onstage, so maybe it seemed like we'd have an easier time than most. When I first heard about the project, I thought it sounded like it might be kind of fun. But I didn't take it seriously at all, and in very short order I discovered that acting was a lot less interesting and enjoyable than I'd suspected.

I should have had some idea what to expect when I got the original script and discovered that I didn't have a single line of dialogue. Not one! Every time my character was supposed to speak, the only thing that would come out of his mouth was the sound of a parrot: "Awk!"

That's exactly what was written on the page. Three capital letters: *A-W-K.*

*"Awk!"*

I guess the writers had picked up on a quirk of my personality, although I'm not sure where they got the information. Sometimes when I'd get loaded and didn't want to engage in conversation, I'd mimic the squawk of a parrot until the other person gave up and went away. Pretty silly, I admit. And that was the Ace Frehley persona the screenwriters wanted to present. Or maybe they just thought I was too stoned or drunk to remember any of my lines, so they tried to keep it as simple as possible. When I first saw the script, I didn't know what to think. Was it a joke? If so, I didn't find it particularly amusing.

"What the fuck is this?" I asked Bill. "I've got no lines in this stupid fuckin' movie? Why am I wasting my time?"

He laughed. "What do you want me to do, Ace?"

"Tell them to rewrite it."

They did, and almost magically I had the ability to talk! I even had amazing superpowers that allowed me to transport the whole band at will to another location. So I took a deep breath and decided to give the project my best shot.

A lot of *KISS Meets the Phantom of the Park* was filmed on location at Magic Mountain, where we actually performed a somewhat staged KISS concert, although most of the interior scenes were done at Culver City Studios. Regardless of where we were filming, I had to be on set at eight o'clock in the morning, which was a complete drag for me in those days. The band was staying at a posh hotel in Beverly Hills, a good forty-five minutes away by car. And it wasn't like I was getting eight hours of beauty sleep each night. I was busy being Ace—hitting the clubs, sometimes partying until the wee hours. Who the hell wants to get up at 7 A.M. with a hangover? Not me, that's for sure. Especially when I never knew exactly how much of my time would be required.

It didn't take long to figure out that most of the moviemaking process was about hanging out in your trailer all day, waiting for someone to tell you that you were needed on the set. A couple of times during the movie I arrived bright and early, threw on my makeup and costume, and got all ready to go . . . and then sat in my trailer. After an hour or two one of the assistant directors would stop by and say, "You know what, Ace? We're doing some close-ups on Gene this morning, so I don't think we're going to need you until after lunch. Why don't you relax for a while?"

That really made me crazy. Here I was, one of the "stars" of the film, and you'd think maybe they could have been a little more considerate? Maybe let me know the night before? Don't these fuckin' people plan? Truth is, I was doing a lot of coke at the time and my nerves were becoming frayed, to say the least. I was getting an ounce of blow delivered to my trailer about once a week! The delivery boy was actually one of the actors on the set (he had a minor role in the film). It was really nuts. We each had our own trailer to hang in. I filled my fridge with cold beer and champagne, and since there was a lot of downtime I indulged in the white powder frequently and followed up with whatever was handy. (You'd be surprised what was handy on a movie set in Los Angeles in the seventies.) The actor supplying me used to put the coke in his character's hat and act like we were buddies just having a cold one together in my trailer. He actually went on to become a pretty well-known character actor down the road, with roles in several big Hollywood hits.

For the most part, I was clueless. I didn't realize that this was the way movies worked, that downtime was a big part of an actor's day—maybe the biggest part. And so the third or fourth time that it happened, I snapped. Totally went off on the producer. When confronted, he really didn't have much to say in his defense in regard to how the shooting schedule was being handled, which didn't make me feel any better.

Fuck this! I said to myself. Then I shouted, "I'm outta here!" (Which, as I realize now, was extremely unprofessional behavior.)

I went back into my trailer, quickly washed off my makeup and changed into my regular clothes, snorted a couple of lines and washed it down with a cold one, and then jumped into my Mercedes. I drove quietly off the lot, trying not to attract too much attention, but in the rearview mirror I could see my bodyguard and road manager in hot pursuit. Well, not so hot, actually. I let them follow me for a while as I bided my time until we got into a more familiar area. The traffic was becoming dense, and I began making lefts and rights, slowly and methodically trying to lose them, until finally I just hit the gas and pulled away, leaving them stuck behind a truck at a red light. The next thing I knew, I was on my own, somewhere in the suburbs of Los Angeles, hanging out at a bar, washing down some tranquilizers with a beer. I calmed down after a while and soon began feeling very guilty about sounding off to the producer. Hell, he'd only been doing his job, and I was making it harder for him. Maybe the script and schedule changes had occurred that morning and there was nothing he could do about it. And I was acting like a spoiled brat! I realize now that all the cocaine and alcohol was really starting to affect my judgment and how I perceived life in general—not just within the band.

But now I faced a dilemma: do I run back with my tail between legs, or skip a day of shooting and hope it all blows over? I had similar experiences at times with KISS. Something would piss me off and I'd lose my temper and disappear for a while. I didn't really like confrontation, so I'd just go off on my own and medicate myself until I felt better. It was typical behavior for an addict. I see that so clearly now; unfortunately, I was oblivious to my actions at the time.

In any case, for some strange reason that day I left the bar and decided to get some fresh air. The sun was shining, but not too hot, and it seemed to improve my mood. I wound up cruising by the La Brea Tar Pits, which is one of the coolest places on earth. I parked the car and got out and began walking around, trying to forgive and forget what had happened earlier; suddenly I noticed a huge sign promoting a new exhibition at the Los Angeles County Museum of Art, which is located just down the block. I stopped in my tracks.

## The Treasures of Tutankhamun

Holy shit! The King Tut exhibit was in town!

A little background is probably warranted here. I'd always been fascinated with the Pyramids and Egyptian culture. I remember reading a book as a teen called *Pyramid Power* that captured my imagination, and since then I'd dreamed of visiting the Pyramids. Well, at this time the Tutankhamen exhibition was touring the United States, and attracting massive crowds wherever it went. Everybody wanted to see the golden mask and the artifacts of the Boy King. People would stand in line for hours in cities around the world. A novelty song by Steve Martin called "King Tut" was a hit single that year. *Tut-mania* gripped the nation! I know, because I had a pretty good dose of it myself.

Funny thing is, I had completely forgotten that the exhibit was going to be in L.A. while we were filming *KISS Meets the Phantom of the Park*, so I was completely taken aback when I stumbled across it that day. I thought to myself, *Wow, if I could just get in there, everything will be all right.* But you couldn't get in without a ticket, and that day's exhibition had sold out weeks in advance.

I wandered around outside the museum for a while, staring at the window, trying to imagine what it looked like inside, until suddenly a young woman approached me.

"Excuse me, sir?" She was probably in her early thirties, with a couple of kids in tow.

"Yes?"

"Would you like to go inside? I have an extra ticket."

"Really?" I asked. "How much do you want for it?"

She smiled and shook her head. "That's okay. You just enjoy the show."

She pulled the ticket out of her purse and placed it in my hand. Then she walked away, leaving me standing there alone, dumbstruck by my good fortune. This lady could have scalped that ticket for a couple of hundred bucks. I would have paid that much. Instead she gave it away, and I don't think she had any idea who I was. I was just a guy with long hair hanging out in front of the Museum of Art, looking like he needed a ticket for the King Tut exhibit.

Who was she, really? Possibly a messenger sent from above intervening in my life? I have no idea, but this kind of thing has happened to me before—too often for it to be dismissed as coincidence. People come out of nowhere to provide assistance or demonstrate kindness. A mysterious luck seems to always pull me out of deep or deadly shit. Luck and guardian angels have always been something I felt were with me, and I believe they still are today.

Five minutes later I was inside the museum, wandering around, blissfully soaking up the Egyptian atmosphere, looking at all these fascinating artifacts, feeling like I'd been transported thousands of years back into the past. By the time I walked out of the museum some three hours later, I felt completely at ease with myself and the world around me. Thinking back now about that afternoon and remembering how upset I was before visiting the exhibit, there are really only two words that best describe what happened to me: *divine intervention*.

I left the exhibit with a feeling of extraordinary well-being and peace. I drove to the set, apologized to the director and producer for my short fuse and absence, and promised that I would behave better in the future.

They accepted my apology and everything seemed to be okay. I didn't learn until much later, when I saw the movie for the first time, that filming had gone on without me that day, including a scene in which our characters waged an epic battle with Frankenstein, Dracula, and the Wolfman in the park's Chamber of Horrors. My character was a big part of that, and in the opening scenes I am present, but once the action starts to pick up someone else takes over. Under the best of circumstances the whole thing would have looked silly, but on top of that the director had enlisted the services of my stunt double to finish the remaining shots in the scene. Usually a stunt double is used only in distant shots or quick cutaways. But in this case my double was a black man. A terrific guy. Hell of a stunt double, too, but he didn't look anything like me facially, and even with all the makeup on it was painfully obvious. I mean, you can see it clearly if you watch the movie. During the fight scene in the Chamber of Horrors with Frankenstein, he gets knocked around and thrown into a pillar with a couple of skeletons tied to it. Just hit the pause button. "Hey, man, that's not Ace. That's a black dude!" Very funny stuff, and let's face it: would you expect anything less from the producers who made the *Scooby-Doo* cartoons?

The funniest day of shooting, though, was probably the one when we did the scene at the pool, in which we are confronted by the park manager and head of security about Gene knocking around a few security guards the night before. In the beginning the park manager rapidly walks into the scene and toward us, from the other side of the pool. Well, on the first or second take he tripped on one of the rocks and took a bad tumble and fell flat on his face and hands. For every take after that I was completely overtaken by the mental image of him stumbling; I must have ruined at least twenty-five takes with my laughter! On the first few takes the other guys joined in, but after that I was pretty much alone. It was very embarrassing for the other actor and me, but I absolutely lost all control of myself. The incident reminds me of when I was a little kid and routinely got busted for cracking up in school or in church.

That was the funniest part of the movie, but the most fun was at night while we were shooting at Magic Mountain. I bought a motorbike while we were out there. The park was closed to the public after dark so I had free rein on the smooth asphalt roads throughout the facility. Between takes I'd jump on the bike with a nice buzz and ride around the whole park without a care in the world. Remember—back in the Bronx when I was a kid we didn't have motorbikes, so it was really my first chance to enjoy myself without having to worry about other traffic. It put a smile on my face, for sure, but I nearly broke my neck a few times.

Typical for me, though. Just being Ace.

Oh, well. Those were just some of the many things that happened (or went wrong) on *KISS Meets the Phantom of the Park.* None of it meant all that much to me. The whole thing was a goof. If you take it in that light, it's okay, almost like a Saturday morning kids' show or a Japanese sci-fi flick. Come on—who doesn't like Mothra and Rodan! From day one I thought it was going to be campy and silly. Gene, unfortunately, took the whole process very seriously and was infatuated with making movies. I also believe it was the spark that got him thinking he could become a movie star. In fact, he did a few more films afterward, too, mistakenly thinking he could act. *KISS Meets the Phantom* . . . was a huge embarrassment for him, I think. For me? I had a few laughs and made some new friends and had a very interesting experience off the set. I didn't really take it seriously from the outset and didn't think much about it once it was over. To be honest, I thought it was a natural step in the devolution of KISS. We got exactly what we deserved, and exactly what most people expected.

By the time the movie came out it was apparent that we all were getting complacent and wanted to do other things. Our two previous albums, *Alive II* and *Double Platinum*, were basically compilations, bringing to nine the total number of KISS albums. All nine were released in the span of four years. I remember at the end of the shoot, sitting around a table with the other guys in the band, with Bill Aucoin and some of our business advisors and accountants, and talking about how we were going to fill the next six months. Bill suggested that instead of making another KISS record, each of us should consider a solo project. I thought it was a great idea. We could all pursue our musical interests, take a turn in the spotlight, and give fans a virtual buffet table of choices from the guys in KISS. Creatively and commercially, it seemed to make a lot of sense, and it had the additional benefit of giving us a break from each other. We had spent so much time with each other over the previous five years that it was inevitable for tensions to arise.

I felt good about my solo project from the beginning, mainly because I knew I'd be teaming up with Eddie Kramer. I had a lot of confidence in Eddie. I respected him and he respected me. We'd been a good team on KISS albums, and there was no reason to think we wouldn't work well together on a solo venture. Apparently, though, no one else shared my confidence. I still remember Gene and Paul saying to me, in front of at least a dozen people, "Hey, Ace, if you need some help on your record, don't hesitate to call."

It wasn't said with malice, but neither was it said with sincerity. There was a tone of condescension to it, like *You're gonna need help.* Remember—Paul and Gene dominated every KISS album. They wrote and sang most of the songs. They were the dominant personalities. I'm sure they figured my album would bomb, or that maybe I wouldn't even get it done. If you want to give them the benefit of the doubt, you could say they were trying to look generous in front of our management team by offering their assistance if I needed it. You know, because I was crazy Ace . . . unreliable Ace . . . the Spaceman. Regardless, I remember walking out of that meeting and thinking, *I'm gonna show these fuckers, and I'm gonna show the world!*

For the first time in a long time, I felt motivated. When somebody says to me, "You can't do that," it makes me want to do it all the more. Even as a teenager, when my parents would say that I was the black sheep, I found it inspirational in a weird sort of way. Yeah, I had a drinking problem. I had a drug problem. I lacked some confidence, but I knew I had the chops; after all I was the lead guitarist in one of the biggest rock groups in the world. I knew I had the ability to make a great solo record. It was just a matter of staying focused and teaming up with the right producer.

Admittedly, focus has never been a strong suit of mine (only later on in life was I diagnosed with attention deficit disorder). I don't work well under the pressure of a deadline and I find it almost impossible to force myself to be creative. Gene once told me, "Ace, I write a song every day." I don't get that. How can you force yourself to write? Writing has to be a creative process, and if you're not feeling creative, it just won't work well. Sometimes I won't write a song for weeks. Then, on a given weekend, I might write two or three songs. When the juices are flowing, you have to be ready. When they aren't flowing, you do something else: hop on a motorcycle, go fishing, have a party, or maybe build a remote-controlled helicopter. Whatever. Fill the time and divert your attention until you feel inspired. I never write by formula, either. Sometimes I start a song with a guitar riff, sometimes with a vocal hook or a melody. It varies. Ideas come from anywhere and everywhere—my personal life, books or magazines, movies, and sometimes even dreams. A good idea is a good idea, regardless of the source.

In the case of my first solo album I was lucky to have a few songs already in the vault, tunes that had been rejected on earlier KISS records. That gave me a head start. I brought them back, did a little rewriting and tweaking, and that helped ease some of the anxiety about going off on my own. Other songs just kind of happened—spontaneous combustion, I guess. It helped, too, that I cleaned up a little bit (although not completely) during the making of the record, usually limiting my alcohol and drug use to the evenings after a long day of recording. I also felt I didn't really have much of a choice. I knew that I couldn't blame anyone else if my solo album bombed. If a KISS record sucked, I could always chalk it up to Paul's or Gene's megalomania. Not now. This time it was all on me. Whatever praise or blame would be heaped on the record, I'd have to take responsibility.

The first thing I did (after getting Eddie Kramer on board, of course) was go out and find a great drummer, since Peter was tied up making his own record. An old friend of mine named Larry Russell (we went to high school together and jammed a little back in the day) came up with this name: Anton Fig. I'd never heard of Anton and wasn't sure if he was right for the project, until I asked Eddie Kramer if he had any suggestions.

"You know," he said, "there's this guy I worked with recently named Anton Fig. He's unbelievable. You should check him out!"

Anton was playing in a band at the time with his two closest friends, Keith and Amanda Lentin. Born in South Africa, he moved to the

States in the early seventies and settled down in Boston, where he studied at the New England Conservatory of Music; he later moved to New York City. When I heard his name from two unrelated sources, I figured it was destiny that we meet. So I invited Anton up to a studio in the North Bronx that was run by my friend Eddie Solan, and we jammed for a while. We hit it off right away, both musically and personally. I immediately hired him for the job and we have enjoyed a lasting friendship in and out of the studios since 1978. (He recently performed on my latest solo effort, *Anomaly*, which was released in September 2009.) Anton has had one of the best steady gigs in show business for the last twenty-five years, as the drummer for David Letterman's house band, featuring Paul Shaffer. He's also one of the busiest session drummers in New York City and has worked with everyone from Mick Jagger, Bob Dylan, and Joe Cocker to Miles Davis, Richie Havens, and Paul Butterfield.

When I first started writing songs for *Anomaly*, one of the compositions was "Genghis Kahn." Listen to the thundering drum work on that song and you'll understand what makes Anton so special. He holds the pocket back, playing a little behind the beat, just like John Bonham of Led Zeppelin would do. If you listen closely to any Zeppelin tune you'll find that what gives it that groove is Bonham's drumming. He's never racing ahead of the guitar; he's always holding back. Same with Anton. It's a unique talent, playing slightly behind the beat. It doesn't come naturally for most rock drummers, but when executed properly it sets up a great pocket and can really make a song swing. Anton is one of the most versatile drummers I've ever met. I bring out the best in him, and he brings out the best in me. We have a musical bond. I don't have to say much when we're in the studio. Usually just a few words about tempo and feel and some suggestions about where I might want a fill. He just gets it, plain and simple.

When I wrote "Genghis Khan," I immediately thought, *Man, Anton is going to kill this song*! I played it with two other drummers prior to Anton, since he was tied up recording, and it just seemed okay, but when Anton got ahold of it he really took the song to the next level. Just as I had envisioned it.

*Ace Frehley* was recorded at the sprawling Colgate Mansion, on the Filston estate in Sharon, Connecticut, right by Lime Rock Park speedway. Once elegant, the hundred-acre estate had been vacant for a few years and had begun to fall on hard times. The grounds were a bit unkempt. Chips of paint and plaster sometimes fell from the ceiling. But parts of it were still very much intact and impressive. I thought to myself, If only these walls could talk. The library, for example, in which we recorded a lot of the acoustic guitar work, had beautifully carved woodwork and turn-of-the-century textured wallpaper, still intact. It was enormous and grand; I found it to be an inspirational and creative workplace. We used several other rooms to create different acoustic effects. On "Fractured Mirror," for instance, we placed microphones at the top of a stairway on the second floor to get a huge, reverberating drum sound.

We did a lot of stuff like that. Eddie liked working with me because I didn't put many restraints on him and encouraged him to experiment with unorthodox recording techniques. With KISS, Paul and Gene usually wanted things done by the book. I didn't even have a book. I was more interested in having fun and taking chances.

I'd say "Eddie, don't be afraid to try some crazy stuff," and "Let's try something you've never done before. Fuck it! Go for it."

I'll never forget the first time Eddie flipped the tape over on a twenty-four-track, two-inch tape machine. I was a little bewildered.

"What are you doing?" I asked.

"Don't worry. Just play your ass off!"

That ended up being my first backward guitar solo and it sounded amazing. I asked, "Where did you learn that" and Eddie went on to tell me what it was like working with Jimi Hendrix at Electric Lady Studios.

Eddie always had interesting stories to tell. Sometimes he'd talk about when he worked with the Beatles and the Rolling Stones, or the Kinks at Olympic Sound Studios in London. Once he talked about what it was like recording *Led Zeppelin II,* including working with Jimmy Page at the mixing board at the Record Plant in New York, and I was on the edge of my seat. Eddie also worked with Dionne Warwick, Peter Frampton, Carly Simon, and David Bowie.

In my wildest dreams I never thought I'd be working with a producer who had worked with so many people that I love and admire. I felt really privileged at that point and I always wanted to give Eddie my very best performance when he hit the record button.

Sometimes we'd put four different amps in four different places and blend them all together in the mix. Crazy shit. Always pushing the envelope. Sometimes even double-tracking drum fills . . . like the drum solos in "Rip It Out." On "Fractured Mirror," Eddie and I achieved a unique metallic bell sound on the guitar. I was playing a Gibson double-neck guitar into a Marshall stack with the volume turned all the way up. I mean, this thing was ready to explode. On one neck I had the pickups on, so if I were to hit the strings on that neck, it would have been loud as hell, but instead I played the picking figure on the other neck, with the pickups off—the sound coming out of the amp was the body resonating through the pickups from the other neck. That's how I got those bell overtones. It's a technique I still use today and you can hear it on an instrumental I recorded and produced for *Anomaly* titled "Fractured Quantum." I was also one of the first guitar players in history to use a synthesizer guitar on record. I used it in the song "Ozone," which was lots of fun, and Eddie and my assistant engineer, Rob Freeman, did a great job transferring that sound to tape. The device was called the ARP Avatar and was elementary in design compared to the synthesizers available on the market today.

Of the songs I wrote for the first solo album, "Fractured Mirror" turned out to be one of my most unique and enduring favorites. So much that since then I've recorded three more instrumentals in the Fractured Series, ending with "Fractured Quantum." What's next? I don't know. The most popular song off that record would probably be "New York Groove," a song I didn't even write and frankly didn't think that much of the first time I heard it. The credit goes to Eddie's assistant, who suggested the song. Originally recorded by a band called the Hello People, "New York Groove" was written by Russ Ballard. Russ had a band called Argent in the seventies and I was lucky enough to see them perform in concert as a teen. Eddie pushed hard to include "New York Groove" on the record. I've always been the kind of guy who will give anything a shot, especially if I respect the person I'm working with, so I agreed.

The signature sound of "New York Groove" is that *acka-acka* crunch at the beginning. It almost sounds as if it's being created on a guitar using a wah-wah pedal. But it's not. It actually was produced by using a device similar to the "talk box" used by Joe Walsh and Jeff Beck, and, most famously, Peter Frampton on *Frampton Comes Alive!* It works like this: A speaker or driver is enclosed in a metal box, into which a tube is inserted. Then a guitar is plugged into an amp, but the speaker output is routed through the box and the signal is routed back from the box into the amp again. The other end of the tube goes into the musician's mouth, allowing him to sing or talk in a manner that sounds as though the words are being produced by the guitar in a weirdly robotic way.

Done well, and sparingly, it's an awesome fucking effect.

I couldn't master the technique well enough to play the part on my own, so I had my friend Bobby help out. Try to picture this: Bobby sitting there next to me, opening and closing his mouth around the tube while I played guitar.

"ACKA-*acka-acka* . . ."

It was pretty funny. But it worked. As did another of Eddie's ideas. He suggested we add loud, rhythmic clapping to the song, figuring it would sound better when the song was performed live. To get that effect we brought in a big, hollow wooden box, and then three or four of us stomped on it together, as hard as we could. And Eddie recorded the whole thing.

It seemed kind of silly at the time, but actually it was brilliant and innovative. They don't do shit like that anymore. Somebody now would just go out and get a stomp box. Or, more likely, they'd grab a digital sample. In those days everything you heard was real. We *created* all the effects. Today you just press a button or click a mouse. It takes a lot of the fun out of the process, really. I'm all for technology, but I do think it has a tendency to stunt the imagination.

After recording the basic tracks in Connecticut, we moved down to Radio City Music Hall. There used to be a recording studio on the top floor. It was wonderful, and I'll tell you why: because the Rockettes used to come up and visit all the time. They would rehearse, take a break, look in, see what was going on. Then they'd go one or two flights up and be sunning themselves on the roof. It was a wonderful, accommodating situation, to say the least.

*Ace Frehley* was released on September 18, 1978. As a matter of fact, all four KISS solo albums were released on that day, a marketing stunt orchestrated by Neil Bogart in an attempt to maximize publicity and sales. I'm still not sure it was the greatest idea in the world; maybe it would have made more sense to roll the records out slowly, over a period of several months, to give each its time in the spotlight. Instead Casablanca pressed half a million copies of each record and flooded the marketplace on a single day.

The results were mixed, to say the least. Critically speaking, *Ace Frehley* was the most successful of the four records. I expected that. My goal was to make a really solid, guitar-based rock album, and I did. The shock, to just about everyone, was that *Ace Frehley* also was the most successful of the solo albums from a commercial standpoint, outselling the other three albums and producing a Top 20 single in "New York Groove."

I was stunned and moved by the response, and especially by the enduring popularity of "New York Groove." It's a great song for a guy from the Bronx, which is what I still am after all these years. It was a total departure from both KISS and my personal style and taste, but it was absolutely the right song at the right time. On every level it works, and I give all the credit to Eddie Kramer. He made it happen, and he's just as responsible as I am for "New York Groove" becoming a hit.

I'm proud of that whole album. It confirmed what I'd always felt: that my musical instincts were strong. For all the success I'd had with KISS, the experience had somehow managed to erode my confidence and self-esteem. The solo project gave me a chance—it gave all of us a chance—to stretch out a bit, to challenge myself artistically. I don't mind admitting that I felt a strong competitive streak during the making of *Ace Frehley*. I guess there's something wrong if you don't feel that. I wanted to make the best record I could make, and I think we did that. I remember hearing all these stories at the time about what the other guys were doing, how they were putting their records together, and what their strategies were. When I heard that Gene was going to have a bunch of guest stars on his record, I couldn't imagine what he was thinking.

*Helen Reddy? Really, Gene? What the fuck!?*

Even in KISS, Gene would sometimes make choices that were so wrong. I know that probably sounds like petty jealousy or envy, given that KISS remains a rock juggernaut even after all these years, but it's really not. There were a few times when I tried to steer the band away from making what I perceived to be terrible decisions. Peter and I were the ones with street sense, with bullshit detectors, if you will. Paul and Gene had no street sense whatsoever. Especially Gene. He had led a very sheltered, straight life. But his take on certain things was incredibly cynical and jaded. Sometimes he'd come up with ideas and I'd say, "What are you, fucking nuts? You can't do that."

It was always about making money, advancing and expanding the brand. It was never about art. Never about music.

Never.

I was dumbfounded sometimes by the stuff that would come out of Gene's mouth. He didn't know the difference between what was cool and what wasn't cool. I mean, come on. How could you not know that Helen Reddy (nothing personal, mind you), in 1978, was a very bad idea? Her presence alone is enough to make any KISS fan say, "Fuck you, Gene. I'm not buying that piece of shit."

The people you choose to work with on a solo album says a lot about you, but I don't think Gene realized it. Or maybe he just didn't care. Half the time I didn't know what was going through Gene's mind.

But I could always see dollar signs reflected in his eyes.

13

# FAST CARS, CELEBS, AND BETTY WHITE

KISS was bringing in millions of dollars in those days, and Jeanette and I did a pretty good job of burning through a lot of it. We got rid of our three-bedroom apartment in Tarrytown, New York, and bought a town house in nearby Irvington, where I built a recording studio in the attic and had a couple of trained Dobermans roaming the yard for protection against unwelcome guests. We moved out after a year because some fans and the press found out I was living there. Cameras would sometimes flash when I walked out the front door. One day I went right back inside and told Jeanette, "We're getting the fuck out of this place."

Next stop was a big spread in Connecticut, in the middle of the woods.

I had just finished recording my first solo album and the Connecticut countryside seemed like just what the doctor ordered: a welcome escape from fans and photographers. We decided to purchase a five-acre estate in Wilton. Things were escalating on all fronts, and it seemed like a good decision at the time. Eddie Kramer's wife, Julie, actually helped us find the secluded place and we made the move in no time.

While living there, Jeanette and I were happily married and a genuinely fun couple to be around—except when we were fighting! We threw lots of big parties and barbecues, and on most weekends we entertained friends and family (they often wound up staying the entire weekend in our home). In July 1980 Jeanette gave birth to our lovely daughter, Monique, which necessitated hiring a nanny. We had already been through several maids by then, so we ended up with two welcome additions to the Frehley household. I'll never forget our housekeeper, Ellie. She was by far the best and funniest of the bunch. I can still hear her talking to Jeanette: "I'm so sorry. I hope I'm not in trouble. I vacuumed up Mr. F's happy powder in the basement!" There was always silly shit going on up there, with no shortage of alcohol and drugs.

Wilton was our main home for more than seven years (although we also had an apartment in midtown Manhattan). I paid only about $350,000 for the house and property, but I put another million into it: beautiful landscaping, stone walls with wrought iron gates and a cobblestone bridge with a waterfall. A small lake on the property I stocked with fresh trout, which made a delicious lunch from time to time. A long driveway led to a circular fountain and rock garden at the main entrance. Marble bathrooms and gold and crystal chandeliers made the place seem that much more luxurious. In the main entrance there was a giant twenty-foot fireplace made out of stone and quartz. In the basement we had the front end of a vintage purple Jaguar above the brick fireplace and a barroom with a giant projection television, pool table, and professionally equipped wet bar.

The driveway in the front entrance was home to a white Cadillac El Dorado, a stainless steel DeLorean, a black Porsche 928, and a brown metallic K-5 Chevy Blazer. They were all fighting for elbow room around the fountain.

The very best thing about the Wilton estate was the recording studio I built right next to the house. It was unique and could be accessed either from the outside through a wall of glass, brick, and an eighteen-foot-tall solid oak door, or through the basement of the house. The basement entrance had a giant plastic bubble skylight above the staircase that led to the control room. Inside, the studio was futuristic and plush, with a lot of glass and poured concrete and wood baffles. The control room was shaped in an octagon and was equipped with one of the first automated consoles available. Eddie Kramer helped me pick out most of the equipment and it was all pretty much state-of-the-art at the time. I worked with several different producers there, and recorded some original material, as well as some great jam sessions yet to be released. I'd like to let everyone hear some of those tapes sometime in the near future.

When KISS wasn't on the road or recording an album, I liked to retreat to Wilton and just hang out with my friends. The place was so big that I didn't even have to see other people who were there if I didn't want to. I could just stay in one corner of the house and isolate. My "friends" were a lot of the same people I'd known for years, people I could trust, or at least thought I could trust. I cherished them, actually, because they knew the real Paul Frehley. Not Ace, not the Spaceman. Just Paul.

Whenever I went out on the road, people treated me differently, because I was a rock star, but most of my friends understood that I wanted to be treated just like any other person. I really needed a vacation from the Spaceman character for a while, because at times I felt like I was losing my identity. My privacy was important to me, and my friends understood that. I liked acting like an idiot without worrying about it ending up on the radio or in a magazine. I treated them well, too. I turned them on, paid for the cocaine, the pills, and got the best beer, champagne, and booze. I gave them money when they needed it, since most of them couldn't afford my lifestyle. I enjoyed doing that for my friends. A therapist, I suppose, could have a field day analyzing those relationships and questioning their health and the motivations of the various people involved. I never went that deep with it. These were my buddies and I liked hanging out with them. I liked getting loaded and having stupid, usually harmless fun.

I wasn't alone in my self-indulgence. Peter bought a Mercedes and a mansion in Greenwich, Connecticut. Gene and Paul bought really nice places in Manhattan. We were all living life in the fast lane, but I was about to break the sound barrier without even giving it a second thought. With each successive tour, life on the road became more bizarre and surreal. When I wasn't touring sometimes I found comfort and refuge in the New York club scene. In the mid-seventies New York's nightlife had reached a pinnacle of decadence. People were busy being fabulous, looking and dressing great, and saying things like "Why not do this?" or "Try a little of that." A lot of money was being thrown around; New York in the mid- to late seventies mirrored somewhat the lives of many stars, writers, and artists of the 1920s and '30s.

I was hitting a lot of clubs—places like Trax, the Cat Club, Max's Kansas City, Area (complete with its shark tank!), Café Central (where my bartender at times was Bruce Willis), CBGB, and of course Studio 54.

Steve Rubell had built the ultimate pleasure palace, and I became a regular guest there. If you were a VIP and liked to party, you made it a point to hang out at Studio 54 when visiting New York. If I ever ran out of drugs there, I could always visit Steve in his office and find a mountain of cocaine on his desk. He was always a friend and a gentleman to me, and was very generous with whatever he had.

I hung out with most of the celebrities and rock stars who walked through the portals of Studio 54; I drank and did drugs with them. Danced with Lindsay Wagner, hung out with Keith Richards, Alice Cooper, Mick Jagger, and John Belushi, to mention just a few. I saw the giant bags of money and people doing drugs and having sex in the bathrooms and up in the balcony. For the right price you could have just about anything you wanted, from drugs to flesh. At that point in time Studio 54 sometimes felt like the center of the universe. Regardless of how decadent the behavior, nobody even batted an eye, because they were all just too fuckin' busy having fun. But even in the middle of the euphoria and glamour there was a strange feeling in the back of my mind that it would all be short-lived—like a beautiful and grand soiree that slowly burned itself out.

I had one girlfriend in those days who bore a striking resemblance to a Hollywood actress. Sometimes just for laughs, I'd call her up and say, "We're going out. I'll pick you up in an hour. We're hitting 54. You know what to do."

"You want me to fix my hair?"

"Uh-huh."

By the time she got into the limo, this gal really looked the part, and when we'd pull up in front of Studio 54 and the doors would fly open, the paparazzi would go nuts.

"Hey! There's Ace Frehley with Natalie Wood!"

It was a riot fooling the fans and photographers who hung out all night outside the club just to get a quick glimpse of someone famous.

Wherever I went, people were doing lines of blow in full view of everyone else; it was just the way the seventies was. It didn't seem unnatural to me, since just about everyone was doing it. I really can't think of anyone I associated with on a regular basis who wasn't at least a casual user. Well, okay, with a couple of notable exceptions: Gene Simmons and Paul Stanley. They were both antidrug.

Peter and I often drank and did drugs together, and as the band progressed it seemed to become more and more of a problem in their eyes. Peter's reliance on painkillers was particularly a big a concern to them, and his car accident in Los Angeles didn't help matters much. I was oblivious to a lot of the chaos, and really wasn't concerned with what most people thought. I was living the quintessential rock star life filled with sex, drugs, and rock 'n' roll and didn't want to stop. I remember thinking that I probably wouldn't live past my early thirties.

Peter and I had some epic nights of partying involving multiple women and enough cocaine to stop the strongest of hearts. The fact that we're both on this earth today, alive and kicking, seems like a small miracle to me.

Peter was my KISS buddy, the only person in the band I ever considered to be truly a "friend" and someone I could trust. Interestingly enough, he's also the only person in the band with whom I ever engaged in an actual fistfight. It happened on an early tour, in Canada. I don't even remember what it was about—I was mad about something and Peter was pissed off about something else. We just butted heads in the dressing room and one thing led to another and fists began to fly. Our road crew broke it up before anyone got hurt. We apologized to each other over a beer and the incident actually brought us closer together.

We'd always come up with crazy ways to entertain each other on the road, some dangerous, some merely ridiculous. For a while Peter would do this character called "Dr. Rosenbloom." He'd dress up like this crazy doctor and put on a fake mustache and slick his hair back and do impersonations. His impression of Sinatra was terrific! When we didn't have guests it was usually just me and our two bodyguards enjoying the show. We'd sit around in Peter's room and get loaded and share lines, laughing our fucking asses off until the sun came up.

On many occasions I also hung out with the guys in the road crew. Roadies and truckers would always be up for a good poker game, and I was always willing to host the game in my suite and cater the festivities. No one in the band ever played poker, so I didn't have much of a choice. I usually ended up winning the majority of those games, but when I lost I tried to be as gracious a loser as I was a winner.

When we toured with other bands, invariably the band members would either end up in my room or Peter's room. The word got out that we had the best stuff and were throwing the best parties after the show. Party animals usually gravitate toward each other, and that was usually the case on a KISS tour.

I have so many road stories, but one that always comes to mind is the tour we did in the summer of 1975 with Rush opening for us. I always liked Rush (and still do). After a few weeks on tour I started to get to know the guys in the band, and their very funny tour manager, Howie. One thing led to another and before long Peter and I were getting visits from the Rush boys. It usually turned into late evenings filled with beer and grass and whatever else was around. Alex Lifeson, the band's guitarist, used to do this hysterical routine with a large paper laundry bag. He'd draw a ridiculous giant face on the bag with a black marker and put it over his head with a couple of holes poked in it so he could see and breathe. Everyone in the room at this point was either drunk or stoned, but usually a little of both. Anyway, Alex would go into this routine with the bag over his head and while smoking a joint out of his eye he put everyone into total hysterics. He really milked the routine until everyone was gasping for air!

The more popular KISS became, the more security we needed, and our entourage swelled accordingly. We had advance men, bodyguards, managers, road managers, valets, etc., along with various girlfriends and wives. For a while (before we began renting private jets) we flew commercially and usually took up all the first-class seating. Our personal bodyguards were guys you didn't want to tangle with. If anyone from coach tried to invade our space (which they almost always did), one of the bodyguards would just flash a look—*Don't even think about it*—and that was usually enough to send them scurrying back to their seats. Our bodyguards were all trained security officers, but they also were great guys, really serious about their work and fun to hang out with. They'd all been around the business for some time and usually knew what to expect in any given situation. I trusted them completely, and put my life in their hands on more than one occasion.

There was the time in St. Louis, for example, in the late seventies. It wasn't at all unusual when we flew into a city for our bodyguards to befriend members of the local law enforcement agencies. It was a smart thing to do, not only because you might need help with unruly fans or with traffic control at a show, but because afterward things sometimes got out of control back at the hotel or at a local club. The bodyguards knew we'd be in a better bargaining position if the local cops were on our side. We'd always accommodate the cops with autographed records, pictures, and T-shirts, and take photos with them and their families as a courtesy for their support. So, this time in St. Louis, while we were in town on a day off, two off-duty cops came back to the hotel to hang out with us. One of them was packing a .45. After a few hours of sitting around and having a few drinks, I said, "Man, let's go out and find some action."

Everyone agreed, but we ended up biting off more than we could chew. We ended up in a bar on the other side of the Mississippi River, which of course meant we had crossed state lines and jurisdictions. We'd been told the place was a rock 'n' roll joint, but it ended up being more of a biker bar and they weren't too fond of out-of-state rockers.

Peter and I stood outside the door, sizing up the atmosphere.

"Ah, fuck it," Peter said. He gestured to the cops and bodyguards. "Who's gonna mess with us?"

So we went inside without reservation, unaware of what was about to go down.

We all started drinking, shooting a few games of pool, and dancing with some of the local chicks. We were just starting to unwind and enjoy ourselves when things began to go wrong. Someone in our group (okay, it was me) supposedly made an improper advance toward one of the bikers' girlfriends. The next thing I knew, guys were squaring off, cursing and threatening to fuck each other up. Usually, in a bar fight, it ends there, with both sides backing out of the brawl before it even has a chance to begin. But not in a biker bar at one o'clock in the morning. Not when you have a couple of cops and professional bodyguards on your side.

Someone made a quick move and fists and bottles started flying. Things went out of control fast, and at one point my bodyguard Eddie pushed me up against the wall and, like a Secret Service agent, shielded me from a guy trying to smash a chair over my head. Eddie took the full impact, but it barely fazed him. Things were escalating and a decision on what to do next needed to be made fast. Everyone fought as best as they could, but after a few minutes it became apparent that we were badly outnumbered. My bodyguards quickly decided it was time to split. They guided us out into the parking lot and threw us into the two limos that were waiting with engines running. The limo drivers burned rubber as we pulled away, and it took a while for everyone to calm down before we began to assess the damage.

A few of us had minor cuts and bruises, but one of the cops had a three-inch gash in his head that was bleeding badly. And that wasn't the worst of it.

"Motherfucker!" the injured cop said. "They got my fucking gun!"

I'd known enough cops in my time to realize that this was a very big deal. Short of an accidental shooting, almost nothing is more embarrassing, and potentially more damaging, to a police officer than the loss of a gun. And when it happens while you're off duty, drinking in a bar, brawling with a bunch of bikers?

Not good. Not good at all.

We got back to the hotel and I let the injured cop wash up in my shower. We tried cleaning out the gash in his head, but it was obvious to everyone he needed stitches to stop the bleeding, so we ran him over to the hospital for some medical treatment. I felt bad that he had lost his gun, especially since he was trying to save my ass! I never found out exactly what happened to him, but I'll never forget what he did for all of us.

I had been so preoccupied with all the commotion at the hotel and hospital that I hadn't realized my favorite motorcycle jacket was missing. Suddenly it hit me. I'd left the fucking jacket back in the bar.

"I need you to go back there and get it for me," I told my bodyguard, Eddie. "And I don't care how much it costs to get back."

"Don't worry, Ace," he said. "I'll get it, no matter what."

I gave him a thousand dollars cash and said, "Don't come back without it."

Like I said, these guys were fearless . . . and loyal. To someone outside looking in, it probably would have appeared to be a suicide mission, but about an hour and a half later Eddie knocked on my door with my jacket in his hand.

"What happened?" I asked.

He told me most of the dudes we'd brawled with had left for the night, but the bouncers were still there. All it took to get my jacket was a short apology and a little cash—all in a day's work for Eddie.

"How much?" I asked.

"I got it for five hundred. Is that okay, Ace?"

I laughed. "I would have paid two thousand to get it back, Eddie. You keep the other five hundred and let's call it a night. Talk to you in the morning, buddy. Good night, and thanks."

Eddie was a good guy, and I know he went to bed that night with a smile on his face.

Thinking back, I couldn't help but wonder how it all happened. When we'd left the hotel, I felt like we were untouchable, like no one would fuck with us. It just made me realize that you're never really safe, especially when you start to get fucked up and women are involved. You never know what's in the stars; but isn't that what makes life worth living?

I'VE COME CLOSE TO DYING ON NUMEROUS OCCASIONS. Car accidents, overdoses, fights. Almost drowned, too. Twice, in fact. Oddly enough, given our love-hate relationship, Gene Simmons came to my rescue. The first incident happened at a hotel pool in Atlanta. It was a day off, on the road, and we were all hanging out poolside, soaking up the sun and enjoying life. I had had one too many beers that afternoon and shouldn't have been swimming. For no particular reason while I was treading water in the deep end of the pool, I remembered this funny old cartoon of Bugs Bunny. It's the one where he's dramatically going through the process of drowning. You know: dipping beneath the surface and holding up one finger. Then bobbing to the surface and going down again, this time holding up two fingers . . . and then three. I saw this in my mind's eye, and I started laughing my ass off, so hard that I began taking in water. All of a sudden I was hacking and spitting and gulping for air.

And then I went under.

*Oh, fuck . . . I'm drowning!*

Luck interceded, as it often has in my life. Gene, sober as always, noticed I was in trouble and within seconds jumped into the pool and dragged me to the surface. Then he pulled me onto the pool deck and pumped the water out of me. Turns out Gene was actually a certified lifeguard when he was younger. Who knew?

I'll never forget waking up with a hangover the next morning and the terrible taste of chlorine in my mouth. Then it hit me. I nearly drowned yesterday! Holy shit! And Gene saved my life! It was probably one of the few times that I was happier than a pig in shit over the fact that Gene was sober. I thanked him and walked away scratching my head, thinking to myself, *Did that really happen?* And as luck would have it, Gene intervened a few years later and rescued me a second time.

It happened one night after a show. I had decided to take a break from all the drinking and partying and just hang out in my room and take a warm bath. I took several tranquilizers to relax and while soaking in the hot water I dozed off. Unfortunately, I had forgotten to turn off the water and before long the tub started overflowing and began flooding the room (much to the dismay of hotel management). Gene must have had a premonition that night, since normally he would have been very busy entertaining one or two lovely ladies in his room, but to my surprise he came busting through the door with a security guard and pulled me out of the tub, butt naked, just as the water level in the tub was about to reach my lips!

"Ace!" he yelled. "What the fuck are you doing? You could have drowned!"

I was even more surprised than everyone else, since I had been awakened from a relaxing sleep; it took me a moment or two to fully realize my predicament. I thought to myself, *My God, I'm so irresponsible sometimes. When will I ever learn?* I thanked Gene a second time for saving my ass and told him I'd be fine for the rest of the night. Gene didn't want to hear any excuses, and I believe he was genuinely concerned for my welfare. Even though I said I was okay, he tenderly helped me into my bed and tucked me in. He decided to sleep in my room that night and keep a watchful eye on the irresponsible Spaceman. The following morning I woke up without any memory of the incident and when I saw Gene in the room I said, "Hi, Gene! What are you doing here? I stayed in last night and just relaxed. What did you do?" He just looked at me in amazement, realizing I hadn't remembered a thing about the night before and was unaware of how close I had come to drowning for the second time.

Even when I got tired of being locked into the KISS formula—with the pyrotechnics and special effects and lighting cues—I still enjoyed performing live. But after a while even that lost some of its excitement, primarily because there was no room for spontaneity. We couldn't deviate much from the plan without risking bodily harm or at least messing up the show. After my accident in Florida, electrocution was always a fear. A bomb was gonna go off over here, or some fire was going to ignite over there. And it was going to happen at a specific time in every performance. So you pretty much had to do the same shit every night, and that became a little tedious. I distinctly remember a few times in the late seventies daydreaming in the middle of a song. This was only halfway through the show, and I became totally detached—my thoughts drifting away from the show as I began checking out chicks in the front row, wondering if I had enough coke and pills for the week, trying to remember if I had met anyone in town the last time I was here, signaling my bodyguards to give out invitations for our hospitality suite.

Once I finished my smoking guitar solo, I usually went on autopilot and thought more and more about events that were going to occur back at the hotel after the show. I don't think the word *bored* applies here as much as the term *spaced-out*. When you know what's always going to happen, you start looking for other things to excite your senses and occupy your thoughts. That started happening to me on occasion, and I just went with the flow.

You can become accustomed to almost anything, and too much of a good thing can sometimes make it seem less appealing. On other occasions, though, I let the good times roll without a care in the world, taking in every sensual experience. I remember playing a big outdoor festival in Atlanta. I was given a gigantic suite in the hotel and I filled it up with a dozen southern belles, all of whom wanted to show me their gratitude for my performance. I wasn't exactly sure how I was going to entertain everyone concerned. Luckily a very popular local DJ assisted me in the selection process and helped me indulge in the fruits of my labors into the early hours of the morning.

I didn't have anything on this guy when it came to staying power. He was over the edge, and the two of us ended up sharing a half-dozen chicks through the course of the evening, drinking and doing lines of coke off their breasts and naked torsos, screwing until we were so numb we had nothing more to give. We both eventually passed out among several naked bodies, only to be awakened by the sensitive caresses of the opposite gender wanting breakfast treats. It was an experience most men will only fantasize about. KISS's popularity was reaching its peak in the South around this time, and even while everything was going on that night, I sensed I'd never have such an over-the-top experience of southern hospitality again.

And I was right.

After months of being catered to by so many different people and visiting so many different places, the road became a blur. Once in a while, though, certain nights would stand out—either because of the pure ecstasy of the event, or because I came dangerously close to losing it all. The next story is an example of the latter and involves an enormous stroke of luck. (No pun intended; or maybe just a little.)

We refer to it as "the golf club affair." It involved me, Peter, and Don

Wasley. (As I mentioned earlier, Don was the VP of artist development for Casablanca Records; Peter and I affectionately nicknamed Don "the Director.") The story begins back at the hotel after a show. We rendezvoused for some drinks and lines, not expecting anything out of the ordinary. The next thing you know we were joined by three chicks. From the looks of these gals it appeared we were in store for a very accommodating evening. Alcohol, cocaine, and quaaludes filled the next hour or two as we savored the fruits of these lovely ladies. Later some of us got hungry and decided to have a snack. Since we were in the hospitality suite there was a long table of food just there for the taking. After we ate we started painting the girls' bodies with the onion dip and salad dressing, thinking it might liven things up a bit. The event quickly evolved into a contest for the best body painting design. Another hour passed, and after a few showers some of us started losing interest. Don, for one, had turned his back on his female canvas and begun practicing his golf swing. Peter had put on a cape and was diving off the furniture into God knows what, pretending to be Superman. I was bent over the table doing a line of blow when all of a sudden I heard a cracking sound, and out of the corner of my eye I watched the girl near Don hit the floor with a thud. Don had been unaware of her approach from behind, and had clocked her on the side of the head with his golf club. She hit the carpet like deadweight!

I remember looking at Don, and I remember Peter saying, "Holy shit! What a fuckin' shot."

Being completely wasted, we all started laughing, but within seconds our laughter quickly turned into deep concern for her well-being, since she wasn't moving. I remember thinking to myself, *What a fucked up way to end such a great party!* I could just imagine the headline: "Groupie Killed in Hotel Suite by Golf Club."

Don had a look of grave concern on his face, since he was looking at a lengthy prison sentence if she was in fact dead. Time stood still for a moment as we tried to revive the fallen angel.

Suddenly a slight moan rose from her mouth as she rolled over onto her back. With half-opened eyes she slowly raised her head, and with a deep breath sat up on the carpet. Seconds later, with a bewildered look on her face, she spoke.

"What the fuck was that?"

I said to her, "Sorry, baby. Are you okay? Don was practicing his golf swing and I guess you eluded his peripheral vision."

Within no time she was back on her feet, bent over the table snorting another line of coke, oblivious to how close she had come to dying. We just looked at each other in amazement, thinking, *Shit . . . what a fuckin' close call!*

Our guardian angels must have been watching over us that night. The sun was coming up and the party continued until we all fell asleep.

So many close calls, so many disasters averted. I have no idea how or why I'm still around. I took so many chances and pushed the envelope of fate so far; sometimes it almost seems like these things never really happened. But they did, and I'm just thankful I lived to talk about it and learned from my mistakes.

There was the time in a large southern city, for instance, when we trashed a hotel room in grand style. Peter was there, getting down with one of rock's best-known groupies, a chick named Sweet Sweet Connie from Arkansas (who was immortalized in the Grand Funk Railroad song "We're an American Band"). I was feeling very lovable that evening and jumped into bed between Peter and Connie, but after a few minutes it was apparent I was an unwelcome guest, so I retreated to the safety of my room, where another party was beginning. My friend Donnie from Westchester showed up (why in the name of Christ was Donnie down there? I have no idea). And the fourth person was a famous stock car driver who shall remain nameless; let's just say he was a big deal at the time. And this was the Deep South, remember, where stock car drivers were treated like . . . well, like rock stars.

So the party progressed as it usually did, with a lot of alcohol and cocaine and whatever, until I came up with the brilliant idea to begin tossing the furniture out the window. Now, I did not invent this concept, but I did almost perfect it. My buddies looked a little unwilling at first to participate, especially since we were twenty stories up and my windows faced out onto a busy street. But once I began the festivities by grabbing a lamp and hurling it out the window, they quickly decided to go along with the plan. Next went a wooden chair, and an end table. Then a desk flew out the window . . . followed by a television set. Each item exploded spectacularly—*CRACK!!*—when it hit the street below, splintering in all directions and terrifying passersby. Next we somehow maneuvered a love seat through the open window. Again, we could have killed someone, but I don't recall thinking it was anything but hilarious at the time. The severity of our actions didn't occur to me, until our road manager, Frankie Scinlaro, came running into the room, panicked and breathless.

"Are you guys out of your fucking minds?" he asked. "The cops are on their way."

"Uh-oh," I said between giggles.

"No, man, this is serious." He pointed at Donnie and the stock car driver. "You guys get the hell out of here."

I started to leave with them.

"It's your room, Ace," Frankie pointed out. "They're going to find you."

"What do you want me to do?"

"Get in bed, get under the covers, keep your fucking mouth shut. Let me do the talking."

The state troopers arrived just minutes later and I eagerly listened to the conversation from under the sheets, while pretending to be asleep. They were ready to take me away without discussion, and who could blame them? There was furniture flying out of my room like missiles. But Frankie, God rest his soul, handled the whole thing like a pro. Frankie was a crazy fuck, and had seen it all and could bullshit with the best of them. Frankie had also road-managed Alice Cooper before coming on board with KISS, so he knew a little something about rock star excess. KISS, though, was almost too much even for Frankie.

"I'm sorry, officer," I heard him say. "Ace had a party with a lot of people in his room, but unfortunately he drank a little too much and passed out in his bed hours ago He's not the guilty party here, and people have been in and out of this room all night. I don't even know most of them. Ace was just trying to give back some Southern hospitality. He had nothing to do with these assholes who tossed the furniture. Believe me, he'll be pissed when he wakes up in the morning."

Incredibly enough, they bought it. Or they didn't buy it, but just didn't care enough to make an example of me. Especially since there were no witnesses, and no one was actually injured in the whole insane episode. KISS had that kind of clout. Either way, without Frankie's intervention, I'm sure I would have ended up in jail that night. Instead I lay there for a while, relieved and thankful for Frankie's skills of persuasion, wondering what adventures awaited me in the next city, and whether I would be so lucky.

During the 1970s and '80s most people who were doing a lot of cocaine usually came up with some sort of code name or alias for the word *coke*, especially when talking about it on the telephone (you never knew if the phone was bugged). In my social circle, names came and went, but the one that remained my favorite over the years was "Betty White." If I was talking to a friend on the phone and wanted to know if there was going to be cocaine at a particular party, I'd just say "Hey! Is Betty going to be at the party?" We always laughed about it when we met face-to-face, and how could you not? I mean it's just too fucking funny for words, and so is the real Betty White. I love her to death, and think she's the most underrated female comedian on the planet.

Alcohol and drugs were my constant companion, my best friend—and worst enemy. Sometimes they were a detriment to my career and personal life. Overall, I guess, you'd have to argue they were mainly a bad thing inasmuch as they nearly killed me. Sometimes, though, being loaded worked to my advantage, as it did on October 31, 1979, when KISS made a memorable Halloween night appearance on NBC's *Tomorrow* show.

Hosted by the friendly and sometimes confrontational Tom Snyder, *Tomorrow* was a popular and successful late-night talk show that attracted some of the biggest names in politics and show business. Hey—John Lennon did *Tomorrow*. How could KISS turn it down? Well, we couldn't, and our appearance was one for the ages.

I was nervous as hell about going on network TV—live!—in front of millions of people. So I started pounding some Stoli in the back of my limo as soon as it passed through my gates on the way to the city. Now, I might have been a formidable drinker in those days, but I wasn't really a vodka drinker. The bottle was nestled in the door of the limo and I reached for it to escape the anxiety I was feeling. By the time we arrived at the NBC studios in Rockefeller Center, I had a pretty good buzz on and all my nervousness had subsided.

When I got into the dressing room, Bill Aucoin showed up with a bottle of champagne, and I had a glass with him and Jeanette. Just before I left the dressing room I snorted a few lines of blow to balance off all the alcohol and give me a little edge. By the time we took our places opposite Tom, on the set, in full KISS costume and makeup, I was feeling no pain. And I was ready for anything.

My amusement began with an introductory voice-over, during which Snyder described our act, and in the process referred to Gene as the "*bass* player." As in, *small-mouthed*, *large-mouthed*, *striped* or *Chilean sea* . . .

By the time he got around to me I could barely contain my amusement. So, when Tom said, "This is Ace Frehley, lead guitarist," I responded with, "I'm not the lead guitarist, I'm the *trout* player!"

And then I cracked up, and so did Tom, much to the chagrin of Paul and, especially, Gene.

Hey, Gene be would the first to admit that he is a control freak. So is Paul. They always wanted to control KISS, and they wanted to control me. But I had talent and a mind of my own, and had different ideas about the direction of KISS. Gene and Paul were caught in this dichotomy: *Oh, fuckin' Ace. We love him, we hate him. We don't wanna put up with his bullshit anymore, and he doesn't wanna put up with ours. But we can't get rid of him because the fans love him!*

"You're supposed to be some sort of spaceman, right?" Tom asked me at one point, while gesturing to my costume.

"No, actually I'm a plumber!"

Snyder laughed from the gut, and fired right back, "Oh, well I've got a piece of pipe backstage I'd like to have you work on."

A hanging curveball if I ever saw one! Regardless, I completed the R-rated joke with the delivery of a major-league all-star.

"Tell me about it!"

There was no live audience in the studio, but just about everyone there, including the crew, doubled over with laughter.

If you watch the video you can actually see me turning to Gene and putting my hands up at one point and quietly saying, "What?" like a child who's misbehaving at a family function and wants his dad to loosen up and join in the fun. Gene was sometimes incapable of that, even in a setting that clearly called for some spontaneity and horsing around. It was all so ridiculous. How seriously can you take yourself when you're sitting there in a superhero costume and full face makeup? Gene missed the whole thing. If he would have allowed himself to be just a little more lighthearted about everything, and stopped fuckin' thinking about money all the time, things might have turned out differently. I love the guy, but he *never, ever got it.*

You could have cut the air in that studio with a knife. Tom picked up on Gene's negativity, and you could tell he wasn't digging it. At one point Gene tried to make a joke about selling Tom some swampland in New Jersey, and Snyder completely ignored him and turned his attention back to me. It was like Gene didn't exist. Tom Snyder may have been a newsman, but he realized very quickly that it was more entertaining to let me laugh and tell jokes than it was to allow Gene to bore everyone with his uptight humor.

Afterward, I got tons of phone calls congratulating me on my "performance."

"You were a fucking riot, Ace! You stole the show!"

Yeah, that was a classic performance, and it might have been the first time that a single appearance so clearly delineated the diverse personalities of KISS. The show speaks for itself and that's all I'm going to say about it. Everyone should judge for themselves what really happened. I enjoyed myself on the show and really wasn't trying to piss off anyone. I was just being the Space Ace. After the interview, Tom came back to my dressing room and we shook hands and had another good laugh. I thought he was very genuine, and he seemed to really enjoy the experience.

Being a rock star provided access to people and relationships I never would have known otherwise. My friendship with John Belushi certainly falls into this category. I met John one night at Peter's pad in the city. Peter lived on the East Side with his wife, Lydia, and I was always a welcome guest in their home. I walked in and John was just kicking back on Peter's couch, having a cold beer and making small talk. We all exchanged greetings, and I cracked open a cold one as well. A few beers later the obvious question arose: did I have any coke? In those days I almost always had at least a few grams of blow on me, but on that particular night I had just scored some really good shit. Once I announced the good news, everyone in the room rose to attention and proceeded to partake of the sparkling powder.

More lines and cold beer filled the next hour or two, with jokes flying back and forth across the room until we were all laughing hysterically. Lydia was always a lot of fun to be around (we had the same sense of humor) and shared a lot of inside jokes about the band. She was with Peter from the beginning, and over the years had become a trusted friend and confidante. I could usually make her laugh at the drop of a hat, but what was more interesting to me was that John seemed to be laughing at almost all my jokes. I had been told for years that I was a funny guy, but to be making a professional comedian crack up felt even more rewarding.

There's a strange bonding process that happens sometimes between two people when alcohol and drugs are involved. That bond was cemented that evening between me and John, and remained that way until the end. We were both famous, and we both loved music and comedy, and we also enjoyed getting fucked up. John and KISS rose to prominence on parallel lines. He was one of the breakout stars of *Saturday Night Live* in its first few seasons, beginning in the fall of 1975. While KISS was selling out arenas and stadiums around the world in the late 1970s, John was in the process of becoming a movie star as well, first with *Animal House* and then with *The Blues Brothers*.

John used to take me down to his private bar, south of Canal Street, which he owned with fellow Blues Brother Dan Aykroyd. What a trip that was. Those guys liked to party (obviously), and yet they really couldn't go out in New York without getting harassed by fans for autographs or photo opportunities, which was another thing we had in common. John and Dan bought their own bar and sealed the windows with cinder blocks; a steel door with a peephole served as the front entrance. To the average passerby, the building looked almost abandoned.

That was the beauty of the club: it was never technically "open." They used it primarily on Saturday nights for a hangout and to entertain guests after the show. Anyone driving or walking by on a Saturday night or Sunday morning might have thought it was a mob hangout, because the street would be filled with stretch limousines, but in reality the bar was filled with the cast and guests of *SNL*.

I was there on some of those nights, and the parties were great, but a little too crowded for my tastes. During the week, though, the place was dead and for me that was a dream come true. I mean just imagine how cool it would be to have your own private bar in Manhattan to hang out in and do whatever you wanted. I'd get behind the bar and act like a bartender for John and any other guests we had invited. Then we'd switch places, tell some stupid jokes, and knock over the drinks. We'd clean off the bar, lay down two-foot lines of cocaine, and try to snort them in one breath. Then we'd dance on top of the bar, or ask some girls I had invited to do a striptease while John and I played the guitar and drums on the little bandstand. It was total decadence, and we enjoyed every second of it.

I can remember staggering outside with John one time in the early morning hours, climbing into my Porsche and driving to a nearby deli for a beer run (yes, we'd drunk all the beer in the bar!), and passing out in the car in front of the deli, only to be rudely awakened by businessmen and secretaries on their way to work. They'd be looking into the windows of my black 928, curiously trying to figure out who the disheveled occupants were. John and I just laughed at them, saying, in effect, "You suckers! Fuck you and your jobs! We don't have to work this morning!"

And so it went on, sometimes for days on end. I remember calling up Jeanette one morning after one or two nights out with John and hearing screams on the other end of the phone. Jeanette was understandably pissed, but I knew she was also a huge fan of both John and *SNL*. I thought to myself, if I put John on the phone with Jeanette maybe he could calm her down and buy me some time.

John got on the phone and launched into his famous Marlon Brando impersonation from *A Streetcar Named Desire*. John started yelling "Stella! Stella! Stella!"

After his routine was finished he also told her he needed me to coach him on an upcoming skit on the show.

Within a few minutes Jeanette's anger had melted away. She told John it was okay for me to stay out for another day. We went back to the bar or my apartment or someone else's apartment and continued the party till we passed out again.

The most memorable story I can share about John is one that reflects the guy's inherent sensitivity and insecurity. You see, like a lot of performers, John wasn't quite the egomaniac he appeared to be onstage. Or, at least, I don't think he was. I was at the Palladium (formerly the Academy of Music) one night in the summer of 1980, shortly after the Blues Brothers movie had come out. Belushi and Aykroyd had embarked on a legitimate concert tour, with a great backup band, and anybody who was anybody in New York was at the Palladium on Fourteenth Street that night to see the Blues Brothers in action. They played for about forty-five minutes, then took a break, with the understanding that they'd come back out and do a second set.

I was hanging out backstage with a date and all the other celebrities when I got the word that no one was allowed in the dressing room to visit the Blues Brothers. Suddenly the promoter, Ron Delsener, came running up to me.

"Ace, we have a big problem."

"What's up?" I said.

Ron told me John didn't want to go back out to do the second half of the show, supposedly because his voice was shot.

"What can I do?" I asked.

Ron said, "Can you try talking to him? I told him you were here."

Delsener paused, then gestured toward my date for the evening, a very tall and lovely New York model. "With your friend."

"Okay," I said. "I'll give it a shot."

As I proceeded to go upstairs to the dressing room, everyone who was milling around backstage looked up at me with amazement. I could hear some of them saying under their breath, "How come Ace can get in to see John and Dan, and we can't?" Paul and Gene were also part of the crowd, looking confused. My model friend was wearing a very short skirt that night, and you could easily see her sheer underpants as we ascended the stairs, adding insult to injury to some of the onlookers.

A minute later I was in the dressing room, asking John how he was feeling.

He shook his head.

"I don't know, man, my fucking voice is shot. I can't sing."

I just smiled.

His voice sounded terribly hoarse and I suggested he drink some hot tea with honey. While he sipped the tea I tried to cheer him up with a few stupid Ace jokes; then I hiked up my friend's dress to lift his spirits.

"Come on, John," I said. "You don't want to disappoint the Big Apple, do you?"

He just looked at me, his face filled with sadness and fatigue.

"I don't think I can do it, Ace."

I chuckled. "Hey, nobody really gives a shit. Stop worrying. I can't sing, either. I just fake it most of the time, but I get out there anyway. Hell, Mick Jagger can't sing. Dylan can't sing. They just kinda talk the words. Everybody does it in rock 'n' roll, especially when they're on tour and they blow out their voice. Remember, the show must go on, and you're a professional."

John smiled.

"I guess."

"Right. Just talk your way through it. Everyone out there loves you. It'll be great!"

We joked around a little more and had a beer and did a few lines of coke. Slowly John's mood began to change for the better. After a few more lines and a little female entertainment, John decided he would finish the show. I told John to knock 'em dead and I'd see him after the show. I left the dressing room smiling, and informed Delsener that the show would begin shortly. Ron was so thrilled he hugged me and said, "I can't thank you enough. I guess that's why they call you the Ace. You really saved the fucking day. I owe you one, buddy!"

In the winter of 1982 I got a call from John, as I did on occasion, usually when he was in town and wanted someone to hang out with or needed some blow. I wasn't available at the time, and here's why: he'd caught me during one of my "cleansing" periods. This was something I did from time to time, probably out of instinct, and I honestly believe it's the only reason I'm alive today. I would take a break from the self-abuse, give myself a chance to come back from the precipice. Even on the road with KISS, I sort of knew how much my body could take before I'd need a rest. Sometimes I'd look at the calendar, notice we were going to be in a particular city for three or four days, and I'd shut everything down. No alcohol, no cocaine, no painkillers, no sex. I'd put a sign on my door saying "Quarantined by the Board of Health!" and then I'd take a bunch of tranquilizers and sleep for two days. My bodyguards gave everyone strict orders not to call or knock on my door. That allowed me to recharge my batteries. I'd usually wake up refreshed, take a hot bath, have some breakfast, and start the whole crazy cycle all over again, feeling as though I'd bought myself a little more time.

When John called me, he had just flown in from California, where he had been working on what would be his last film, *Neighbors*, and was going to be in town for only a couple of days.

"Come on, Ace," he said. "Let's hook up in the city."

"Sorry, John. Can't do it. I'm cleaning up for a while. I just need a break from the insanity."

I remember him laughing on the other end of the phone. I suppose it did sound funny, the idea of me not wanting to party. A break from the insanity?! What do you mean? I was Mr. Insanity . . . from Outer Space! I must admit his offer was tempting, and I hadn't seen him for weeks, but I had been burning the candle at both ends and just wanted to stop feeling like shit for a little while. I also wanted to relax and hang out with my two-year-old-daughter, Monique, and be Daddy for a while. Also, don't forget—I'm a Taurus through and through. Once I've made up my mind, that's it. I very rarely reverse a decision.

We had a few more laughs and eventually he decided to give up and make other plans. He told me he'd call when he got back from L.A. on the next run, and then said good-bye.

I didn't realize that would be the last time I'd ever speak to John. If I had known, I would have dropped everything and met him in the city, no questions asked. A few weeks later I was watching the news when I heard that John had died of a drug overdose in Los Angeles. I was in complete shock; an overwhelming feeling of sadness came over me. I was never going to see him again. I had become very fond of John, and suddenly I realized all the fun we had together was over. He had told me a few months earlier that he wanted to put me in his next film, since I was one of the few people who could always crack him up. Now it was just a dream.

We had a mutual admiration. John Belushi was a great guy and a gifted performer. I feel very lucky to have known him. His death was a tragedy and was the catalyst for me to clean up my act for several months afterward. I still think about the crazy times we had together and get a smile on my face; I just wish things could have turned out differently. John was a comedic genius and no one has ever been able to fill his shoes. He was unique. I miss him. I think everyone does.

# 14

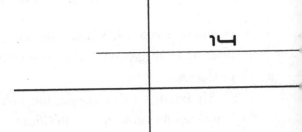

# APPLE WINE AND AIRPLANE GLUE

While some critics blasted us for indulging our egos with solo albums, I believe the interlude provided a crucial artistic outlet for all concerned. If I hadn't been given the opportunity to record *Ace Frehley*, I probably wouldn't have lasted as long as I did with KISS. The success of my solo album gave me significantly more confidence as a writer when KISS reconvened to record our next album, *Dynasty*.

The production process began changing with *Dynasty*. There was very little collaboration among band members. Each of us went into the studio on our own to record demos that we later presented to each other and the producer, Vini Poncia. This process created more of a power struggle within the band, since several of the songs would have to be rejected. I wanted more of my work represented on KISS records, and for the most part, I was accommodated.

I have mixed feelings about some of the tunes on *Dynasty*. On one hand, I think it's one of the better KISS records, with a lot of hard-driving rock. Vini did a terrific job of making a record that would appeal to hard-core KISS fans. I also liked the fact that he was willing to listen to my suggestions and even encouraged them, unlike some other producers.

My buddy Chris Cassone, the in-house engineer at North Lake Sound Studio, came up with the idea for me to cover the Rolling Stones song "2000 Man." On first listen, it didn't really sound like a KISS song, but I made short work of that. It was the title that originally caught my attention, and with a major overhaul, and slight rearrangement, I changed it into something special. I've always loved the Rolling Stones, and *Their Satanic Majesties Request* was a brilliant record. From what I can remember, it was their answer to the Beatles' release of *Sgt. Pepper's Lonely Hearts Club Band*. Vini loved the idea for the remake of "2000 Man," and it became one of the premier tracks off the record, as well as a signature song for me in concert.

Besides "2000 Man," there was "Hard Times," a song about my high school days in the Bronx, and "Save Your Love," which was a slight departure from my normal straight-ahead rock 'n' roll. For the first time in "KISStory," I sang more songs on a KISS record than Gene.

There were problems that surfaced during the making of *Dynasty*. Peter had been involved in a bad car accident in L.A., and had become increasingly reliant on pain medication. Sometimes it affected his drumming and gave him mood swings, which provoked internal conflicts within the band. When his performance in the studio became questionable, the band opted to use a studio drummer, and we chose Anton Fig, whom I had worked with on my solo album. At the time I wanted to believe that Peter's absence in the studio would only be temporary, but it turned out to be permanent.

The situation deteriorated over the course of the next year, and when we recorded *Unmasked*, Peter's spot on drums was again filled by Anton, even though Peter's image appeared on the cover. Technically, *Unmasked* was the last studio album to feature the original lineup.

Even though *Unmasked* wasn't as big a commercial success as its predecessors, it still had some memorable tracks. I again aced three songs on the record: "Two Sides of the Coin," "Torpedo Girl," and "Talk to Me." The latter became a big hit in Australia, and I performed it live in concert around the globe.

Even though Peter was absent during the *Unmasked* recording process, he did return to film the video for the album's first single, "Shandi." Peter was obviously very upset at the end of the taping, and I felt some of his pain, knowing it would be his last time wearing the KISS makeup and costume. I don't believe Peter really wanted to leave the band, but Paul and Gene were dead set on replacing him. I wanted to give him another chance, but my hands were tied. I was outvoted, and the decision was made to move forward without him, so I accepted the decision reluctantly.

Before Peter left the band, there had always been a certain amount of creative and personal tension. For the most part, though, it was manageable. Yeah, it's true that we often played two on two—me and Peter against Paul and Gene—but when tempers flared, I usually tried to be the peacemaker. In the wake of arguments I'd sometimes tell a stupid joke to make everyone laugh and clear the air. Chemistry and balance allowed the band to function in spite of the quirks and egos of its members, but with the loss of Peter, I soon realized things would never be the same.

Finding someone to fill Peter's shoes wasn't an easy task. We auditioned several great drummers, but settled on a relatively unknown kid from Brooklyn named Eric Carr. Eric was a solid drummer who had played in a variety of local bands before he joined KISS. He was a very good replacement; he just wasn't Peter.

Here's an example. There was a time when we were touring in Canada, not long after Eric joined the band, and one day Eric and I were out shopping and ended up in a big toy store at a mall. As we passed the model airplanes and cars, I was overcome with a feeling of nostalgia.

*Wow . . . been a long time since I sniffed glue!*

I knew there was a difference between the glue in this store and the glue they were selling back in the States. The regulations in Canada were different. This shit was the real deal, like the glue I'd sniffed as a kid back in the Bronx. My curiosity got the better of me, so I decided to ask Eric for a favor.

"Hey, man. Could you buy some glue for me?"

Eric looked at me like I was fucking crazy.

"Why can't you buy it yourself?"

A fair question, and one I couldn't readily answer. It had more to do with paranoia and the feeling that with my well-documented reputation for getting loaded, if anyone recognized me, there might be repercussions. Hardly anyone knew what Eric looked like without makeup. He could buy a few tubes of glue without so much as raising an eyebrow. And he agreed reluctantly. We went back to the hotel, and after a few drinks, I decided to satisfy my curiosity. I emptied the tube into a paper bag and got down to business. I wasn't sure what to expect and my memory was hazy. I remember hearing that sniffing glue was one of the most toxic things you could do to your body and brain. Like most drugs, the chemicals in glue are metabolized through the liver. I knew all of that, but I figured that one more time wouldn't kill me. Hell, I knew plenty of guys who had sniffed hundreds of times and they were still walking around, although missing millions of brain cells. Hey—I'm not advocating glue sniffing. I don't recommend that people try any of the crazy shit that I did. But it's my history, and it is what it is. Mainly I was curious as to whether sniffing glue was the terrifying experience I recalled.

Luckily, it wasn't. I got dizzy and reached a short-lived euphoric state. At its hallucinatory peak, I saw pink elephants floating across the ceiling, like in Disney's *Fantasia*. The high lasted only about fifteen minutes, and then it was gone. Disillusioned and frustrated, I tossed the bag into a nearby garbage can and cracked open another beer.

So what's the point, you might reasonably ask? Just this: If it had been Peter with me that day, we'd have been sniffing glue together. Eric wasn't quite as straight as Gene and Paul, but he sure wasn't a party animal. He was just a good kid from Brooklyn trying to fit in at his new job, which happened to feature several unusual coworkers.

*Job* is the right word, too. Eric was a hired gun, brought in to replace Peter, but not to be an equal partner. This was a drastic change in the fundamental structure of the band, and one that had a profound impact on all of us, but especially on me. In the past, we had all been equal partners, and we voted on all important issues. More often than not, when we disagreed, the voting was split: me and Peter on one side, Paul and Gene on the other. But now Peter was gone, and I was in trouble. The balance of power shifted heavily in favor of Gene and Paul. I realized quickly that they usually voted one way, and I voted another. Four was a good number. With four there was fairness and democracy. If a tiebreaker was needed, we turned to Bill Aucoin. He was like the fifth member of KISS. But eventually Gene and Paul got rid of Bill as well. They were control freaks, and Peter's departure allowed them to exercise that control to an extent I hadn't anticipated.

I should have seen it coming.

Bob Ezrin is a brilliant producer, but when it came to the ninth KISS studio album (and what would turn out to be, for all practical purposes, my last KISS album for a while), *Music from "The Elder,"* I disagreed with him and the band on many issues. I could see it from the beginning. I had the street smarts and common sense to take a giant step back and look at the project with an objective eye, and I knew it was a colossal mistake in judgment. Paul, Gene, and Bob didn't get it. They went forward with the whole ridiculous concept.

To be perfectly candid, I never fully understood what the hell this record was supposed to be about. Gene had written some kind of story, and there was talk of turning it into a feature-length movie or animated film or something. Even after the *Kiss Meets the Phantom* . . . catastrophe, Gene was fascinated with Hollywood culture. Ezrin stoked the fire by suggesting that Gene's little story be used as the basis for some sort of big multimedia, cross-platform vehicle for KISS. Part of the plan, apparently, was a "concept" record.

As anyone who knows rock 'n' roll can tell you, concept records can be career killers even for the most talented bands. The problem is that instead of ending up with a masterpiece like *Tommy*, you could end up with *Saucy Jack*, Spinal Tap's unproduced rock opera about Jack the Ripper.

I cowrote two songs for the record. One was called "Escape from the Island," and the other was originally called "Don't Run" but was later renamed "Dark Light," after Lou Reed rewrote some of the lyrics. I didn't understand the concept, and I didn't give a fuck about the central character (some old fart nobody knew anything about). It was ludicrous. I kept trying to tell the guys that if we released an album of self-indulgent nonsense, complete with spoken dialogue and haunting wind instruments, we'd be slaughtered. Our core fans would get pissed, and serious rock critics would laugh at it. It was doomed from the beginning.

Didn't matter what I said, though. I was outvoted.

Ezrin has willingly taken considerable heat for that album over the years and admitted he was doing a lot of drugs at the time, which clouded his judgment. Dammit! I was doing a lot of drugs, too, but I could still see that the project was going to be a flop. At one meeting after another, I went on record against it, but the other guys insisted on moving forward.

Even weirder was the fact that we recorded a big chunk of *Music from "The Elder"* at my home studio in Connecticut, but I avoided being in the studio most of the time. If I wasn't doing vocals or laying down a guitar track, I was usually upstairs shooting pool and having a cold one and a toot. Granted, that's not the way it's supposed to work. If you're enthusiastic about a project, you want to be there as much as possible, but I was so opposed to the album's direction that I went into avoidance mode.

After the project moved up to Canada, I decided to remain behind most of the time and continued to work on guitar solos and overdubs at home. To my dismay, a lot of the solos I recorded were missing from the final mix. Go figure.

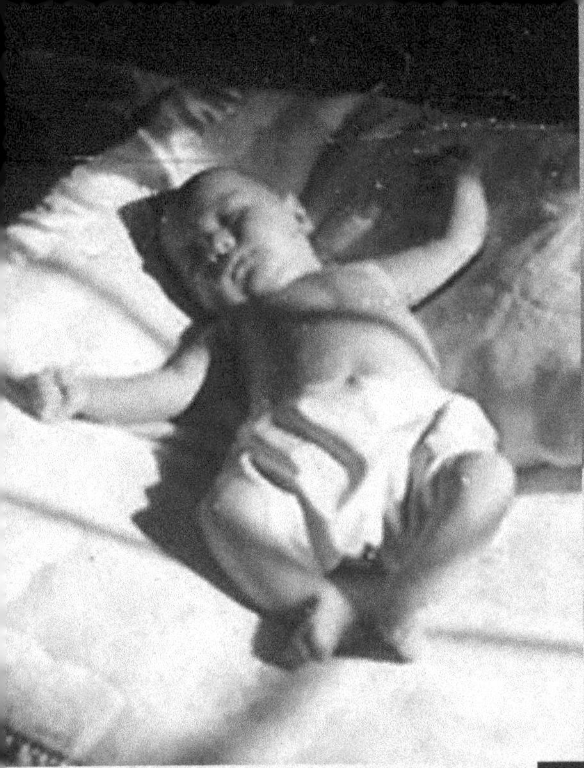

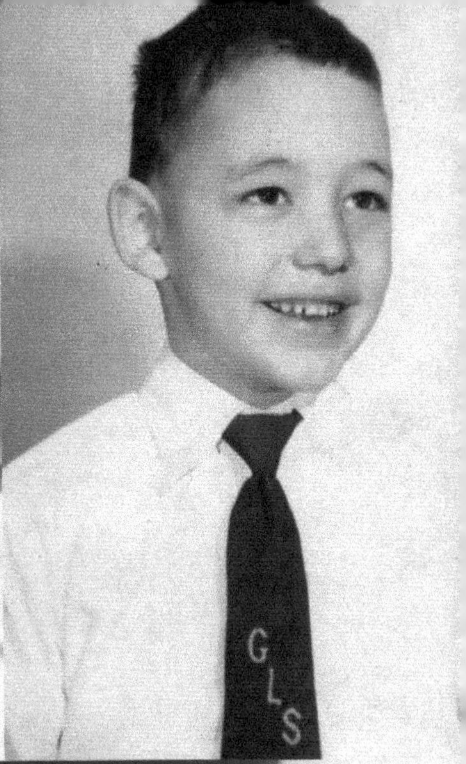
GLS

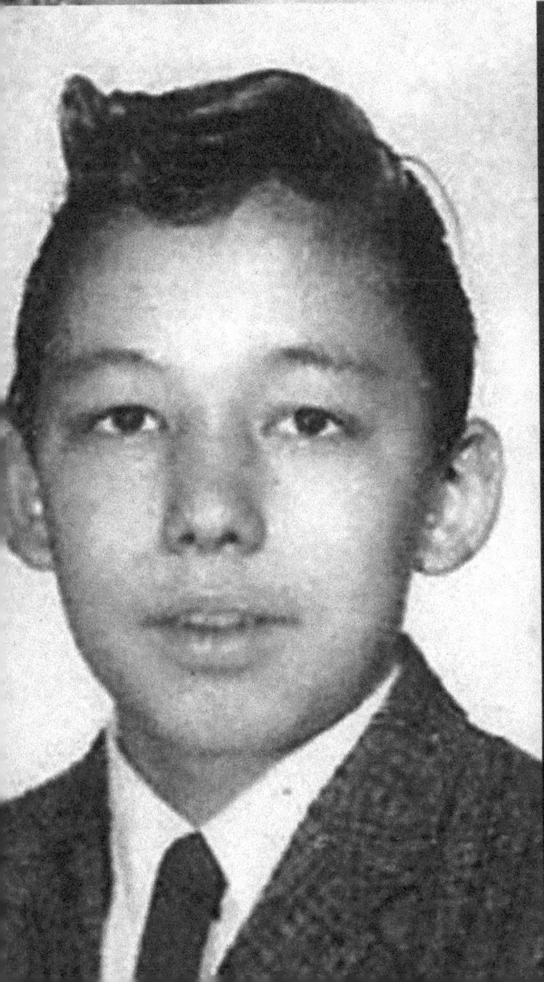

IGNORE THIS BUTTON
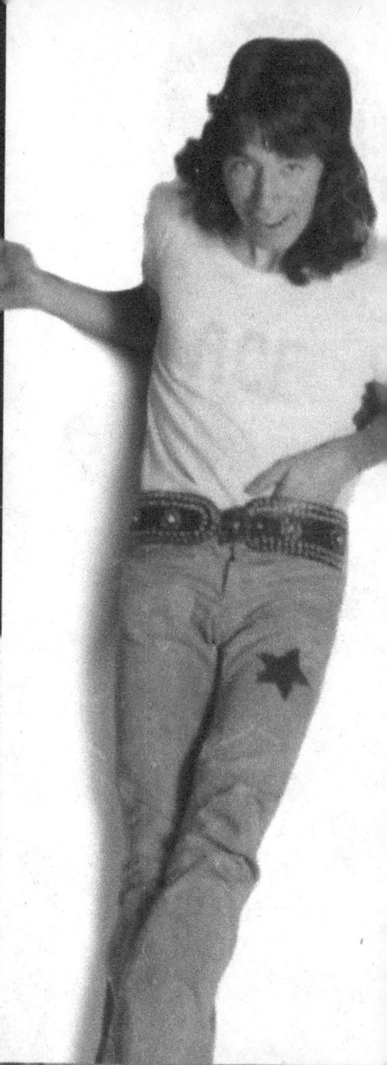

LANEY
LANEY
ACE
ACE

REST ROOMS

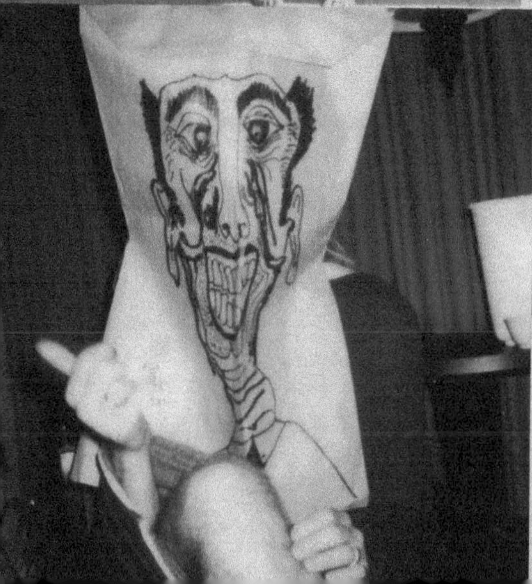

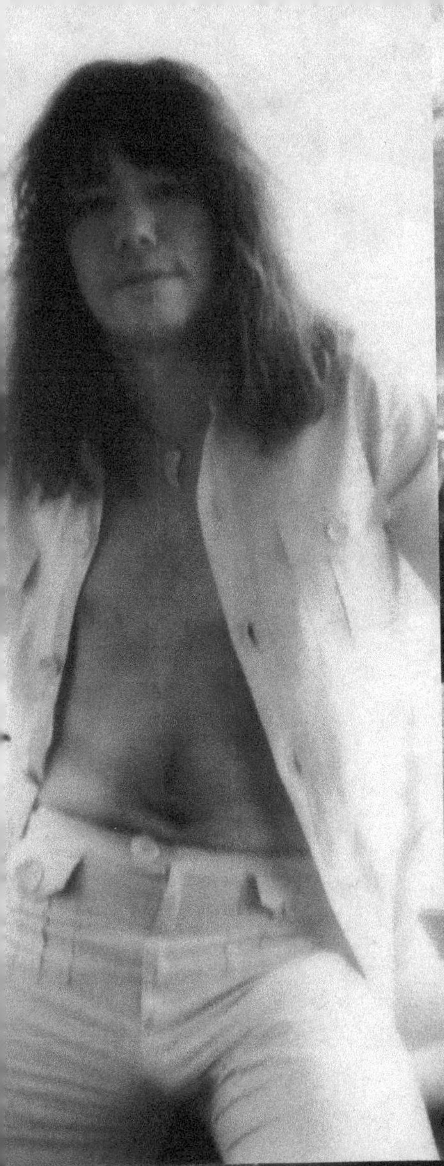

GORDON

YOUTH DISSENT
AT THE
Rustic Pub
FRIDAY AND SATURAY!
DRINK & DANCE TO THE SWEET SOUNDS OF
LOCATED ON BLONDELL & FINK AVENUES
1 BLOCK EAST OF WESTCHESTER SQUARE
KISS
WORLD-TOUR
2009-2010

STOP
CROSSING

RHINO

COULD U COME BACK IN A FEW BEERS?
FREHLEY
TALENT

& FITCH

All Limitations are self inflicted...

One of the biggest tragedies during the recording of that project (bigger even than the album itself, as far as I'm concerned) was the death of my dog, a shepherd-Lab mix named Seamus. He was the most friendly, loyal dog I had ever owned and a great watchdog as well. Sometimes he barked excessively, but if you're a dog person, that's no big deal. Not everyone is a dog person. Paul fell into that category. He was afraid of the dog, and so I agreed to keep Seamus out of the house and studio whenever Paul was around. I had a dog run next to the house, off the garage, bordered by a chain-link fence, and I used to put Seamus in there for only brief periods or when there were workers on the property and I wasn't around. He normally didn't like being separated from me—I think he was worried about me and may have thought someone was trying to hurt me. One day Seamus tried to tunnel his way out to get closer to me, and he wound up getting stuck underneath the chain-link fence. By the time I found him, he had choked to death. I was devastated. If you're a dog lover, you can probably understand how much that blew my mind. Seamus was not just a pet; he was my best friend and companion. I used to prop him up on the couch next to me when I was loaded and talk to him. And I swear to God, it seemed like he understood everything I was saying. He'd just look back at me and nod his head. Now he was gone, and I secretly blamed Paul for the whole incident.

The thing is, *Music from "The Elder"* is not really a terrible album. It's just a terrible KISS album. The songs themselves aren't all that bad, but some of them simply aren't appropriate for a KISS album.

We changed the costumes and cut our hair, and I went along for the sake of consistency. The whole thing was ridiculous. When I see video footage of KISS performing songs from that album on television, trying to look so serious and self-important, I don't know whether to laugh or cringe. Like I've always said, I'll try almost anything once, but if I had a do-over, I'd take a pass on *Music from "The Elder."* I think we all would, and the KISS Army would be grateful.

---

I remember one time when Monique was just a baby, and I was home in Connecticut, waiting for a limo ride to the airport. When the car arrived, I was in the bedroom packing my bags. I could hear Jeanette yell, "Come on, Paul! You're going to be late!"

We had a big, sloping, circular driveway, with a fountain in the middle, and when I finally got outside, the limo was parked just off the edge of the driveway. I knew right away the guy was in trouble. The driveway was made out of asphalt with a cobblestone border, and the driver had managed to back the car into the rock garden and get the undercarriage stuck on some of the larger rocks.

"Sorry, Mr. Frehley," he said nervously. "I'll get us out of here in no time."

No time is about what I had. Here I was, already late for a flight to a KISS show, with my road manager calling me, and everybody else freaking out because I'd missed flights in the past and had made it pretty clear that I was becoming disenchanted with my role in KISS.

"Get the fuck out!" I shouted.

Then I jumped in the car and hit the gas. The wheels started spinning like crazy, but the car didn't budge.

"Idiot limo driver," I muttered under my breath. "Where do they get these fuckin' guys?"

The driver began to panic. For all I know he'd only been on the job a day or so and he was worried about getting fired.

"We're going to have to get a tow truck, sir," he said.

"Bullshit!" I yelled. "I'll drag you out of there."

I ran down to the garage and fired up the four-wheel drive—a Chevy K-5 with monster-truck wheels. I pulled up in front of the limo and tied the bumper of the car to the back end of my truck using a thick nylon rope.

The limo driver's eyes widened.

"Mr. Frehley, I'm not so sure this is a good idea."

"It'll be fine. Get behind the wheel and put it in neutral. I'll pull you right out of there."

I had a little hangover from the night before, and I had popped a few quaaludes to ease the sting. I began revving the engine. The car started to move, accompanied by an awful scraping sound—the undercarriage being dragged along the rocks. The sound, I later discovered, had spooked the driver, prompting him to throw the car back into park. Physics took over from there. The rope snapped and my K-5 was catapulted forward—right into the front of my house! The car smashed through a wall and came to a stop in the closet of my baby daughter's bedroom (she wasn't there at the time, thank God).

I got out of the car, dazed and bleeding from my chin. Jeanette was screaming, "Paul! For Christ's sake, you're in Monique's bedroom!" The limo driver was in shock, and the next thing I knew, paramedics were on the scene, examining me in my living room.

"You need to get to a hospital, sir."

"Not possible," I said. "I have to get to a concert or twenty thousand people are going to be really pissed."

Eventually they relented and agreed to let me go, but not until I had signed a waiver declining medical attention. I called my road manager and explained sheepishly that there had been a slight mishap at the homestead, but that I was on my way to the airport. He booked me on a later flight, and I remember getting on the plane and washing down some Valium with a Bloody Mary. I fell asleep for most of the flight, and upon arrival, jumped into a waiting limo and headed straight for the venue, where I quickly threw on my makeup and performed a great show—as usual.

All in a day's work.

In April 1982, shortly before KISS went into the studio to begin recording *Creatures of the Night*, I was home in Connecticut, preparing for my inevitable departure from the band. What I mean by "preparing" is simply this: I wasn't writing songs for KISS and I wasn't participating in most band business, including public appearances. Simply put, I had lost interest. The days passed in a blur of drinking and drugging, interrupted by the occasional outing with friends.

On opening day of trout season, I went fishing with Anton Fig and an acquaintance of mine named Alf, whom I'd met through my guitar roadie. Alf, who lived in Ridgefield, Connecticut, not far from my home, was brilliant when it came to finding and catching trout (which is not the easiest thing to do). Alf led us around half of Connecticut to just about every little backwater creek in the state. We caught a dozen good-sized trout and then went back to his place to get a cold drink (or two . . . or three). Alf was also a home brewer whose specialty was apple wine that he stored in big fermenting barrels in his basement. He used a lot of sugar, so the wine was really sweet, but it was also strong—"probably twenty-five percent alcohol," Alf boasted. "So go easy on it, boys."

Anton and I each had a couple glasses of this shit, which would have been enough on its own to provide a nice buzz. On top of the beer we'd been drinking all day (hey, come on—who doesn't drink beer when they're fishing), it left us damn near shitfaced. Not that we were concerned. We climbed into my Porsche and headed back to my house.

The last thing I remember before the accident is telling Anton to buckle his seat belt. Then, according to the accident report, we must have hit a patch of sand on the shoulder of one of those serpentine New England country roads and lost control of the car. We careened into a stone wall, which slowed the Porsche just enough to prevent us from being killed, and then slammed head-on into an oak tree. If it had been a cheap car we likely would have died instantly.

At first we weren't sure how bad it was. My face and head were bleeding slightly, and my lower leg was sore; Anton's back was aching. But we both got out of the car and walked away—amazing, considering the car had been crumpled to half its normal size. We both declined medical treatment, and the police officers who investigated the accident were incredibly nice and accommodating, offering to give us a ride back to my house.

"Wait a minute," I said. "We have a cooler full of trout in the car."

I popped the rear hatch of the Porsche, not sure what carnage would present itself. But the cooler was intact, so we moved it to the patrol car for the ride home, which was only about five minutes away.

Incredibly enough, there were no tickets dispensed as a result of the accident. The damage appeared to be limited to personal property: my car. The local police were not ball-busters. I lived in a small, affluent community, and the cops believed their job was to protect the taxpayers, rather than harass them. They did that in those days, especially in a tight-knit community where people have money, and where cops don't have much to do except make sure everyone is okay. Times have changed, obviously.

So the officer dropped us off at my house, where Jeanette and Anton's wife were waiting for us.

"What happened?" Jeanette asked.

"Nothin'. Never mind."

She reached up and gently dabbed at my face.

"Your nose is a mess."

I pulled away and laughed dismissively, then put the cooler on the counter. "Let's just cook the fish, alright?"

"You guys look like hell," she said.

I'm sure we did, but between the beer and the apple wine, we were feeling no pain. I gave them both a little story about the accident, leaving out the part about all the drinking, said we were fine, and then commenced cleaning the trout. For the next few hours we cooked and ate and drank. It wasn't until around eleven o'clock that night that the throbbing started, first in my ankle, and then in my head.

"My back is killing me," Anton said. "What the hell is going on?"

The answer, of course, was that we had been in shock, attributable partly to the body's natural response to pain and trauma, but also to all the chemicals coursing through our systems.

"Come on," Jeanette said. "We're going to the hospital."

We went to the emergency room, where doctors informed me that

I'd broken my nose and suffered a hairline fracture of the ankle. I'd feel like crap for a while, maybe a long while, but I'd be okay. Anton, meanwhile, had sprained his back. And what did they prescribe for our discomfort? Percocet and Valium.

Jackpot!

We went back home, loaded up on painkillers and tranquilizers, and passed out.

It wasn't until the next day, when I got another look at the car, that I fully understood how lucky we'd been. If his seat belt hadn't been buckled, Anton probably wouldn't have survived the accident, and I don't think I could have lived with that—killing a friend because I was loaded. I thank God I never seriously hurt anyone (other than myself) because of my stupidity. As it was, Anton would experience back problems for some time afterward. If not for the fact that he was such a good and loyal friend, he probably would have sued, but that's not the way Anton rolls.

The injuries I sustained in that accident affected me for several months and contributed to my lack of enthusiasm over getting back into the studio with KISS. Really, though, I had no interest in remaining with the band. The breakup was not nearly as explosive as you might think. It happened over the course of several months, with numerous conversations and meetings involving me and the guys, as well as our management team. Paul actually came up to the house and we hung out and talked for a while. We went to a mall in Stamford, Connecticut, did some shopping, and tried to recapture some of our old friendship. I look back on that now and realize it was a generous gesture on his part. Paul tried very hard that day to talk me out of leaving, but there wasn't much he could do to change my mind.

"Paul," I said, "I'm really unhappy. It's not that I want to leave, but I feel like I have to leave."

I remember a conversation with my attorney, in his office. He struggled to convince me that quitting KISS was the stupidest thing I could do.

"I know it feels right to you at this moment," he said. "But it's not. It's a terrible business move."

I knew that if I didn't leave the group, I was going to die. Everything about my life was in disarray at that time. I felt no connection to KISS anymore and wasn't happy with the direction the band was taking. I distinctly remember waking up one day and having a cup of coffee in the kitchen while glancing out at our beautiful dining room with marble floors. I suddenly became filled with despair and began entertaining suicidal thoughts.

*Shit! Is this it? Is this what I worked for and dreamed about my whole fucking life? Is this how it's going to end?*

I felt trapped, and so I did what I always did when I was anxious: I escalated my alcohol and drug use to numb myself.

It's hard to point a finger at one particular problem. Each thing fed something else: the drugs, the drinking, the band, my marriage. Obviously if I wasn't drinking and doing all the drugs, my judgment wouldn't have been so clouded and I might have made a more intelligent and sound decision. But it wasn't like I decided overnight. I'd been thinking seriously about leaving KISS for more than a year, maybe longer. After the success of my solo album, I knew I was more creative when I had some distance from other guys in the band, so it was probably only a matter of time before we split. And again, it was all about the money for them; it was never about the money for me. I sat in my attorney's office one afternoon and listened to him make his case. The numbers were staggering. We'd just renegotiated our record deal to the tune of nearly $15 million. That didn't include merchandising or concert revenue, which, combined, were probably worth another $20 million.

Per person.

"Please, Ace," my attorney said. "Think about this very carefully."

I had been thinking carefully, if not clearly. Here I was, a kid from the Bronx, a guy who had known what it was like to get by on practically nothing, and now I had a mansion in Connecticut, a fleet of cars, and more money than I could spend. But who did I know up there? Who were my friends? My coke dealer? I was suffering from an assortment of maladies, culture shock and loneliness among them. I was spinning out of control and I didn't know how to stop. About the only place where I felt like I had any power was my professional life. Maybe if I quit KISS, everything else would fall into place. To this day I still believe that if I hadn't left the band, they would have found me dead somewhere. I would have OD'd or driven my car into a tree and ended it all. I told that to my attorney and his response was one of disbelief.

"But Ace . . . it's fifteen million dollars! That buys a lot of therapy."

I just shook my head. "You're not listening to me, and I don't know how else to explain this to you. I'm going to kill myself if I don't get out of this situation."

Gene eventually weighed in as well, tried to convince me that there was plenty of opportunity for me to do side projects even while working with KISS.

"Go off and do your own records," he said. "We don't care. Have fun. But don't quit the band. It's not necessary."

No one understood. I needed to get away from them. They didn't approve of my lifestyle, and I didn't approve of what they were doing with the band. I couldn't be a part of it anymore. What's worse than having a ton of money and not having a good time? I would gladly have given up millions to walk away. In fact, I did. Although it wasn't officially announced until 1983, I quit the band in '82, and I think it saved my life.

Barely.

15

# SMOKEY AND THE BANDIT (REVISITED)

**May 21, 1983**

It started on a Friday afternoon, around five o'clock, with a phone call to Buddy, a close friend and drinking partner who ran a successful jewelry business in Manhattan.

"I'll be there in a little bit," I said.

"You bringing the DeLorean? I haven't had a ride yet."

"Sure, why not."

We met at Buddy's place at Nineteenth Street and Sixth Avenue, and then headed to a little bar called Harvey's a few blocks away. I'm not sure exactly how long we stayed there, but I know that by the time we walked out, I was already too high to get behind the wheel of any automobile, let alone a DeLorean, but I was oblivious to it, and so was Buddy. You'd think I would have learned a lesson after nearly killing myself and Anton when I smashed up my Porsche, but it never really sank in. Even though I had moved on with my career, my reckless behavior continued.

On our way back to Westchester, we passed through upper Manhattan, driving wildly. A police car spotted us and gave chase, but luckily we eluded them by taking side streets and running a few red lights. Somehow we made it back to Buddy's house without having an accident or getting arrested. When we walked into his joint I quickly passed out on the couch. The following morning we got up and started drinking beer for breakfast, and the whole process started all over again. Later that afternoon we ended up in White Plains at a bar called Cheers, which was owned by Buddy's cousin. It was the day of the Preakness horse race, and everyone was having a good time, but we started to have a little too much fun, and realized we needed to split to avoid a confrontation—or worse. By the time we left the parking lot, I had already smashed into two cars. As we pulled into an intersection on Post Road, I ended up rear-ending a third car ever so gently. Unfortunately, at the same time a police car was passing us in the opposite direction and witnessed the love tap. The impact was so slight that I presumed there was no damage to either car, but the other driver got out of his two-hundred-dollar piece of shit looking pissed.

I also got out of the car, but I couldn't find any damage. At that point the police officer approached and asked for my license and registration. Since I had been driving with a suspended license for DWI, I knew I was going to be arrested, I went back to my car and pretended I was retrieving it from the glove compartment. My survival instincts kicked in, and I made a judgment call.

"Buddy, get out of the car."

"Huh? What are you talking about?" he said.

"Just get the fuck out of the car!"

"Ace, man . . . don't do anything stupid."

"I laughed. Don't worry about it. I'm outta here!"

As soon as Buddy got out, I pulled down my gull-wing door and put the pedal to the metal, leaving a patch of burnt rubber in my wake.

Now, I've done a lot of crazy things in my life, but this one was one for the record books. For the next hour I played a real-life game of Grand Theft Auto, leading police on a high-speed chase through Westchester County. I flew through red lights, bouncing off other cars and embankments, narrowly avoiding a major catastrophe. Although I was pursued by a half dozen police cars, only one cop had the balls to pull up alongside me. I was going about sixty miles an hour against traffic on the Bronx River Parkway. He simply pointed a finger at the shoulder of the highway—a universal symbol for "Pull over, asshole."

The officer couldn't keep up with me in his unmarked Chevy Nova. As I shifted into fifth gear, I politely smiled and waved bye-bye . . . and left him in the dust.

After losing the cops I pulled into a deli to make a phone call. Steam and smoke were rising from the hood and the undercarriage, and the car looked like it had been through a war zone. I surveyed the damage and just laughed to myself.

*Hey, I pulled a "Smokey and the Bandit" and got away with it!*

In my insanity, I figured I would just walk into the deli, call up one of my friends, and have them come pick me up. I'd report the car stolen and let the cops spend the next few days chasing around some phantom thieves who took my DeLorean for a joyride. What I didn't realize was that the owner of deli had called the cops after observing me and the condition of my car outside.

I called my buddy, Crazy Joe. "Yeah, pick me up in a few minutes. I'm reporting the car stolen."

What I had failed to notice was that the street was filling up with police cars. As I exited the deli, I was confronted by a dozen or more cops with gun barrels drawn and aimed at my head. It reminded me of a scene from *The Blues Brothers*.

"Put your hands up!" one of the officers shouted. "Don't move!"

I froze in my tracks, as they cuffed my hands behind my back. I wondered how I was going to explain the more than six grand I had in my pockets at the time. I mean, who carries that much cash, aside from someone looking to buy drugs, which of course was exactly what I had in mind.

Luckily, I hadn't succeeded. Six grand could buy a lot of blow in those days, and I can only imagine the charges I might have faced if I'd managed to make a score before the cops gave chase. As it was, they booked me on charges of drunken and reckless driving. I was fortunate, though. A couple of the cops knew who I was and immediately started making conversation. When we arrived at the police station in White Plains I was treated like a celebrity by several of the younger officers. I posed for pictures and signed autographs. Then they took my mug shot—a keeper if ever there was one. In the photo I'm wearing a T-shirt with an Andy Warhol silkscreen of Marilyn Monroe on the front. Marilyn's eyes were made of clear plastic with floating pupils and everyone got a kick out of it. Most of the officers and detectives were friendly, but one cop wasn't even slightly amused. He was a black sergeant, new on the job, and he quickly became agitated by the special treatment I was apparently receiving from the other cops.

"Put this guy in a cell!" the sergeant shouted. "I don't care what group he's with."

The room fell silent for a moment. I tried to break the tension with the following line:

"Yo! I'm with the Temptations!"

Everyone cracked up. Well, everyone except the sergeant, who stared at me disdainfully, in much the way he probably stared at any wiseass drunk. He was about to throw my ass in a cell when another young cop stepped forward and intervened. His name was Jimmy Jenter, and he was the cop in the Chevy Nova who had signaled for me to pull over earlier.

"Hey, Sarge," he said. "Can I take him back to my office and see if I can get someone to bail him out?"

The sergeant said nothing at first, then waved a hand dismissively.

"Yeah, sure. Get him out of here."

Jimmy took me to a back room, let me make a phone call, and gave me a cup of coffee. He seemed like a pretty serious guy, a little older than he looked, but he wasn't pissed at me. His demeanor was calm and professional. While I was waiting for my ride, he told me that he was a recovering alcoholic and had been sober for three years. He'd recently lost a nephew to a drunk driver, which should have made him want to kick my ass, but he revealed not a trace of anger.

"Look, I'll probably never see you again," he said before I left the station. "But if you ever get tired of living like this, and you want to do something about it, give me a call."

He handed me an Alcoholics Anonymous card with his name and phone number on it. Out of courtesy, I tucked it into my wallet, thanked him for all his help, and left with my buddy Joe, who had bailed me out. Little did I know at the time that Jimmy would end up being a lifelong friend.

There were consequences to the DeLorean incident. My license was revoked, I had to pay a large fine, and I received a bunch of negative publicity that made international headlines. In a way, I was fortunate. Had this been twenty-five years later, the fallout would have been much worse: mug shot on TMZ.com, video clips of my courtroom appearance on CNN, and cell phone footage of the car chase drawing millions of hits on YouTube. The worst sort of notoriety: a celebrity falling hard. Not to mention the harsh legal ramifications that would have come down on me. The other consequence was a court-ordered two-week stint in a hospital detox unit, and some mandatory AA meetings. At one of the first meetings I was approached by a guy who looked familiar. He walked up to me, extended his hand, and said, "Hi, Ace. You remember me?"

Not sure what to say, I merely shrugged.

He smiled.

"I'm Jimmy—the cop who gave you the card when you were arrested."

*Holy shit!* I hadn't recognized him out of uniform.

"How you been?" he asked.

I laughed. Seemed pretty obvious how I'd been.

"Working the program, I guess. We'll see how it goes."

Jimmy eventually became my sponsor in AA and one of my closest friends. We've been to hundreds of meetings together over the years, and we've spent a lot of time hanging out and chatting. The difference between us is that Jimmy never relapsed. He was a rock; I was a rocker. But I thank God that he came into my life. He never gave up on me, through good times and bad.

Especially the bad.

Once I embarked on my solo career, I paid little attention to what was happening with KISS. There were financial and legal matters I should have handled more professionally, but I simply wanted to move on with my life and put the KISS years behind me. But I wasn't really moving. At best I was treading water. In my heart I realized that nothing takes you out quicker than resentment. And yet I was filled with it. I didn't want people to even mention KISS when they were in my presence, which was ridiculous, of course, since the band had been such a huge part of my life. I couldn't just pretend it had never happened. In a very real sense, the early eighties were troubled times until I formed my new band, Frehley's Comet. They were years largely wasted on drugs and alcohol. That entire period went by in a blur, as I isolated myself up in Connecticut. I tried to keep my nose clean (so to speak). Since I was still on probation, I knew that any future transgressions would not be dealt with lightly. It's really serious to get in trouble when you're on probation. You go right to jail, and jail is not a good place for celebrities.

I'd walked away from the twelve-step world after only a handful of meetings. "This is for the fucking birds," I told Jeanette one day.

From time to time, I rented out my studio to friends and other artists, simply because it was there and it was such a terrific, state-of-the-art facility. A diverse group of artists passed through its doors: the 1960s folk-singer Melanie; Neil Smith and Dennis Dunaway from Alice Cooper's original band; Rolling Stones producer Chris Kimsey; and the late Bob Mayo from Peter Frampton's band, to name just a few.

On one occasion I had a song idea I wanted to lay down, but I had rented out my studio to some friends. When that happened I usually went to North Lake Sound in White Plains. This particular studio was only forty-five minutes away and had become sort of a hangout for me in the late seventies. It was owned by Chip Taylor (the singer and composer), Jon Voight (the actor), and Joe Renda. (Incidentally, Chip and Jon are brothers.) While I was putting down my song idea, some friends of mine stopped by to see what was going on. I decided to take a break, and after a few drinks and some lines I decided to call it a day without any more recording.

Instead I invited my friends up to Wilton so I could check on how things were progressing at my place. I was driving Jeanette's Corvette and somehow all three of us squeezed into it. Me, my friend Richie Ayers, Tommy, and a quart of Stoli vodka, to boot! Needless to say, while driving up the Merritt Parkway we all indulged in the Russian spirit and some blow, and by the time we got off the parkway in Norwalk, we were all pretty loaded. My judgment was somewhat impaired by that point, and I almost ran over a cop directing traffic at an intersection. When I realized what I had done, I panicked and hit the gas. The police soon showed up at the gates of my property to arrest my ass, but I didn't respond to their calls. Instead I called my attorney and pleaded with him to feed the police some sort of excuse. Somehow my attorney pulled off a magic act here. He called the local police and calmed them down to the point where they left the front gates and decided not to arrest me. To this day I'm still not sure exactly what bullshit explanation prompted their retreat, but I do remember making a large contribution to the local PBA that year!

But the party didn't end. After my nerves settled down I became frisky with a .357 Magnum. Escaping the clutches of the law had made me feel invincible, so I proceeded to go downstairs with my trusted

Smith & Wesson just outside the entrance to the studio and conduct an experiment. I was interested in figuring out how many times a .357 Magnum bullet would ricochet off concrete walls before coming to a halt. I felt like I was being scientific, figuring out the trajectory of the bullet, where it would strike, and the geometry of the angles its path would follow. Attempting all this, mind you, under the influence of God only knows what else I had consumed since escaping the clutches of the law.

I got off at least two or three shots without killing anyone, thank goodness, but I did succeed in emptying out the whole recording studio and house! I remember thinking, *Where did everybody go? I'm not dangerous; I'm not trying to hurt anyone.* Fortunately, that was the end of ballistics training for the day, as I went upstairs for a nap. My recollection of this event was a little foggy, but when consulting with my friend Richie Ayers, he confirmed every detail. Incidentally, Richie's dad is the famous Marvel Comics artist Dick Ayers. Richie told me, "I couldn't believe all the precise calculations you made before firing the first shot! It was as if you were a mad scientist on a quest!"

Thinking back, I thank God for getting my friends and me through that day without any injuries. I can't help but wonder, in amazement, how the human brain works. It can still retain with accuracy events that occurred while under the influence over thirty years ago. It's really quite fascinating.

I WORKED INTERMITTENTLY ON NEW SONGS, BUT I WAS RARELY focused. Friends would come up to the house and we'd jam and drink and watch TV. Slowly, almost painfully, I put together enough material for an album, but I was in no condition to make a record. I'd wake up in the morning, and if I wasn't too hungover, I'd vow to spend the day writing and recording. Invariably work gave way to fishing and drinking and getting fucked up. I'd crack open my first beer mid-morning and wash down a few painkillers to ease the hangover from the previous night's festivities. If I started to feel tired, I'd do some blow. Then tranqs at night to fall asleep. Pretty soon my drug use was out of control. Prescription drugs were relatively easy to obtain in those days. Physicians routinely handed out prescriptions for tranquilizers and painkillers with little trepidation. Feeling anxious? No problem, here's a script for ninety Valium. With five refills! Shoulder acting up from playing guitar? Don't sweat it. Take some painkillers. Can't sleep? Take a couple of sleeping pills.

Around this time I met a pair of doctors in Manhattan. I can't remember who recommended them, but I knew other rock stars who also were their patients. These doctors were young and somewhat reckless. They both did blow, and sometimes they'd even accept cocaine from me as payment for an office visit. Our relationship escalated to the point where we started spending time together on occasion. I specifically remember hanging out with them one night at the Limelight club on Sixth Avenue in Manhattan. It was very crowded, and I think Alice Cooper was playing that evening. These guys had been prescribing me some of the most potent cough syrup you could get, called Hycodan. It was like drinking liquid codeine, but it looked and tasted like cherry syrup. We'd all order club soda and go into the bathroom and spike it from my prescription bottle. I remember cracking up about it, since everyone in the bar assumed we were drinking vodka and cranberry juice. Under the circumstances, I didn't feel like I was doing anything all that bad, but eventually it caught up to me.

It happened on Mother's Day. On the way to dinner, I walked into a pharmacy to pick up a prescription, and the next thing I knew I was being handcuffed and taken away by federal narcotics agents to the Westchester County Jail. Getting arrested on a Friday sucked because the chances were pretty good that you'd be spending the entire weekend behind bars. Judges and district attorneys don't like to work on weekends, so if you hope to post bail, you'd better know someone in high places.

I was booked and put in cell A-27, and that made everything seem that much more surreal to me. Twenty-seven has always been my lucky number—I was born on the 27th, after all. Anyway, at this point the

Aceman started to worry. I was scared and nervous, but not for the reasons you might think. I didn't have any drugs on me, and it was only a matter of time before I would start kicking. Inside my cell, I tried to appear calm and collected, but in reality I was beginning to panic. I decided to lie down and try to get some sleep, but soon enough I was awakened by a guard shining a flashlight into my cell.

"Hey, Ace," the guard said with a laugh, "How was the concert?"

I tried to ignore him, but it happened on and off through the night, and I didn't sleep a wink. By morning, my withdrawal symptoms had really kicked into high gear. Then I remembered something a friend once told me. If you ever get stuck in jail, throw a fit, and they'll put you in the forensics unit. It's generally safer there, with trained medical personnel who are primarily concerned with making sure no one gets killed. Best of all, they hand out medication to inmates. So that's what I did. I became hysterical, screaming obscenities, crying my eyes out, pleading for help, telling everyone I wanted to die. Now, the truth is, I was feeling more than a little anxious, but this was a significant embellishment. In my mind's eye, I was Jack Nicholson in *One Flew Over the Cuckoo's Nest*, faking his way to a diagnosis of schizophrenia so he could do easy time in the psych ward.

Of course, things didn't turn out so well for ol' Jack, and they didn't turn out so well for me, either.

They ended up putting me in the forensics unit, all right, but it wasn't quite the country club I expected. Rather, it was a smaller and creepier version of where I had just been—with one major difference. All the crazies and suicidal inmates were also on my cell block.

In general population, I had my own cell, but in the forensics unit I was tossed into a cell with three black guys. Here I was, a fallen rock star and fraudulent nut job, surrounded by legitimate psychotics and the criminally insane! Nearly everyone knew who I was, too—the guards, the inmates, and the hospital staff—but most of the time I just got the cold shoulder.

"See that?" one guard said to me, pointing to the unit's lone elevator. "When you leave this place, you have two choices. You go out through that door standing up, or you leave feetfirst in a fuckin' box. Your choice, asshole."

By midday, finally, we were told to line up to receive our medication. And not a bit too soon for me, since my body was craving drugs. Eventually I made it to the counter, where a nurse handed me a small paper cup with two small pills rattling around at the bottom. I gasped as I looked down at them.

"Benadryl? That's what you're giving me? Fucking Benadryl?! What the fuck am I supposed to do with this?!"

"Sorry," the nurse said. "That's the best we can do without a prescription, and the doctors have all gone home for the weekend. You'll have to wait until Monday for anything stronger."

I couldn't believe it! I was totally fucked, far worse off than if I'd stayed in cell A-27. Here I was, no drugs, feeling like shit, and locked up in a cell with a trio of guys who looked like they wanted to fuck with me.

Later that afternoon, my father-in-law, Vinny, came to visit, and I remember telling him, "Dad, you have to get me the fuck out of here."

"We're trying, Paul," he said. "But you have to be patient. Hang in there. Jeanette's been very worried about you, as well."

That night, after dinner, when we were all locked in our cells, I heard a couple of my cellmates plotting to kick my ass. They spoke just loudly enough for me to hear. Their idea, obviously, was to scare the shit out of me. At that point my street smarts took over, and I remember saying to myself, *If they're gonna try and take me down, I'm gonna go down swinging!*

I decided to strike up a conversation with the third black guy, who was older and seemingly less agitated than the other two. He was probably close to forty years old, while the other guys were in their early twenties.

I figured that if I formed some kind of bond with him, maybe he'd help me out if things got too crazy. It turned out that he was also a dad with a young daughter, and we shared a few stories about our kids. He was also an addict, and as our conversation progressed I got the feeling that he was becoming sympathetic to my situation.

A change in work shifts after dinner brought a second glimmer of hope, in the form of a female officer who happened to be a childhood friend of Jeanette's. I told Kathy what had happened to me, and she appeared to be concerned. Talking with her lifted my spirits.

*Here it is. Another visit from my guardian angel. Someone to watch over me.*

Or so I thought.

At first Kathy appeared friendly and glad to see me, but she quickly changed her demeanor after getting dirty looks from the other guards. I realized then that her hands were tied and she wasn't going to be able to give me much help. Protocol dictated that she back off and not show much compassion toward me.

Around 10:45 P.M., one of the guards came by and announced that lights would be turned out in fifteen minutes; that meant the ward would be locked down for the night. My heart began racing. I curled up on my bunk, trying to remain calm. My only thought was about surviving through the night, and I began to pray. I started counting the minutes in my head, preparing for the inevitable. I was overcome by a feeling of total hopelessness. Then, just two minutes before lockdown, I heard a voice. I swear to God, this really happened.

"Let's go, Ace."

I sat up, feeling bewildered. I couldn't believe my ears!

"Go where?"

"You made bail. You're out. Come on."

It seemed too good to be true. Almost a miracle. On wobbly legs, I stood up and followed the guard through the ward. While exiting I received sneers from the other inmates. I got a strange feeling, as though I were part of a movie or something, and I'd been granted an eleventh-hour reprieve. I gathered my belongings and slowly walked out of the jail and into the parking lot. When I saw Vinny and Jeanette waiting next to a running car, I expelled a sigh of relief. In short, it turned out that Jeanette's grandfather, Joe T., the Teamsters vice president, had called in a favor and gotten a local judge to get out of bed and sign the papers necessary for me to make bail. None of us said very much as we pulled away from the county jail and drove off into the night.

After we got home I pounded a handful of Valium to relax and cuddled up next to Jeanette. I began to wonder: Had all this really happened, or was it just some bizarre psychotic episode brought on by a drug-induced stupor?

Reality set in all too quickly the following morning, as I peered through the kitchen window and spotted a patrol car staking out the house.

16

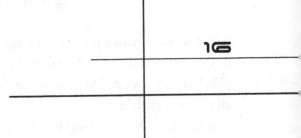

# ROCKET RIDES AND REHABS

One of the worst things about addiction is that it makes you weak and vulnerable. That's probably the most important lesson I learned during my brief incarceration at Westchester County Jail. It also taught me to prepare for the unknown. If I was going away on a trip I'd make sure I had enough medication to last until I returned. I'd count all the pills twice and make sure all my prescriptions were legal. I tried to have a connection set up at my destination rather than carry anything that was illegal. Being addicted to drugs is a lot of work and occupies a lot of your time.

Sometimes it didn't matter how well I'd planned. I'd somehow run out of medication anyway. One time I got really sick in Japan. I ran out of Valium halfway through my stay. I didn't want to be seen drinking in public, and I didn't want alcohol on my room service bill, either. Interestingly enough, it's socially acceptable to be drunk in public in Japan. It's a big part of their culture (or at least it was back then). But at this point I was trying to project a sober image. I needed something to relax me, so I drained the entire minibar, guzzling mostly whiskey like it was water. And here's the thing: I never even liked whiskey! But it didn't matter. I wanted to anesthetize myself in some way, and that was all that was available.

I finally ended up going to a Japanese doctor and told him I had chronic panic attacks and extreme anxiety. He wasn't quite sure exactly what I was talking about, since his English left something to be desired, but finally (with a little pressure from my road manager) he wrote a prescription for Valium; unfortunately, the maximum legal dose of Valium in Japan at the time was only five milligrams (half the amount readily available in the United States), so I had to double the dosage and ran out again in no time. This pattern was typical of the way I had to live my life; as a result, I stopped enjoying the pleasures of drugs rather quickly. All I was doing was maintaining my addiction, and I always lived with the fear that if I ran out, I'd become ill.

There was one method of smuggling coke I devised that seemed to work flawlessly, although I never tried it outside the continental United States. I probably shouldn't be revealing this, but here goes . . .

I'd get a large prescription of antibiotics from my doctor and make sure they came in capsule form. Then I'd empty out a dozen capsules and very carefully refill them with cocaine. After the capsules were reassembled, I'd mark them with a tiny dot so I could tell them apart from the rest. If anyone tested the capsules for illegal drugs, the chances were better than 6 to 1 in a prescription of ninety pills that the coke wouldn't be discovered. This type of insane planning surely sounds obsessive to an ordinary person, but if you're strung out, this amount of meticulous preparation for a trip is almost commonplace.

Traveling out of the country was always the worst, because it was simply too risky to attempt to pass through customs while carrying illegal drugs or any other medication without a legitimate prescription. I toyed with the idea from time to time, but never had the balls to follow through with it. And here's the reason why.

One time I was traveling from the States to a foreign country and decided to take a gamble and tape an eight ball of coke inside the sole of my sneaker. It was a long flight and I dozed off on the plane after a pill and a couple of drinks. While I was dreaming I got a terrible premonition that when I landed and got off the plane, I would be busted inside the airport and thrown in jail to rot. I woke up in a pool of sweat and decided no drug was worth the risk of incarceration. Especially in a foreign country. I remember the stewardess announcing over the intercom, "We'll be landing shortly. Please fasten your seat belts."

In a panic I jumped up and ran to the bathroom. The stewardess intercepted me and instructed me to return to my seat.

"If I do, I'll piss in my pants," I said.

Reluctantly, she allowed me to enter the lavatory, saying, "Only if you're quick about it. We're on our descent, sir."

Once inside, I locked the door and quickly pulled off my sneaker. I ripped the inner sole out and peeled off the tape that was holding the coke in place, and proceeded to flush it down the toilet. At first it appeared to get stuck in the bowl and I began to panic. The intercom went off again.

"Please prepare for landing."

Desperate, I stuck my hand in the toilet bowl, pushed the coke down, and watched it finally disappear into the darkness. When I looked at my hand it was slightly stained from the blue liquid in the toilet. I rushed to wash it off, just as the stewardess interrupted by knocking on the door and directing me once again to return to my seat. I hurriedly dried off, slipped my sneaker back on, and unlocked the bathroom door. The crew was giving me the evil eye, so I rushed back to my seat and fastened my seat belt. Within minutes we were on the ground. I took a few deep breaths and waited patiently for the seat belt sign to go off. Then I grabbed my carry-on bag and exited the plane with everyone else. It was extremely hot and humid in the airport, and I began to perspire heavily.

When I entered the customs area there were two officers with drug-sniffing dogs screening everyone getting off the plane. I tried to remain cool but couldn't help but feel apprehensive. As soon I passed by the agents, one of the dogs started barking. The agent allowed the dog to approach me and it immediately began sniffing my sneaker! The first thing that passed through my mind was that perhaps there was some residue left over from the coke in my sneaker. For a second, though, I wondered if I had forgotten something. Had I put one or two eight balls in my sneaker? Momentarily unsure, and more than a little anxious, I must have appeared suspicious to the officer. He politely asked me to remove my sneakers and started to inspect them thoroughly. The nightmare that I envisioned on the airplane suddenly began racing through my head. I was about to come up with some sort of excuse when the customs agent handed me back my sneakers.

"Okay, go ahead. Sorry for the delay."

I was totally drenched, sweating so profusely that it reminded me of the day I wrote "Rocket Ride" with Sean Delaney. . . .

It must have been at least 90 degrees and the air-conditioning had just broken down in our town house in Irvington, New York. Since heat rises, my studio in the attic was becoming unbearably hot. We were sweating our balls off up there, but we kept working because our creative juices were flowing—as were the ice-cold beer and two eight balls of uncut cocaine. Sean and I had decided that nothing was going to stop us in our quest.

"Rocket Ride" was a song that over the years has become a favorite among fans worldwide and I want everyone to know exactly how it was born. I had this great guitar riff and Sean started coming up with a few lyrics and melodies. I can still see Sean's face, red as a beet, covered in sweat, but completely frozen from all the blow, as he chanted, "She wants a rocket ride! She wants a rocket ride!" I was laughing hysterically and hitting the record button on my eight-track reel-to-reel tape deck at the same time.

"Hey, Ace. That rhythm part works great," Sean said.

"Yeah, good idea. Let's double the length of this part!"

On and on we went, at a frantic but productive pace . . . until we had completed a decent demo of the song. We finished at around dinnertime and were so exhausted from the heat and pace of the session that we both passed out on the couches downstairs in the living room and slept till the following morning.

The next day we put together a rough mix that was good enough to give "Rocket Ride" a resting place on the next KISS record, *Alive II!* "Rocket Ride" went on to become the second KISS single on which I handled lead vocals; it peaked at number 39 on *Billboard*'s Hot 100, making it KISS's seventh Top 40 hit.

When I think back on that day it still amazes me how the whole creative process developed. Sean and I must have sweated away at least five pounds apiece and were almost delirious from the heat and everything else we had consumed by the end of the day. Somehow, though, it all worked out and we created magic that afternoon. Sean went on to work with Peter and Gene on other projects and we never got the chance to work together again on a song. "Rocket Ride" will go down in KISStory as the only Frehley/Delaney composition, but I'll never forget the experience and I'm sure he never did, either.

I'll always have fond memories of Sean; he was a character, to say the least. Sean was with us practically from the inception of KISS. He contributed ideas for our costume designs and stage sets, and also came up with most of the moves we did onstage; he basically choreographed those early KISS shows in our formative years. Sean was always there to lend a helping hand when anyone needed it. He had a limitless amount of energy and never turned his back on us when something needed fixing, on or off the road.

Sean was always there for me and Jeanette, too, and we treated him like family. I'll never forget the time he planted a big kiss right on the mouth of my father-in-law, Vinny, on our wedding day! Vinny was so taken aback that he just stood there for a second in shock. Then he burst out laughing. I mean, what else could he do, especially with so many people standing around watching?

Sean knew how to break the ice with people and defuse any tension in the air. He was Bill Aucoin's live-in lover and he had the gift for making people around him feel at ease, especially about his sexuality. Sean never tried to hide the fact that he was gay, and neither did Bill. They were both very open about it in our inner circle. Sean was a good friend and trusted confidant, and I'll always miss his big smile and grandiose personality. He was one of a kind.

From working with Sean and Bill I learned never to judge people by their bedroom tastes or fetishes. As far as I'm concerned, if it feels good and doesn't hurt anyone else, go ahead and enjoy yourself. Life is just too short to worry about what other people are thinking. There are just too many people out there who are leading miserable lives because they didn't have the balls to take some risks when they were younger.

Regrets are a son of a bitch. Thank God I've learned to live my life without them!

One day back in Wilton, I received a call from Buddy. He invited me to go out on his boat, which was docked on Candlewood Lake in Connecticut, about thirty minutes from my place. He hadn't checked on his boat in a couple of weeks, and he figured we could also do some fishing and get a little R&R. Buddy brought a cooler full of beer and I supplied the blow. After checking out his boat, I started laying out long lines of coke on the deck. A few minutes later Buddy remarked, "Wow, this is really good shit. I can hardly feel my face!" I was pretty frozen myself, and just laughed while guzzling a can of beer from the cooler.

Before long, minutes turned into hours and the sun began setting in the distance. We never even untied his boat from the dock to go fishing. We were too occupied with just having a good time. Once it got dark we started getting a little frisky and decided to come up with Plan B. Buddy told me he had two cute friends who lived not far from the lake and they both loved coke. I told him to give them a call, and with a little coaxing (which meant letting them know we had some dynamite blow) they decided to invite us over. When we got there, they were just sitting around looking disinterested. I decided to lay out a bunch of lines, and pretty soon the party was in high gear. We still had half a cooler full of beer—icing on the cake, you might say—and we continued to party until the sun came up. That morning, after thanking the girls for a very nice stay, Buddy picked up his Rolls-Royce and we invited two other gals to go waterskiing back at the lake. We finally succeeded in getting his boat away from the dock, but we really weren't too interested in waterskiing with the girls. Instead we indulged in other forms of entertainment, which of course included drugs and alcohol. As the hour grew late, Buddy thought it would be a good idea to head back to the marina. Everyone was pretty loaded and I somehow talked Buddy into letting me drive his boat back to the dock. Unfortunately I'm not a very good sailor even when I'm sober; under the influence I'm even worse. I confused reverse gear with forward and ending up taking out his neighbor's dock! The police showed up, but we somehow talked our way out of it by blaming the accident on the boat's faulty transmission. I think the cops suspected foul play, but when they discovered who I was, and saw the big silver Rolls-Royce in the parking lot, they just decided to let it go.

Little did we know that many years later a funny coincidence would take place. In 2008 I had asked Buddy to help me out with security at an autograph signing I was doing in New Jersey. He agreed, and ended up working security on the line of fans waiting to greet me. Suddenly a fan struck up a conversation with Buddy. The kid was going on and on about what a big fan he was, and eventually told Buddy, "Nobody knows this little tidbit of information, but when I was a little kid Ace destroyed my dad's dock on Candlewood Lake!" The kid wasn't sure that Buddy really believed him, since Buddy was grinning from ear to ear after hearing his story. The kid started offering even more details about the incident, thinking Buddy didn't believe him, when Buddy interrupted.

"Hey, that was my fuckin' boat!"

When the kid finally got up to meet me, we all had a good laugh about it. I signed some of his stuff for free, feeling a little guilty about what had happened all those years earlier, but it seemed like he wasn't holding any grudges. He was just really happy to finally meet his favorite guitar player in the flesh, so we let bygones be bygones.

My drug dealer in Connecticut turned out to be a real character. When I wanted to score a large amount of blow, he'd usually deliver. When he showed up at the house he'd often try to hang out for a while, but I'd always come up with some sort of an excuse to get rid of him. He wasn't much fun to be around, since he always appeared paranoid and edgy. I tried to complete our transactions as quickly as possible, but when I was buying five thousand dollars' worth of coke, I liked to test it chemically for its purity and weigh it on my scale to make sure I was getting the right amount. One day he showed up at my door with his shirt turned inside out; he was covered in sweat. He told me he thought he was being followed by narcs. I just laughed.

"Don't be ridiculous. You're letting your imagination run wild. Nobody's out there. Relax."

I gave him a beer and a couple of Valium, and sent him on his way. About two weeks later I called him and told him I wanted another ounce of the same stuff. He said he'd just gotten a new shipment in, and that it was even better than the last batch. The only hitch? His car had broken down, and if I wanted the coke right away, I'd have to come pick it up. I started to get a little suspicious, but my desire outweighed my fear. I told him I had to stop at the bank and get some cash, and then I'd be over.

I got a little sidetracked shopping and ended up being a few hours late. When I arrived I found him acting crazy and paranoid. He thought he was being watched, and that whoever they were, they were closing in on him. To ease his anxiety I told him that I had looked around outside before I came in, and hadn't seen anybody watching the apartment.

The whole scene was weird, and I thought to myself, *It's probably a good idea if I just make the exchange quickly and get the fuck outta here.* I dropped the cash on his living room table and grabbed the ounce of blow, and off I went. As I exited his place I started to get anxious, but I had taken a lot of Valium that day and decided to ignore any of my reservations. I jumped into my Chevy 4x4 and made a beeline for my place. I kept checking my rearview mirror to see if anyone was following, but there was nothing there.

A few days later I got a call from a friend who informed me that my dealer had gotten busted. He said the guy had been under surveillance by Drug Enforcement Administration agents for some time, and that his apartment had been raided and he'd been taken away in handcuffs. I started envisioning scenes from all the movies that dealt with this sort of topic, and how they played out. You know—where a cop tries to make a deal with the criminal, extracting information in exchange for a lighter sentence. I started to panic.

*What if he talks? What if he tells the cops that I'm a customer?*

I started throwing away all my drug paraphernalia: my scales, chemical testing kit, coke vials, etc. I buried whatever coke I had left in the woods behind the patio under a big rock. The days passed slowly, eventually turning into weeks. Finally I decided that I needed to clean up. And not just for health reasons. I figured that if my dealer had in fact ratted me out, it would look much better to a judge if I was actively seeking help.

My first and only real experience with traditional rehab was a mental hospital called Silver Hill, in New Canaan, Connecticut. They also specialized in alcohol and drug rehabilitation. This was classic inpatient rehab—a monthlong stay at an extremely expensive facility in a lovely country setting.

Silver Hill was an interesting place, and mostly catered to the rich and famous. At Silver Hill I was led to believe that a rebirth was right around the corner, and the journey would be conducted in a spa-like atmosphere, complete with gourmet meals, a pool, tennis courts, and even arts and crafts.

The first order of business upon arriving at rehab was filling out a ton of paperwork. They needed my signature on at least a dozen documents. Next came an evaluation—physical and psychological. The primary purpose of the evaluation was to determine the patient's level of dependence, so that the detox process could begin immediately and be handled as efficiently and comfortably as possible. Some people naturally lied about how much medication they were taking, thinking they'd be started on a much higher dose to help ease the weaning process. I took a different approach. I decided that honesty would be the best policy. Because I was taking such a large amount of Xanax, I figured any exaggeration would make me appear to be dishonest from the outset. When I told the nurse I was taking around twenty 1-milligram pills of Xanax a day, she stopped writing for a moment and tried to size me up.

"Around twenty? You sure about that?"

"That's right."

She sighed deeply and continued writing, unfazed by the reports of my alcohol and cocaine use, which by comparison must have seemed reasonable. After the consult I went back to my room and rested for a while, until one of the doctors stopped by for a visit.

"Mr. Frehley," he said with a wry smile. "How much Xanax are you taking . . . really?"

I shrugged.

"Like I told your nurse. Around twenty pills a day. Really."

The smile went away as he gave me a hard look.

"That dosage would kill most people."

"What can I tell you, doc? I'm here."

He nodded. "So you are. Okay . . . I guess we'll have to take the Ativan Challenge."

The Ativan Challenge was something devised to test a patient's drug tolerance. It basically involved feeding a prescribed dosage of Ativan in consecutive intervals until the patient showed signs of impairment. This would allow the staff to determine the true level of drug dependence.

After dinner they started me on two Ativan every forty-five minutes. Three hours into the challenge, I was stone cold sober, talking smoothly, walking a straight line with ease. Four hours passed, then five. Around midnight the doctor came in and examined me. I still seemed relatively sober and at that point the doc became frustrated and quickly walked out of the room and shouted to the nurse.

"Start him on a hundred and twenty milligrams of Valium tomorrow and we'll see how he does."

The following day he stopped by to look in on me.

"I've never seen anyone with that kind of tolerance to tranquilizers," he said. "It's remarkable."

"Well, doc, being a rock star is a very stressful occupation."

The dosage the doctor prescribed kept me floating around the joint for a while and made the whole process more tolerable. After a few days someone mentioned that my cottage was the same one Gregg Allman had once occupied. I guess it was reserved for VIPs, but that really didn't make it any more appealing. What did make it more appealing was that it was occupied mostly by women. In fact, the only other guy on the premises was about seventy years old. He had been dropped off by his family a week before I got there. The poor old guy was detoxing off alcohol and appeared to be very shaky. I felt bad for him since he looked like he had been drinking most of his life and may have been experiencing the DTs.

Among my fellow residents in the cottage were two girls in their mid-twenties and a couple of housewives: one in her thirties, the other in her early forties. The only other woman in the cottage besides the nurses was an older woman in her late sixties. An interesting and diverse group of characters, but we were all in the same boat. I obviously gravitated toward the two gals in their twenties, and they both were quite eager to get to know me. There really wasn't a chance for any real fooling around, but I enjoyed flirting with the younger gals and we all became quite friendly over the next few weeks. After dinner and an AA meeting we usually watched TV together or played cards. Sometimes we exchanged some of our drug and alcohol stories and laughed about what we were experiencing.

Once they began lowering my dose, I started feeling the sting of withdrawal, but it was manageable. And it worked. I left Silver Hill without the physical craving for alcohol and drugs. My body was clean for the first time in several years, but my mind remained addicted to my old ways and lifestyle. I really wasn't sure if I could follow through with a life of complete abstinence, but I was willing to give it a shot.

Please don't misunderstand me. I really don't want to sound like I'm preaching or making a stand against drugs and alcohol. The fact of the matter is, I don't believe that there's anything wrong with either of them. Unfortunately, in excess, they're just not very healthy for you. But many people function quite nicely while using drugs or alcohol on a recreational basis. The trick is moderation. If you can handle it, go ahead. Knock yourself out! Believe me, if I could have just one or two beers I'd still be drinking today. I've accepted the fact that I can't, and I'm finally okay with my decision.

That's really the whole thing in a nutshell. I believe it's a personal choice, and one that shouldn't be taken lightly. The only reason I'm talking about any of this stuff is because I'm a celebrity, and have influenced millions of people over the years. I just want to set the record straight and tell it like it is:

*This is what happened to me.*

If hearing my story has a positive influence on someone—if they're at a crossroads in their lives and decide not to go down the same path I did, and make some of the same mistakes—then that's good enough for me.

17

# COUGH SYRUP, FISH SANDWICHES, AND VOODOO

When I got home from Silver Hill, I felt a renewed sense of commitment to my music and career. The guys in KISS had been saying some pretty awful shit about me in the wake of my legal and personal problems. Talk about hitting a guy when he's down. I usually just ignored it or used it as a motivating factor.

A fresh start was in order, and part of the process involved legally separating from my wife. Jeanette had decided to move on, and was involved in a relationship with a local guy. I decided to move out of Westchester and set my sights on the Big Apple. I chose a new high-rise on the Upper West Side. Living on the forty-third floor had its advantages. Not only did I have a spectacular view of Manhattan, but most of the hustle and bustle of the city was far below me. When the windows were closed, sometimes I even forgot where I was.

I was pretty familiar with the neighborhood, since Anton Fig and

Lydia (Peter Criss's first wife) lived only a couple of blocks away. My favorite Japanese restaurant was just around the corner and most of the restaurants in the area delivered. I liked the fact that, unlike in Westchester, you didn't have to drive everywhere. You could walk to most of the stores, and other places were just a cab ride away. Studio 54 was closed by now and Manhattan wasn't quite the pleasure dome it had been in the seventies. That was a good thing, since I hoped to spend most of my days writing and recording. Sometimes I'd go for rides in Central Park on my ten-speed bike or work out at the gym in my building. I really wanted to discover the healthy side of New York, and finally see how the other half lived.

Part of the plan was to reassemble Frehley's Comet. The original lineup included Anton Fig on drums, John Regan on bass, Arthur Stead on keyboards, and Richie Scarlet on guitar, as well. That lineup recorded several demos and played some gigs in the tristate area in 1985.

My good friend Ed Trunk had an A&R position with Megaforce Records and approached me about a record deal. He introduced me to Jon "Jonny Z" Zazula, the label's founder, and I decided to sign on the dotted line.

I recruited my favorite producer, Eddie Kramer, and we went into the studio and began cutting basic tracks. By this time I'd made some changes to the original lineup, dropping Arthur Stead and replacing Richie Scarlet with Tod Howarth, who had previously worked with Ted Nugent and Cheap Trick. Tod was from California, so he actually moved into my apartment temporarily while we worked on the record. I was intensely active with the first Frehley's Comet record, coproducing with Eddie and writing or cowriting eight of the album's ten songs. Before it was even finished I knew that I'd done some of the best work of my career, and I was looking forward to seeing how it was going to be received by the public.

After the album was finished, I spent several long days doing interviews in support of the record. On one particular day, Ed Trunk picked me up in a limo. He had scheduled several radio interviews in the New

York/New Jersey area. In addition to his A&R duties at Megaforce, Ed was also a disc jockey at WDHA in New Jersey, and that was our last scheduled stop. During the course of the day I had taken a few tranquilizers to relax and had also forgotten to eat. To Ed's dismay, I ended up passing out in the back of the limo. We were already running late, and he got very nervous when he couldn't completely revive me. As we pulled into the station's parking lot, I could see the panic on Ed's face.

The limo was immediately surrounded by fans seeking autographs. What made matters worse was the fact that Ed's boss was also there, waiting impatiently. I gestured for Ed to come closer, and I whispered two words:

"Fish sandwich . . ."

Ed replied, "What?"

"Two fish sandwiches! *NOW!*"

Upon my request, Ed instructed the limo driver to make a beeline to the nearest McDonald's. Luckily there was one just down the road; when we arrived Ed sent the driver in with instructions and a twenty-dollar bill. I couldn't help but laugh to see Ed making such a fuss. As usual, though, he had my best interests at heart. On the drive back to the station, he started feeding me one sandwich after another. By the time we got there, I was completely revived. Remarkably, I ended up doing a great interview. And to this day, Ed has never downplayed the rejuvenating qualities of a McDonald's fish sandwich.

*Frehley's Comet* sold over 500,000 copies and peaked at number 43 on the Billboard album chart. Critical response was strong, as well. The most successful single off the record was "Into the Night," written by Russ Ballard, who also wrote "New York Groove." But the song that has endured over the years and is loved by most fans is definitely "Rock Soldiers." Cowritten by Chip Taylor (an accomplished musician and writer whose biggest hits were "Angel of the Morning" and the Troggs' "Wild Thing"), "Rock Soldiers" was inspired by my ill-fated trip in the DeLorean but also evokes images of the crash that nearly killed me and Anton. It is, more than anything else, a song about rock star excess, and was written very honestly about my own life experiences, which, as it turned out, were far from over.

*It was back in the summer of '83*
*There's a reason I remember it well*
*I was slippin' and slidin', drinkin' and drivin'*
*And bringin' me closer to hell*

*And the devil sat in the passenger's side*
*Of DeLorean's automobile*
*He said: Hey Frehley, Frehley let's not be silly*
*There's a life out there to steal*

*Rock Soldiers come*
*Rock Soldiers go*
*And some hear the drum*
*And some never know*

*Rock Soldiers! How do we know?*
*ACE is back and he told you so*

*With a trooper in the mirror*
*And Satan on my right*
*We went wrong way down a one way road*
*Hittin' everything in sight*

*I cried I am invincible*
*Said I was high above the law*
*But my only high was just a lie*
*And now I'm glad I saw*

*Calling Rock Soldiers*
*You! Rock Soldiers*

*Calling Rock Soldiers*
*Hard Rock Soldiers*

*Hup! Two three four*
*Rock! Two three four*
*Hup! Two three four*
*Rock! Two three four*

*Friends say they'll stay with you*
*Right through the danger zone*
*But the closer you get to that fiery hole*
*You'll have to make it alone*

*When I think of how my life was spared*
*From that near-fatal wreck*
*If the devil wants to play his card game now*
*He's gonna play without an ACE in his deck!!*

The video for "Rock Soldiers" was shot in Canada. We used about fifty fans as extras, all playing guitar along with us in the chorus. It was produced by Geddy Lee's brother, Allan Weinrib, and I had a lot of fun on and off the set.

When we hit the road after the release of *Frehley's Comet*, I couldn't have been more excited. I toured the United States and Canada, and one of the shows that stands out in my memory was the night we played at the Beacon Theatre in New York City. I always enjoyed playing in old theaters, since the acoustics made everything sound that much better. And with a hometown crowd, the energy was just amazing. Several celebrities showed up for the show and after-party, including Paul Stanley and Atlantic Records president Ahmet Ertegun. I remember being greeted warmly by Paul at the party.

"Great show!" he said. And I believe he meant it. He was really happy for me. Ahmet seemed equally impressed with my performance.

I was glad I finally got a chance to talk with such a legend in the recording industry.

While I was performing down in Florida, I had a chance meeting with a fashion model. We were playing a local theater in Miami and everyone was revved up for the show. We had arrived in town early, and I ended up hanging out by the pool, soaking up the Florida sunshine. I noticed a few models doing a photo shoot by the tennis court, but I didn't pay much attention to it until I saw this really striking blonde. I had to get back to my room and get dressed for sound check, but before I left the pool I decided to invite all the girls in the photo shoot to the concert. They accepted the invitation and I quickly went back to my room and then headed over to sound check. We put on a great show that night, and after three encores the crowd still wanted more. I couldn't help but notice the cute blonde I'd invited to the show, since during the concert her eyes were mostly focused on me. After I got back to the hotel, I couldn't remember if the girls I'd invited were actually staying at the hotel. I did what I usually did in those days. I cleaned up and headed down to the hotel lounge to see if anything was going on. There I found Kim, the gorgeous blonde. We talked for a while and then I invited her back to my room, along with her girlfriend and Tod Howarth. After a few drinks, I left Tod alone with his newfound friend, and we headed over to Kim's room, where I ended up spending the night.

The attraction between us was undeniable; amazingly enough, I discovered she lived only a few short blocks from me back in the Big Apple. When I got home we began dating, and by the end of the month we had decided to move in together. One of the fringe benefits of our relationship was that other fashion models were always visiting the house and sometimes spending the night.

On one weekend, one of Kim's girlfriends stopped by, and I ended up shooting a video of the girls lip-synching to "Rock Soldiers." They were both sitting in a small rubber raft in my living room, playing guitars in their underwear. We all had a great time that night, and over the years that video became affectionately known as "The Seahawk."

While Kim and I were living together in New York, I began recording the next Frehley's Comet studio album, *Second Sighting*. It was my only solo album on which Anton Fig didn't play drums. Someone suggested using Jamie Oldaker, and when I learned that he had worked with Eric Clapton, I decided to give him a shot.

Megaforce also wanted me to put out a live video, so we flew over to England and recorded a live performance in London at the Hammersmith Odeon. Around the same time period, we also shot a video for "Insane," the first single released off *Second Sighting*. It was shot at SIR studios in New York and featured more than a dozen models dressed up as nurses. I asked Kim to participate, and she agreed. Unfortunately, the pressure of touring eventually took its toll on our relationship, and we went our separate ways later that year.

Since Kim was out of the picture, I ended up spending a little more time with my other friends in the city. One day I went over to Anton Fig's house and we started drinking. His wife was out of town on a trip, so . . . well, you know how it is: *When the cat's away, the mice will play!*

I had previously given Anton a taste of my favorite cough syrup, and he enjoyed it as much as I did. I had just gotten a new prescription, and told Anton about this harebrained scheme I had concocted. Luckily there was an empty bottle lying around, which was all I needed to complete the task. We took a walk down the street to the local pharmacy to see if it would work.

In those days cough syrup bottles were made out of glass instead of plastic. I figured that after I had the prescription filled, I could quickly run around the corner and pour most of it into the empty bottle, then smash the original bottle inside the bag, and immediately run back into the pharmacy yelling, "I almost got killed by a fuckin' cab."

Upon handing the pharmacist the paper bag, which was dripping with cough syrup and broken glass, I asked him if he could please replace it. This entailed a little bit of further acting by me, but after a few seconds of deliberation, he bought the story. He handed me a freshly filled bottle and we headed back to Anton's place, laughing at our good fortune.

"I can't believe it fuckin' worked!" Anton exclaimed. And for the rest of the evening, we had twice the fun.

In support of *Second Sighting*, we went out on the road with Iron Maiden, but they canceled the tour prematurely. The last show was in New Orleans, and the band and crew boarded the tour bus back to New York. I never enjoyed taking long bus rides, so I opted to stay behind and fly out the following day. I was feeling a little down since the tour had ended so abruptly, and by the time I got back to the hotel my feelings of despair had escalated. I started drinking and took some sedatives to relax.

As far back as I can remember, I had always sensed a strange voodoo vibe in New Orleans. It was nothing tangible, but being a sensitive guy I could pick up on that kind of shit. As the evening progressed, I became really fuckin' depressed; by midnight I was toying with thoughts of taking my own life. Everyone, from time to time, has experienced moments of despair and sometimes even fleeting thoughts of suicide, but this was different. It was something I couldn't shake, and I almost felt possessed.

In my darkest hour, I remembered that I could always draw strength from a higher power. I was brought up in a religious household, and even though I had stopped going to church regularly a long time ago, I still kept in conscious contact with God. I opened the drawer of the nightstand and reached for the Bible. As I began reading some of my favorite passages, all the feelings of hopelessness began to dissipate, and eventually I came to my senses. After saying a few prayers, I fell asleep. I woke up the following day and thought to myself, *What the fuck was I thinking?! Thank God for Gideon!*

In 1989, I went back into the studio with Eddie Kramer to record *Trouble Walkin'*. I decided to bring back Richie Scarlet on guitar as well as Anton Fig on drums. The album also included some very special guests—most notably Peter Criss, along with Sebastian Bach, Dave Sabo, and Rachel Bolan from Skid Row. My old friend Eddie Solan (KISS's original sound mixer) assisted Eddie Kramer in the production process, and my buddy from the Bronx, Peppy Castro of the Blues Magoos, added some great background vocals. I also invited Eric Carr to play drums on one track, and he instantly accepted. He was really excited about the prospect of working with me again. Unfortunately, a few days later, I received a phone call from Eric, who sounded very upset. He informed me that Gene and Paul were opposed to the idea; therefore, he had to regretfully decline the invitation. I was also upset, as Eric's situation brought back unpleasant memories of how fucked up they could be at times.

The album's first single was a cover of the Move's song "Do Ya," and I had the pleasure of shooting the video at the historic Apollo Theater in Harlem. I also covered a track called "Hide Your Heart," which was written by Desmond Child, Holly Knight, and Paul Stanley. During the mixing process I received an interesting phone call from Gene Simmons. I couldn't believe he had the balls to request that I take my version of "Hide Your Heart" off the record. His reasoning was that they had recorded a version of it as well and were planning on releasing it as the first single off their new album. I informed him that I had invested a lot of time and money in the recording process and was thrilled with the results, so I wasn't about entertain his request. I was dumbfounded. Un-fucking-believable!

After the release of *Trouble Walkin'*, I embarked on a successful tour, during which it was a real treat performing again with Richie Scarlet. I opted not to record another studio album for quite some time, although I continued performing live on the "Just 4 Fun Tour" in 1992 and the "Kick Ass Tour" in '94.

During this period, I began spending much of my downtime in Danbury, Connecticut, hanging out with Richie Scarlet and his circle of friends. I was introduced to a cute hairdresser named Colette, and we began spending a lot of time together. Colette was good friends with Richie's wife, Joanne, and we all enjoyed hanging out and having a few laughs. Eventually, Colette and I decided to get a place together.

One Sunday afternoon, while we were out a ball game, I locked my keys in my 4x4. I had to smash the side window to unlock the door, and when I got home I sealed the hole with gaffers' tape and quickly forgot about it. The following night I hung out with Richie and some other buddies at a local bar. We ended up leaving around closing time. The cops must have been staking out the place and watching my SUV, thinking it might have been stolen because of the broken window. I got only a few blocks from the bar when I spotted flashing lights in my rear-view mirror and was directed to pull over. My survival instincts kicked in; without even batting an eye, I threw my push-button knife and a vial of coke under the rubber floor mat.

I was approached by two officers and asked to produce my license and registration. After some checking, there appeared to be a problem with the paperwork, and I was asked to exit the vehicle and place my hands on the hood. While I was being questioned, the other cop began searching the interior of the SUV. I remembered what was under the floor mat and feared it would be discovered; then the officer who was questioning me told me to put my hands behind my back. He pulled out a set of handcuffs.

"Hey, what are you doing?" I exclaimed. "I'm Ace Frehley! This is my car, and I was the one who smashed the window!"

The other cop, whose interior search was now moving perilously close to the floor mat, suddenly stopped.

"Are you serious?" he said.

I told him to check the glove compartment and he'd find some 8x10s and a couple of CDs. After checking it out and seeing that I was the guy in the photos, both cops realized that I wasn't a car thief. A few minutes later, after asking for some autographs, they decided to let me go. As I pulled away from the side of the road, I couldn't help but imagine what would have happened if I hadn't opened my mouth as quickly as I did.

I would have been charged with possession of a lethal weapon and an illegal substance. Either charge alone would have been sufficient to get me thrown in jail; together they would have sealed my fate.

As I continued down the road, I realized that my guardian angel had once again intervened. And I couldn't help but wonder: *How many more close calls will I have before my luck runs out?*

18

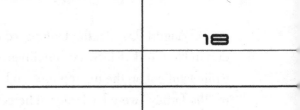

# RETURN OF THE BAD BOYS

In 1995, I embarked on a co-headlining tour of the United States and Canada with Peter Criss. It was billed as the Bad Boys tour. Each night, at the end of my set, Peter would return to the stage and joined me for one of the encores. Around this same time, Paul and Gene began a tour of "official" KISS conventions. When the tour hit Los Angeles, Peter made a special appearance with his daughter, performing "Hard Luck Woman" and "Nothin' to Lose."

Peter and I were both invited to attend the New York KISS convention in late July, but our tour scheduling made it impossible. A month later, KISS was scheduled to appear on MTV's popular *Unplugged* series. Peter and I were again given an invitation to participate, and we decided to accept. We headed to New York after finishing the Bad Boys tour, and our first actual reunion with Paul and Gene took place at SIR studios, where we began rehearsing for the show. The event was well documented on video, and it is part of the *Unplugged* DVD that was released a few months later.

On August 9, 1995, the *Unplugged* concert took place at Sony Studios in New York. KISS's current lineup kicked off the show, and after a while Paul got on the microphone and announced that some members of "the family" were backstage. The crowd immediately started cheering, and as Peter and I walked out, they went crazy! After getting a hug from Paul and Gene, I greeted some of the cheering fans in the front row, including my daughter, Monique. After taking a seat next to Paul, I grabbed the microphone and yelled, "I don't think anybody expected this, did they?" We immediately broke into "2000 Man" and followed it up with an acoustic version of "Beth."

After a few more songs, we ended the show; then some fans in the audience began yelling, "Reunion tour!"

After the *Unplugged* performance, negotiations started between both camps in hopes of a possible reunion tour. The fans wanted it, and I thought it might be fun to throw on the Spaceman costume and makeup for old times' sake. Discussions went on for several months, culminating with a meeting in Manhattan, at which Peter and I talked to Paul and Gene in Los Angeles via videoconference. It was the first time I'd ever experienced that type of technology, and I found it fascinating. During the meeting we discussed various subjects, and by its conclusion we'd come to a verbal agreement to move forward with the reunion tour. The final details of the contracts would be handled by our respective attorneys. In retrospect, I realize I could have negotiated a better deal for myself, but I agreed to their terms for the benefit of all concerned, and especially for the sake of the fans.

Nothing was announced to the press at that point. Instead we built upon the excitement of all the rumors by making an unannounced appearance at the Grammy Awards in full makeup and costume. We finally dropped the bomb at a huge press conference aboard the USS *Intrepid* in Manhattan. It was hosted by Conan O'Brien, and broadcast via satellite around the world. The response was overwhelming, and when tickets went on sale for the first show at Tiger Stadium in Detroit, all 40,000 tickets sold out in only forty-seven minutes.

The anticipation leading up to that show reached epic proportions among our fans, and they weren't disappointed. Opening night was electric! I decided to fly in Jeanette and Monique so they could be part of the whole experience. I was especially excited for Monique since she was just a baby when the KISS phenomenon was at its peak, and I had always wanted her to better understand exactly how crazy the whole thing was. When Monique was growing up, I'd sometimes show her pictures and videos, but I don't think she ever fully understood it. Tonight was her chance, and I was more excited for her than I was for myself. This was my second time around, after all.

The closer it came to showtime, the more a strange sense of déjà vu permeated the air. From the moment we hit the stage, 40,000 screaming fans stood up, and the excitement continued until the final encore. When the show was over, we congratulated each other backstage; there was a genuine feeling of camaraderie in the dressing room. The tour continued throughout the year and was the highest-grossing tour of 1996.

By the time we finished the Reunion Tour and went into the studio to begin recording *Psycho Circus*, Paul and Gene had already been pushing my buttons by not including me in several decisions that affected my life. The plan was for all four of us to reunite in the studio for the first time since we recorded *Dynasty* in 1979. I remember presenting three or four demos to the producer, Bruce Fairbairn, and the band. Before I sent them off, Jeanette warned me by saying, "Don't send them that many songs; they're gonna steal your ideas!" I just laughed it off, but while doing research for this book, I revisited her statement and remembered one of the songs I submitted was titled "Life, Liberty, and the Pursuit of Rock 'n' Roll." Upon closer examination of the lyrics, I realized that some of them mirrored one of Paul's songs on *Psycho Circus*, "I Pledge Allegiance to the State of Rock 'n' Roll."

It eluded me at the time because I was more focused on another song I had written, "Shakin' Sharp Shooter." I felt this song was the best of the bunch, but it still received resistance from everyone. I was determined to get at least one song on the record because I wanted to be represented as a writer. The other guys liked the music but had problems with the lyrics, so I offered to rewrite them. Gene actually came up with the new title of the track, "Into the Void." It was the only *Psycho Circus* song on which all four original members performed, and it was very well received by the fans. I also performed it live on the *Psycho Circus* tour.

While out on tour in support of the record, we were involved with a feature film called *Detroit Rock City*, which was about KISS fans on their way to a concert in Detroit. Paul, Peter, and I had minimal participation in the film except for a live performance at the end; it was mostly Gene's baby. During the shooting of the movie, Gene had specifically approached me and asked whether Monique would be interested in doing a cameo. I figured since his girlfriend Miss Tweed and Paul's wife were being included in the cast, why not Monique? I thought it was a really nice and friendly gesture to invite her to fly to L.A. and be in a scene with the lead character, Edward Furlong. So I called her and told her about the invitation. She loved the idea, so we made hotel and flight arrangements for her, and she came out to L.A. when it was time to shoot her scene.

Everyone on the set was extremely nice to Monique, and she was catered to as if she were a star. She really enjoyed the whole experience and made some new friends as well. It was like a dream come true for her since she'd long been interested in acting, and this was her chance. Monique stayed in L.A. for four or five days and we were lucky enough to get in a day or two of quality time for ourselves. When she got back to New York, she told everyone about the fun she had on the set. I remember how anxious and excited she was to see the final cut of the film. She kept saying, "Dad, it's gonna be my acting debut!" I was really happy for her, and I enjoyed seeing her so excited about something that I was part of and had helped make possible.

Eventually we got a final copy of the movie. I'll never forget the look on Monique's face as she waited with anticipation for her scene with

Edward to materialize on our giant TV screen. When we got there, to our surprise, it had been edited out. She was heartbroken. All that work and preparation—flying three thousand miles to Los Angeles, learning her lines, talking with the director, being made to feel like she was part of the team—only to have the rug pulled out from under her. She just couldn't hold back the tears, even with others in the room. I'll never forget the look on her face when she turned to me.

"Daddy, why?"

I knew it wasn't an accident. Gene had been involved in the editing process on a daily basis. I even remember getting tapes from him, early on, with alternate scenes and endings, but Monique's scene was always included. I knew Gene was probably pissed at me for something I had done, but to get back at me by hurting my daughter? I mean, it was *his* idea in the first place, so what the fuck was he doing?

I never felt the same about Gene after that. He had reached an all-time low with me, and this particular snub contributed greatly to my second departure from Kiss.

In the summer of 2000, I was in Dallas, Texas, during the Farewell Tour. On my day off I received an invitation from my cousin Bill for a barbecue. He had a ten-acre spread in the suburbs, and I was excited about the prospect of going shooting since I knew he had a gun collection. Bill had been in the air force and knew a lot of interesting characters. When I got to his place I was greeted by Bill and my cousin Scott, along with a friend of theirs who was a Vietnam vet.

After a few beers and a joint we ventured into the backwoods of his property on a search-and-destroy mission. I tried out several of Bill's automatic rifles and settled on an Uzi. We set up a bunch of targets, and after going through several hundred rounds we took a break and began catching up. Bill's buddy told me he'd been a demolitions expert in the war. I was quite fascinated by some of his stories and asked if he could give demonstrate any of his bomb-making techniques. He agreed, but since we didn't have any dynamite or C-4, we ending up going to a supermarket and picking up a few household items. We came back to the ranch with a gallon jug of Clorox, several boxes of mothballs, and some baking soda.

Before long he had concocted a recipe with the ingredients, packing the mixture tightly inside a gallon jug. Upon sealing it with the cap and installing a fuse, he informed everyone of the potential danger, since it had become a very powerful explosive. I was a little skeptical at first, but when I looked at Bill and Scott and saw their reaction, I realized that this guy wasn't fucking around.

"What should we blow up?" I asked excitedly.

Bill suggested an old dam that was on the far corner of his property. It was constructed of big logs and railroad ties and didn't have any real practical use. When we got there, his buddy crawled down into the riverbed and placed the makeshift bomb at the base of the dam with the fuse exposed. Since it was deep in the riverbed, and I couldn't see it, I figured I'd be safe just a few yards away.

"You're going to have about a minute to get the fuck out of here after I light this thing," he said.

The other guys nodded.

"Don't fuck around," he said. "I'm not kidding."

When he lit the fuse, Bill and Scott took off immediately and yelled "Paul! Fuckin' move it!"

I quickly followed Bill, eventually stopping about fifty yards from the riverbed behind a tree. While waiting patiently for the explosion, he told me to cover my ears. Suddenly there was a thunderous explosion, like nothing I'd ever encountered. The ground shook for a few seconds, and I noticed Bill looking up.

"Watch out for falling debris!"

Within seconds, large chunks of wood and pieces of railroad ties began raining from the sky. I couldn't believe the amount of destruction the device had unleashed. It also made me realize how deadly this concoction would be if it fell into the wrong hands. Half the dam was obliterated; all that was left were mangled logs and railroad ties thrown randomly about, as if some child had become frustrated with his Tinkertoys.

After the explosion, we had a few more beers and decided to finish off the rest of the ammunition. I had several clips for the Uzi and began shooting relentlessly. The gun finally overheated and jammed. I kept squeezing the trigger in frustration, until suddenly a round exploded inside the chamber, sending shrapnel out of the hole where the casings are ejected. A fragment must have hit me in the chest, but I was so numb from everything I had consumed, I barely felt any discomfort.

After that incident, my cousin decided it was probably a good idea to call it a day, and we headed back to the house for the barbecue. While I was eating, Bill noticed that my T-shirt was covered in blood. I was perplexed, because I still didn't feel any significant pain. So I removed my shirt and wrung it out. We were all amazed at how much blood poured onto the ground.

"Shit," Bill said. "What the fuck happened?"

"I must have been hit with something when the Uzi jammed."

Bill wanted to take me to the hospital, but I declined. I told him I was okay, and I asked him to take me back to the hotel so I could take a nap.

I woke up around midnight feeling disoriented and nauseous. I started getting really worried—maybe I'd actually been hurt worse than I had realized. I decided to call the front desk and ask for assistance.

"Can I help you, Mr. Frehley?" the clerk asked when she picked up the phone.

"I think I've been fuckin' shot!"

I probably should have chosen my words more carefully, as it wasn't long before the sirens were wailing outside the hotel and my room was overrun with emergency medical technicians and police officers, all naturally thinking that there had been a shooting in my hotel room.

"Where's the victim?" one of the cops said as he entered my room.

"Right here! It's me!"

The detective seemed confused.

"Where's the perpetrator?"

"It was an accident," I tried to explain. "Could you please just get me to a hospital?"

With the help of our manager, Doc McGhee, everything was smoothed over in fairly short order, and I was whisked away by ambulance to a nearby emergency room. Doc followed in his car to give me support. Upon arrival at the hospital, I was examined and X-rays were taken, revealing small bullet fragments in my chest.

"You're lucky," the ER doc explained. (Man, how many times have I heard that one?) "Another inch to the left and one of these would have pierced your heart; you would have bled to death."

Apparently my rib cage had impeded the shrapnel. That was the good news. The bad news was, the fragments had to come out. Drunk and anesthetized, I could still feel the doctor trying to dig out the little fuckers. At one point the surgeon asked a nurse for a magnetic probe to help locate the fragments.

"I don't think that'll work," I slurred.

"Excuse me?" the doctor said.

"Bullets are made out of lead, right? How you gonna find 'em with a fuckin' magnetic probe? Lead isn't magnetic!"

I might have been a little out of it from the injection they gave me for pain, but I could still remember basic science from high school.

Eventually they gave up and left a few pieces in my chest. Then they sent me back to the hotel, armed with some painkillers and antibiotics. I slept for about twelve to fourteen hours and put on a show the next night. The other guys knew what had happened but didn't seem too fazed or concerned. I guess they were accustomed to the insanity.

---

## NO REGRETS

Following a short break in the tour, I flew home to New York for a visit. On the day I was preparing to fly back to California for a concert, we had a big problem in our backyard. A deer had fallen through the canvas cover of our swimming pool and drowned. The incident was very upsetting, and it took a while for me to calm down everyone in our house. We called the police and the emergency unit, and it was a huge ordeal getting the dead animal out of our pool. The whole thing got me sidetracked to the point where I ended up missing my flight. Everyone on the West Coast became concerned about whether I would make the concert. At the last minute I asked Monique to fly with me since I didn't feel like traveling alone that day. She quickly packed a bag and we headed for the airport. Somehow we had missed the second flight, and at that point everyone began to panic. We managed to book on one last flight, but it would really be cutting it close. On the plane, Monique and I had a few drinks. She had just done her hair and was wearing really large sunglasses. I remember the stewardess thinking Monique was my girlfriend, and she played the role to the hilt as a joke.

Before we had taken off, I told Doc that we'd need a helicopter waiting for us if I was going to make the show, so when the plane landed, the copilot was at the gate and quickly directed us upstairs to the heliport. That night we were doing a sold-out show at Irvine Meadows. We took off in the helicopter and landed in the parking lot. I ran into the dressing room and was told that the show was scheduled to go on in roughly thirty minutes. I was surprised to see my road manager, Tommy Thayer, in my costume and makeup. I guess they really didn't think I was going to get there on time, but I was determined to do the show. I quickly threw on my makeup and costume and we hit the stage. The show pretty much went off without a hitch, which I think surprised just about everyone.

After the concert, we went back to the hotel and crashed. Since Monique had had very little time to pack, she had forgotten several items. The following day I decided to take her shopping on Melrose

Avenue. After a few hours we wound up at a Japanese restaurant. I drank a little too much sake, and upon leaving the restaurant must have been spotted by some cops. We got in the car, I started up the engine, and a police car immediately pulled up behind us with its lights flashing. Two cops—one male, one female—got out and approached from behind. The female officer asked Monique to come sit in the patrol car with her while the male cop asked me for my information. While the female officer was questioning Monique, there was a case of mistaken identity. Just like on the plane, the female cop assumed Monique was my girlfriend and started questioning her about alcohol and drugs.

"He's not my boyfriend!" Monique exclaimed. "He's my daddy!"

The female officer was so embarrassed that she began feeling bad for Monique and decided to give me a break. She approached the car with Monique and said, "Mr. Frehley, we're not going to arrest you, but we can't allow you to drive the car in the condition you're in. You'll have to leave it parked here and get a ride."

After making a few phone calls without any luck, I decided to try my cleaning woman, Wendy, who took care of my apartment in L.A. (I was living bicoastal at this time). She hurried down to the scene and gave us a lift. Monique looked at me and said, "Daddy, that was a close call!" I was very embarrassed about what had happened, especially since Monique was with me. I apologized to her for my shortcomings.

She just looked at me and smiled.

On April 13, 2001, the tour ended with a sold-out show at Carrara Stadium in Australia. We had a standing rule that no girlfriends or wives were allowed in the dressing room before or after a show, but from time to time during the course of the tour, when Gene's girlfriend or Paul's wife flew in for a show, the rule would be broken. When this happened, I decided to look the other way for the sake of the show and band harmony.

On this night, after the show, I was sitting in the dressing room, taking off my makeup, when my girlfriend, Shannon, showed up outside the door. Paul and Gene had already gone back to the hotel, so I figured, *What the fuck? Everyone's gone, and it's the end of the tour.*

"Come on in, honey," I said. "It won't be a problem."

"You sure?" Shannon said.

"Yeah, it'll be fine."

With that, Shannon came into the room and waited for me to get dressed.

Within minutes, Tommy Thayer walked into the dressing room and did a double take.

"Come on, Ace. You know she's not supposed to be in here."

I thought, *Well maybe she isn't, but does it really fuckin' matter at this point?*

"Mind your own business," I said. "The tour is over."

Tommy stood his ground. "No, she has to get out."

At that point I walked right up to him and punched him in the jaw. He went down for a moment, more stunned than actually hurt.

From time to time during the tour, Tommy and I would have minor disagreements, but I usually shrugged them off and went on with my day. I always felt that he was unhappy in his position as road manager and secretly fantasized about replacing me in KISS, since he had dressed up in my costume and makeup earlier in his career while performing in a KISS cover band. Toward the end of the tour, I even sensed a hint of resentment. When he sounded off in the dressing about Shannon's presence, I felt it was completely unwarranted, and it infuriated me.

My reaction was swift and deliberate. It was the culmination of ill feelings I had been holding in for quite some time, and my Bronx-born instincts took over. But not long after punching him, I began feeling remorse. I later apologized on our jet, but he seemed reluctant to accept it.

Within months of the incident, Tommy finally got his wish. I had declined Gene's invitation to perform on yet another KISS tour, so Paul and Gene hired Tommy to dress up in my costume and makeup and perform in my absence. I felt very uncomfortable about their decision, since I had originated the Spaceman character and designed the makeup. My first reaction was, "Isn't anything sacred to those guys?" But I soon realized that their lust for money outweighed any sense of fairness or logic on their part.

Many KISS fans were outraged, but over the years Gene and Paul have tried to rewrite history by downplaying my contributions to the band. On several CD releases, they even deleted my songs from the playlists; on DVD releases, they edited out a lot of my close-ups, focusing primarily on themselves. It seemed like they were trying to erase me and my songs from the minds of KISS fans. New fans were completely unaware of this subterfuge, and older fans either turned their backs on the band or just bit the bullet.

At first Gene and Paul even tried to hide the fact that I had left the band. In promotional ads and merchandise, they still continued to use my likeness instead of Tommy's, and my whole departure from the band was minimized in the press. I remember getting several awkward phone calls from acquaintances looking for tickets to local KISS concerts.

"I'm not in the band anymore," I explained. "Actually, it's been a couple years now."

"I'm so sorry, Ace," they would respond in amazement. "I had no idea you left the band."

If anyone reading this thinks I'm exaggerating or trying to distort the truth, please do your own research and examine the facts. Since 2001, every move KISS has made has been premeditated and part of a well-orchestrated plan. Nothing, including their attempts to minimize my contributions, has been left to chance.

So, you might wonder now, "How does Ace feel about Kiss today?" Fair enough. Here's my response:

At this point in my life, I just need to let things go. Holding on to resentments can really make you ill, so I'll leave the dirty work to my attorneys. I can sum up the KISS situation in just five simple words: "What goes around, comes around." No matter what happens, I'll be just fine.

That being said, in reality, I think they're just a bunch of dirty rotten whores. *Awk!*

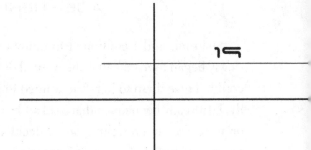

19

# INTO THE VOID

When Shannon and I returned to the States from Australia, I felt not only like I had finished the Farewell Tour, but also that I wanted to bid farewell to KISS for good. I was feeling much the same as I did in 1982: completely disenchanted. The idea of working with them again became less appealing to me as the days went by.

Within weeks of returning, my publicist notified me that I was being inducted into the "Bronx Walk of Fame." It was a prestigious honor, and I became very excited about it. The ceremony would take place on the Grand Concourse, in front of the Bronx Courthouse, just a few blocks from Yankee Stadium. A plaque with my name on it would be placed atop a lamppost, about twenty feet from the street. I was being inducted with several other celebrities, including Academy Award–nominated director Stanley Kubrick, actor Burt Young, retired New York Mets player Ed Kranepool, actress Diahann Carroll, and U.S. Secretary of State Colin Powell. Following the afternoon ceremony, there was a black-tie affair in the evening, during which each of the honorees got up and said a few words to the audience. I enjoyed the whole event, and I had fun meeting such an impressive and diverse group of VIPs.

Shannon and I continued to enjoy our break from touring, but I slowly began to realize that she wanted different things out of life, and I couldn't give them to her. She wanted to get pregnant and raise a family; I'd already been down that road and was more interested in focusing on my career and traveling. So we decided to call it quits that year, and she moved back to Canada. Shannon eventually got married and had a couple of kids, but we've remained friends over the years.

After Shannon left, I reconnected with my old girlfriend, Ronnie. I was seeing her at the time my father passed away in 2000, and she really helped me get through a rough period in my life.

I still remember the morning I got the call from my brother, Charlie. I knew my dad wasn't doing well after his stroke, but I'd been so busy working in L.A. with KISS, I was unaware of just how much he had deteriorated. The night before I received the call, Ronnie and I had been up late entertaining some friends. Normally it would have taken me at least thirty minutes to crawl out of bed after a party, but the day my dad passed away was very different. I remember jumping up in bed early that morning as if someone had shaken me. Even stranger was the fact that I remember being wide awake at the time. I also remember feeling a strange presence in the bedroom, like a cool breeze entering through the door and slowly moving past my bed and finally exiting out the window. At the time I had no inkling that anything had happened to my dad, but when my brother told me exactly what time he had passed away, I did a little math in my head and realized it was around the same time I had been awakened so abruptly. I remember my mom telling me some family secrets about paranormal experiences, and I always believed that I had the ability to communicate with the other side.

Upon getting the news, I booked a flight back to New York and helped with some of the funeral arrangements, although my brother and sister handled most of that. I was on a very tight schedule since a KISS tour was about to commence, and the band needed me back out west. Most of it really went by in a blur, but I remember Jimmy Jenter being there for me the whole time. Driving me around and giving me a shoulder to lean on.

The scene at the cemetery was surreal. Fans were outside the mausoleum where my dad was being laid to rest. All I wanted to do was pay my respects to my father's memory and be there for my mom and family, but the crowd outside the service made it hard for me to relax and stay focused. After the service was over, Jimmy quickly cleared a path through the onlookers and whisked me away in a limo to Westchester Airport. When we arrived, a private jet had its engines running; Jimmy gave me a hug and I was gone. Five hours later I landed in California and began filming a Pepsi commercial that seemed to go on forever. The tour began the following day. I never really did get a chance to mourn the death of my father.

After I was back in Westchester, Ronnie arrived with a dozen suitcases and moved into my place without any reservations. Things started off fine, but as the weeks progressed it became apparent to both of us that we had lost something over time and weren't going to recapture it. One night we had a big fight, and she started punching me. I really wasn't in the mood for any nonsense that night, and I've certainly never believed in hitting a woman. So I called my bodyguard Mac and asked him to deal with her. He took her away to his place on my request and things got a little sticky after that. Mac wasn't in the mood for any nonsense, either, that night and decided to let the cops deal with her. That wasn't the best way to handle the problem, but he told me she had become too violent for even him. The cops came and decided to drop her off at the psych ward. I'm not exactly sure what crazy story she told the doctor and local authorities, but they were planning to arrest me pending an investigation of the facts. I had no idea of their plans, but God bless Jimmy Jenter!

When Jimmy and my buddy Mike found out the police were planning to raid my place, they quickly intervened and explained that her accusations were not credible. Now, in most cases that wouldn't have changed anything, but Jimmy and Mike were both federal marshals and very well respected by their fellow officers and peers. They explained that they knew me personally, and that I had entertained both of them in my home. After a few tense moments on both sides, the police decided to take their advice and call off the raid. After I regained my composure, I decided to try to help her. We made a deal with her doctor at the hospital. He said if I secured a rehab that was willing to accept her as a patient, they would release her in my custody. I made some calls, wrote a check, and got her into a facility. I called Mac and asked him to pick her up at the hospital and escort her on the plane, and deliver her to the rehab. He did as instructed, and she's doing much better today.

As I wrote this story, I tried to imagine how my life would have turned out if I hadn't met Jimmy back in 1983. It's something I can't even begin to visualize. But he's not the only one who has been there for me.

There was another guy who ended up saving my ass on more than one occasion. Chris McNamara (the aforementioned "Mac") used to date my sister-in-law, Anita. When I found out he was a bouncer and bodyguard, I didn't wait long before inviting him to work for me in a similar capacity. I brought him out on the road to watch my back when I was touring with KISS. We've had some close calls over the years, and this story is about one of them.

One night on tour, we had a day off, and I felt like going out and shooting pool, so Mac found a place right up our alley. It had dozens of pool tables, arcade games, a mechanical bull, a bar and restaurant, and a strip club—all under the same roof! I remember telling Mac, "If we had places like this back east, they'd be packed all the time!"

We had a few beers and played several games of pool. Later on, a couple of buddies joined us. We grabbed a quick bite to eat and then thought it might be fun to check out the strippers at the other end of the club. I normally wasn't a big fan of strip clubs. I never liked the idea of being in a situation where if I got excited, I couldn't do anything about it. I always found that frustrating.

Well, as the evening progressed, I ordered champagne for everyone, and we started getting very silly and loud with the girls. It was beginning to get late, so Mac wisely suggested it might be a good idea to head back to the hotel. Within the last ten minutes of our stay, I bumped into an old girlfriend, Audrey, and decided to invite her back to my room. I had a limousine waiting for us in the parking lot, and as we were leaving I ran into the bathroom for a minute while everyone went outside. When I walked out, Audrey looked upset.

"What happened?" I asked.

She pointed to a tall guy leaning against the wall and explained that he had said something nasty to her. I immediately walked over and confronted the guy. I asked him what he had said. As soon as he started talking, I gave him a solid shot to the head, and he went down for the count. What I hadn't noticed, unfortunately, was that he wasn't alone. The guy had several buddies with him, and the biggest one was marching straight toward me. Mac, though, saw what was happening. He quickly intercepted the approaching guy and gave him a hard right hand to the chin.

*Crack!*

Everyone in the parking lot heard the sound of the poor guy's jaw breaking. The rest of his friends stopped cold in their tracks. Mac scared them off just long enough for us to jump into the limo. In the process, though, a security guard in the parking lot sprayed Mac with pepper spray, and he was temporarily blinded by it. We slammed the door shut and I yelled to the limo driver, "Let's get the fuck outta here!"

When we got into the street, we headed for the on-ramp to the expressway, but at the end of the street our path was blocked by a black BMW and a black Mercedes. The limo driver seemed reluctant to go forward, but I quickly threw two hundred-dollar bills in his lap.

"Hit it!" I shouted. "Go up on the fucking sidewalk around them, or we're dead."

The driver acted on impulse and did exactly what I told him to do. We narrowly made it past the two cars and shot up the entrance ramp onto the highway. I turned around and saw the two black cars spin out and follow us up the ramp in hot pursuit. I looked around the limo. Everyone seemed okay—except for Mac, who said he could barely see. I told the limo driver to floor it, and not to stop for anything. Then I called 911 and told them we were being chased by two cars with guns. I gave them our location on the highway and waited patiently. The two cars were approaching and things were getting tense in the limousine. I wasn't sure if they really had guns, and I didn't want to find out, either. A few seconds went by. Then, miraculously, a police car flew up the on-ramp in front of us with its lights flashing, quickly followed by a second police car. I looked through the rear window and saw the Mercedes and BMW slow down and pull U-turns. I told the limo driver to pull over immediately. I wanted to go explain to the cops what had happened at the bar, and thank them for saving our asses.

When I explained who I was and what had happened, the officers were quite sympathetic. They even escorted us to the hotel just to be safe, a gesture I really appreciated. By the time we got back, Mac's vision was clearing up, and he did a quick inspection of the limo. He said he had thought he had heard a few shots during all the craziness, but I wasn't so sure; I hadn't heard anything. Upon closer inspection, though, we discovered two bullet holes: one on the side fender and one in the radiator, which was now beginning to emit some steam. I looked at Mac and began to laugh.

"Shit! That was a close one."

One day in November 2007 I came home and found a message on my voice mail. To my surprise, it was Gene Simmons extending an invitation to be on his television show. He went on to say that he was going to be roasted on the show, and that he wanted me to be part of it. It was going to be a very big deal, he promised, with Cher and Steven Tyler among the list of celebrities who were going to take part.

I listened to the message a few times, and with each playback I became more convinced that I could sense a slight tone of desperation in his voice. I thought to myself, *Gene, desperate? Probably not.* But I decided to do a little research and find out exactly what was going on with the show. His producer sent me several e-mails requesting an answer, but I didn't want to reply right away. I thought about some of the roasts I'd seen in the past, and remembered being invited to Hugh Hefner's roast, at which I sat on the dais between Patty Hearst and Deborah Harry.

I ended up losing my temper at a party following that event. I'd been chatting with Hugh and his entourage of Playmates when out of the corner of my eye I saw some guy pouring a bottle of champagne over my daughter's head! I dropped everything and darted over to Monique. I grabbed the guy and started punching him in the face. I only got three or four shots in before the bouncers intervened. Having seen the whole incident, they just pulled the guy out of my hands and dragged the half-conscious asshole out of the club. They apologized to me for the incident, but I was far more interested in my daughter. Luckily, Monique was okay; she was just a little shaken up.

Most of the roasts I recalled consisted of people who were lifelong friends or coworkers of the person being "honored." That's when it suddenly hit me: Gene doesn't have any friends! Never did—as far back as I can remember. And everyone who has ever worked with Gene in the past has either been fired or quit. The only person who's remained with him over the years is Paul Stanley. At that point I decided to give Paul a call and see if he was going to be involved with the show. We shot the shit briefly, and then I hit him with the question.

There was a slight pause as Paul carefully considered his response. "I'm not doing the show, Ace. It's not in my comfort zone."

I didn't press him on the matter. We chatted for a few more minutes, wished each other well, and said good-bye.

The next few days I continued making calls in an attempt to find out who else was going to be involved. Peter said he'd received an invitation from Gene, "But I told him I was busy." It didn't occur to me to call Eric Singer or Tommy Thayer, since they were just hired guns wearing our makeup. After a few more calls to some of the other people who were supposed to be involved, I decided it was probably better if I just bowed out gracefully.

When I finally replied to Gene's producer, declining the invitation, he seemed somewhat agitated. I figured he was getting frustrated with the whole idea of a Gene Simmons roast, since most of the people I had contacted had no intention of taking part. I wasn't going to let it bother me, though. I decided to put the whole thing out of my mind and concentrate on recording. Several months passed. I had forgotten about the roast until a friend called and said the program had already aired.

"How was it?" I asked, not really caring about the answer.

My friend laughed.

"Pretty bad."

He went on to explain that most of the guests involved appeared to be comedians paid by the network to appear on the show. For a moment I almost felt bad for Gene. I mean, really. How embarrassing.

It's been documented in more than a few publications that I've had some alien encounters and sightings in my life. One of my homes is located in the lower Hudson Valley, a well-known UFO hot spot where thousands of verified sightings have taken place over the years. I've seen some very strange stuff at times (sober and under the influence). Most of the people in the area just kind of take it for granted, and I, for one, am not fazed by it in the least.

My most memorable encounter happened in 2002. At first I thought the whole experience was a dream. What changed my mind was what happened afterward. I woke up one morning and found myself lying on the ground in the front doorway of my home, my body half in the house and half in the driveway. I'd woken up in a lot of strange places in my life, but this took the cake. I slowly got up and went inside for a cup of coffee. As my head cleared, I could recall a strange dream about being inside a spaceship. It didn't seem that weird, since I dreamt about UFOs and aliens from time to time in the past, without ever giving it a second thought. This time, though, seemed different . . . more *real*. Maybe because I'd never woken up in the doorway before.

The more I thought about the dream, the more vivid it became in my mind's eye. After breakfast I decided to go outside and look around the yard. I stumbled upon a circular impression in the grass, almost like a giant burn. It appeared to be about thirty feet in diameter, but after inspecting it more closely with a tape measure, it actually turned out to be twenty-seven feet.

27 . . .

My lucky number!

Later, in the shower, I checked my body for marks—some sign of having been abducted. But there was nothing strange to be found. By the next day the impression in the grass had disappeared, and I just went about my business like nothing had ever happened. I figured if what I had dreamt really had taken place, there wasn't much I could do about it.

Close encounters—real, imagined, or manufactured—had long been a part of my life. Sometimes they were merely a source of amusement, like the time I was on a hunting trip with my buddies Frank and Bob.

It all started with an invitation from Frank, whose family owned about seventy acres of land in upstate New York. Hanging out there was my first real experience with hunting and handguns. Frank was a very good marksman, and later on in life he became a licensed federal firearms dealer. He was the guy (with the help of his older brother Kenny) who taught me how to shoot. Since the seventies I've had a love affair with guns, and I shoot just about every chance I get (which isn't really that often, due to my hectic schedule).

This particular incident occurred on probably my second or third visit to Frank's place. All three of us, at the time, enjoyed our drugs and alcohol, and we weren't exactly amateurs at it. It was the last day of a long weekend trip. We had used up all of our ammunition and blown up a few other things on Frank's property, and now we were looking for something different to do. I remembered that I had a few weather balloons in my trunk, and the whole crazy charade began from there.

We had been drinking all day, and Frank and I decided it might be fun to dress Bob as an alien, and see how authentic he would look! Since we didn't have any silver space suits, green makeup, or ray guns, we decided to improvise. We just grabbed some ordinary household items: a white sheet, a cork, and a flashlight.

And the weather balloon.

One of my favorite science-fiction films is *Invaders from Mars*. Most of the film lacks authenticity in terms of special effects, but I always loved the appearance of one particular character, an alien leader encased in a glass sphere. If you've ever seen the movie, you'll remember that the alien had a large forehead and brain, characteristics we hoped to replicate with Bob. To get the desired effect, we stretched the weather balloon over Bob's head, which was no small task. At first he had it around his neck and none of his features were visible. He looked so ridiculous that Frank and I completely lost it. We laughed so hard that I actually threw up!

When we finally regained our composure, we helped Bob reposition the balloon just above his eyes. At first there was too much air in the balloon, but after letting some out, he began to look the part of an alien: totally looked totally fuckin' weird. To finish off his costume we wrapped him in the sheet, burned the cork and rubbed it around his eyes, and handed him a flashlight.

We helped Bob get through the cabin door, which was harder than you might think, since we had to squeeze the balloon and direct him without popping it. Then things got really interesting. We led Bob down the hill and told him to walk along the side of the road, but not too close. Maybe ten yards or so. While he was slowly walking, he put the flashlight inside the sheet and under his chin. From a distance, in the dark, he looked like, well . . . *something not of this earth.*

Soon enough a car went by. Frank and I were hiding in the bushes. The car slowed down momentarily as it passed Bob, then sped away. This happened a few more times with similar results. Eventually an eighteen-wheeler came along, and when the driver spotted Bob on the side of the road, he slammed on his brakes and almost jackknifed the truck.

That was a little more than we had bargained for.

"We'd better get him inside before somebody takes a shot at him," Frank said.

A few minutes later we were approached by a pickup truck—one that had already passed by earlier. There were two guys in the cab and a shotgun rack in the bed. Clearly these guys wanted a second look. Maybe they were out to do a little alien hunting.

"Turn off the flashlight!" I yelled to Bob.

The road suddenly went dark and we all hid quietly until the pickup truck drove off. Then we whisked Bob back into the cabin and called it a night.

A few days later the local newspaper ran a story bearing the following headline: "Local Man has Alien Sighting Outside Port Jervis."

We couldn't help but laugh about the whole experience. Apparently Bob had been even more convincing than we'd realized.

Once I got my studio up and running, I continued writing and recording new material. In mid-2007 I once again hooked up with Anton Fig, along with a new bassist, Anthony Esposito. The first track we worked on was "Pain in the Neck," and within a few short months the songs really came together. In October, Ed Trunk called and asked if I wanted to perform at a Halloween party he was hosting at the Hard Rock Cafe in New York. I talked it over with Anthony and he agreed to help me assemble a band for the performance. I hired Scott Coogan on drums and Derrek Hawkins on guitar to round off the new lineup.

I told Ed I'd love to do it, but in reality I was a little apprehensive. This would be my first live performance in more than five years with my own band. And I'd been sober only a year (following a relapse in Las Vegas). But all my fears were put to rest that night at the Hard Rock. I hit the stage with a powerful set and the show turned out to be a big success. Anton Fig sat in on drums for a song, to the delight of the fan, and reviews reported that I looked and sounded better than ever.

When I got home that night, I was happy and thankful for the outcome, which seemed all the more remarkable considering what a struggle I'd gone through just eighteen months earlier.

The difficulty had begun one night in early February 2006, when my sister, Nancy, called to say that my mom was very sick; she was in a nursing home in Saginaw, Michigan, where my sister lived with her husband, Ron.

From the sound of Nancy's voice, I knew the situation was serious, so I decided to jump on a plane the following day. Complicating matters was the fact that it was Super Bowl weekend and the game was being played in Detroit. Most of the flights were booked solid, but I managed to get a ticket and fly into Detroit that Friday afternoon. On the plane, before we landed, the pilot mentioned that a snowstorm was moving into the area, and I became concerned; I thought my plan might be in jeopardy. After we landed, though, I succeeded in renting a car and got on I-75 headed toward Saginaw. Normally this is about a two-hour drive, maybe less. But the snow had already begun to fall, and shortly after we got on the road, the weather took a dramatic turn for the worse. There were some tense moments on the highway, but I finally arrived at my destination—several hours late, but in one piece, thank God. I got a chance to see my mom briefly that night, and my worst fears were realized: she was close to death. The doctor said she probably wouldn't last through the weekend.

I was overwhelmed with grief, but also very thankful that I had a chance to say good-bye to my mom. I spent the weekend at the nursing home, and had to return to New York on Sunday. Before leaving, I told my mom it was all right for her to join Dad up in heaven, and that he was waiting for her. I was holding her hand at the time, and even though she couldn't talk, she squeezed my hand and appeared to understand what I was saying. I kissed her good-bye and told her I loved her, and then drove back to Detroit for my flight home. I later heard from my sister that she passed away just hours after I left.

A few weeks after my mother's death, I got the news that KISS was being honored by VH1 as part of the network's first Rock Honors award show in Las Vegas. I wasn't sure what role I would play in the ceremony, since Tommy Thayer had been wearing my makeup and costume and performing with KISS. I remember Ed Trunk calling me up and saying, angrily, "I can't fucking believe those guys! That's your award. You were a cofounder of the band, and you designed the Spaceman makeup and costume!"

I wasn't sure what to think. As I told Ed, "Well, I guess I'll be getting a call from Paul or Gene?"

The phone never rang, so Ed came up with the idea for me to play with an all-star band that was also performing on the show. At the time I was a little reluctant to even go to Las Vegas for the taping without a formal invitation from KISS, but Ed convinced me.

"You have to go, Ace. Don't let them get away with it. They're always trying to make it seem like you never existed. Fuck 'em!"

So I agreed and booked a flight to L.A. and started rehearsals with Slash, Gilby Clarke, Scott Ian, and Tommy Lee. We rehearsed a couple of days and then jumped on a private jet and were flown to Las Vegas by VH1.

There was a lot of excitement revolving around the show. In addition to KISS, Def Leppard, Judas Priest, and Queen were being honored. When I arrived on the set, I realized that it was a much bigger deal than I had anticipated. As usual, Ed Trunk had given me the right advice. I was still wondering why I never got a call from Paul or Gene concerning the show, but I really didn't want to think about it. I just pretended that everything was fine; when I saw the guys from KISS, I greeted them like nothing had ever happened, posed with them for a few pictures, and acted like we were long-lost friends. The truth, though, is that I started feeling ill about the whole production and how my contribution to KISS was again being minimized. I'd been sober for some time, but before the show I started feeling even more anxious, and when Slash offered me a drink backstage, I just couldn't say no. I didn't want to feel my emotions anymore and was still very upset about my mother's passing.

Rob Zombie joined us on lead vocals, and together we performed a kick-ass version of "God of Thunder." Right before the show I suggested to Slash we throw in the riff from Led Zeppelin's "Bring It on Home" between our guitar solos, and he agreed. It blew my mind that we pulled it off flawlessly, in harmony, without any prior rehearsal. That was a rush!

The show progressed; eventually KISS played a few songs. I wondered if they felt strange during their performance, knowing I was watching their every move. We all posed together at the end of the show for the press, and then it was over.

I went back to my hotel suite knowing I had lost my sobriety, and even though I wanted to blame KISS or my mom's passing away, I knew deep in my soul it was my own fault. Later I heard from Slash, who apologized for handing me my first drink. He was feeling somewhat guilty, since he had also struggled with addiction, but I assured him that I was planning on getting fucked up anyway, and if it hadn't been him, it would have been someone else.

I stayed in Vegas a few more days and continued to party, and then headed back to New York. I should have called some of my sober buddies and told them what happened, but I didn't want to face the music. I continued drinking and self-medicating and slowly began spinning out of control. By the end of the summer I was a mess. If not for my daughter Monique's intervention, I'm not sure what would have happened.

One day Monique called and expressed concern for my well-being. She had been told I was getting fucked up, and she was well aware of my destructive behavior. Monique had also been in the same place herself, and she realized I was going down a road from which I might not return. She started crying, and somehow got through to me. When I got off the phone with her, I looked in the mirror and said, "Well, now what?" I knew I was at a point where I hadn't gone over the edge with what I was taking, but I was very, very close. I had only been drinking and doing pills, but I was seriously thinking about getting some coke. If I'd taken that step, I probably wouldn't have been able to stop. I would have been on the merry-go-round again, without any desire or strength to get off.

That evening I did some praying and self-examination, and decided to call Monique and tell her I was going to get sober. She was thrilled with the prospect, and I promised I would follow through with my decision. In the next few weeks I opted to slowly decrease the dosage of all the junk I was consuming. Finally, by mid-September, I was completely done with everything. I called Jimmy Jenter and told him I'd like to hit a few meetings that week. I believe he may have heard through some of our mutual friends that I'd fallen off the wagon. He agreed to join me, and I slowly began regaining my sobriety—one day at a time. As of today, I haven't had a drink or any opiates or tranquillizers since September 15, 2006. By the time this book is released I will have celebrated five years of sobriety!

Life is full of twists and turns, but there are only two roads you can follow. The choice is up to you.

Even though I was working on my new album at the time, I got the itch to hit the road and perform live with my newly formed band. I hired an agent and we quickly put together a U.S. tour. I realized performing sober was lots of fun, and we kept adding dates to our tour schedule.

I wanted to prove to everyone else in the business that what Gene Simmons had said about me was a lie. He had basically slandered my name in the press by telling everyone I was still a drunk and a drug addict. Furthermore, he said I was unreliable as an artist . . . and unemployable. It wasn't the first time this had happened, and I needed to show the world that Gene had his head up his ass. The tour continued in the States and then went through Canada without any mishaps. I appeared at every show and met every contractual obligation that was required of me. I've always been the kind of person who draws strength from adversity, and this was just another example of my resiliency.

Later that year we did a sold-out show in London at the Hammersmith Odeon and received rave reviews across the board. With the tour under my belt and some positive press to rebut Gene's negative campaign, I decided to go back into the studio and finish my new studio album.

Despite the many ups and downs I had with KISS over the years, I couldn't help but remember all the fun we shared in our formative years. We achieved greatness in the music industry and had several groundbreaking achievements well into the new millennium. To this day I still consider them my brothers in rock 'n' roll and love them.

When I got back to New York, I went into the studio and recorded the rest of the songs for my new studio album. After completion of the overdubs, I set my sights on California and hired Marty Frederickson to mix and master the CD, with an assist from Anthony Focx. The tracks were sounding great, and while mixing in Burbank, California, I started getting lonely and decided to call up an old acquaintance.

# NO REGRETS

I met Rachael Gordon in 2008 while I was appearing at the House of Blues in San Diego. Her good friend Victor (who was a big fan of mine) brought her to the show not knowing what to expect. Upon meeting Rachael, I was immediately intrigued and invited her to come back to my hotel for a visit. When she appeared at my door with a group of friends, I asked her to leave the rest of her entourage outside except for her girlfriend Vanessa. My guitar roadie, Mark, was in the room, and he expressed a desire to meet Rachael's friend. They politely entered my room, and after a few minutes I cornered Rachael and engaged in a conversation to try to get to know her better. While I was talking to her our eyes locked, and I had a very strange sensation. It felt like I had known her my whole life. But how could I? We'd just met. The only thing I could surmise was that we must have had a relationship with each other in a past life.

As we continued talking, the phone rang. It was my road manager. I had a show in Los Angeles the following night, and he informed me that everyone was heading up there now; he suggested I leave as well. I told Rachael I had to split, but not without inviting her to come to L.A. for the weekend. Unfortunately, she declined.

"I'm not that kind of girl," she said.

We kept in touch sporadically over the next several months, but our schedules wouldn't allow for a reunion until more than a year had passed. In April 2009 Rachael accepted my invitation to join me in Burbank, where I was finishing my new CD. We spent the entire weekend together and formed a solid bond. She returned a few weeks later and we spent another weekend together. Slowly but surely, we fell in love. Rachael was the first woman I'd met who I felt really understood me; she's also taught me how to enjoy life again without the use of alcohol and drugs.

I was surprised to discover that Rachael was also a singer. She'd released a few CDs and done some touring, too. With so much in common, our relationship blossomed, and by July we decided to get a place together in Los Angeles. In the fall she accompanied me on a long European tour. Upon returning to the States we decided to recuperate in Las Vegas for the holidays. After giving it some thought, we decided to get engaged on New Year's Eve, 2010. We've been together ever since.

My latest album, *Anomaly,* was released on September 15, 2009, to rave reviews, exactly three years after I became sober. It debuted at number 27 on the Billboard 200, which was again special (remember—27 is my lucky number).

But that fall was a time of both celebration and sadness. Shortly before *Anomaly* was released I got the call from a friend at Gibson Guitars who informed me that the great Les Paul had passed away. I had met Les many years earlier and thought he was just a delight to be around. I was lucky enough to have had the pleasure of jamming with Les, and I'll never forget that day. Les was always up and positive and never had a bad word for anyone. Sometimes he'd even crack silly jokes. For example . . .

"Ace, you know why I like women with small hands?"

"I don't know," I said.

"'Cause they make my pecker look bigger!"

Les was a great human being and a creative genius. He was the inventor of multitrack recording and the electric guitar . . . and so much more.

Some time later I got another call and was asked if I would make a presentation at the New Jersey Hall of Fame to Les Paul's son, Russ. The ceremony honored New Jerseyans who had made invaluable contributions to society with a Lifetime Achievement Award. Along with Les the honorees included Danny DeVito, Susan Sarandon, and Jack Nicholson, to name a few. I thought it was such an honor to be asked to present the award to Russ Paul, and I quickly accepted.

Rachael accompanied me to the ceremony, along with my manager,

Dave Frey, and my assistant, John Ostrosky. It was a star-studded event, and I enjoyed every minute of it. I walked out with my Ace Frehley Signature series Les Paul and explained to the audience that it was one of Les Paul's creations—with a little help from me. It was a night to remember. And I know Les was up in heaven, looking down at us with a big smile on his face.

# EPILOGUE

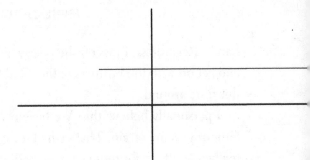

**New York City**
**October 5, 2010**

Now here's a curious moment.

I'm wandering around backstage at Carnegie Hall—*Carnegie fuckin' Hall!*—waiting to take my turn at the mike. How improbable is it that I'm here, participating in something called Redemption Song, an event billed as "an evening of conversation and performance exploring the relationship between artistry, dependency, recovery and longevity"?

How unlikely?

How remarkable?

Not that I don't belong . . .

*Artistry, dependency, recovery and longevity.*

I certainly know a few things about the first couple of items on that list. And I'm learning about the third. It's the last one—*longevity*—that still has me a little stumped. There are times I wake up in the morning and feel like I can easily ponder the inner workings of quantum mechanics, but other mornings I'm lucky if I can find my ass with both hands. Regardless, I toss off the covers, greet the new day with a smile, and get on with the business of life. God knows I'm trying to do it right this time around.

I personally believe this: We have only *today;* yesterday's gone and tomorrow is uncertain. That's why they call it the *present.* And sobriety really is a gift . . . for those who are willing to receive it.

A few years ago I made an appearance at the Rock and Roll Hall of Fame in Cleveland, where they were honoring Les Paul, shortly before he passed away, with a weeklong celebration of his life achievements in the music industry. I had met Henry Juszkiewicz (CEO of Gibson USA) about twenty years earlier and we had become good friends over the years. I got up in front of all these people, talked about my career and my sobriety, and told them about the last time Henry and I had spent any time together.

"Henry is a very generous guy," I said. "He threw a big birthday party for me. I was supposed to be there are at seven-thirty, and I think I showed up around one o'clock in the morning."

The audience laughed, which was fine, but the memory made me cringe—all those people waiting for me to arrive, but I was just too wasted and kept missing my flights. Henry and my other friends at Gibson had taken the time to organize a birthday party, and I was just oblivious to all their hard work.

I apologized publicly that night at the Rock and Roll Hall of Fame. "And now that I'm sober," I added, "I don't have to worry about things like that happening anymore."

I paused.

"I mean, I'm still late all the time . . . but at least I'm straight."

Everyone laughed again, then burst into applause. It felt good to get that off my chest, since I'd been holding it inside for years.

I still work on my sobriety and attend meetings when I can. I need to remember what I used to be like, and how lousy I felt both physically and mentally toward the end. How irresponsible I was, and how it affected my coworkers and loved ones. I believe all the mistakes and dangerous detours were things I needed to go through to get where I am today.

I draw strength from the pain I went through, and only now am I beginning to realize it was part of a much larger plan that is continually unfolding, every day. I'm very thankful I was given a second chance at life. Today I enjoy performing live, writing and recording, and traveling more than ever before. I feel like my eyes have been opened.

After attending Bill Aucoin's funeral last year in Florida, Rachael and I decided to go on a road trip and drive cross-country back to Los Angeles. Even though I'd been to most of the places we visited while on tour with KISS and the Ace Frehley Band, I saw everything in a different light, and made discoveries that totally blew my mind! Visiting Monument Valley and Mount Rushmore made me feel like I was ten years old again; now we're planning a trip to visit the Pyramids at Giza.

Which brings us back to Redemption Song and Carnegie Hall, and a night I never could have imagined. My sponsor, Jimmy, also is in attendance, offering a little monologue about the night we met following my wrong-way trip through White Plains back in '83, and the unlikely friendship that arose from that encounter. The story is by way of introduction. That's the format for the evening—a little talking, and a lot of music, performed by an eclectic group of artists: Rickie Lee Jones, Guns N' Roses drummer Steven Adler, Run DMC frontman Darryl McDaniels, and me. We're very different people, of course, with different backgrounds, different tastes in music, and different points of view on any number of subjects. Our commonality—our bond—is that we all are addicts.

But we're musicians, too, and now it is my turn to play the part. The crowd applauds warmly as I take a seat on the stage, guitar in hand. There are only two of us out here, me and my buddy Eddie Ojeda, from Twisted Sister, also on guitar. I start to tune up a little, when suddenly it dawns on me: this is the first time I've performed this song live, with just acoustic guitars.

"We're gonna need your help on this," I tell the audience. "Because we don't have a drummer."

Everyone laughs. It's a friendly room, that's for sure. Suddenly the laughter melts into applause as Steven Adler appears to my right.

"What am I?" he blurts out. "Chopped liver?"

I give Steven a little nod, then slowly begin to tap my foot. Eddie does the same. The tapping grows louder as Steven takes up the cue and stomps about the stage, pumping his fists in time, and finally putting his hands together. The audience joins in, and soon the entire room is rocking.

I look over at Eddie and smile, and together we begin to play. I can't remember how many times I've performed this song in my hometown, but that night seems magically different. I'm overcome with emotion and my eyes begin to water as I glance around the entire room. I start singing the first verse, and the energy in the air becomes electric. As I approach the chorus I am filled with a new sense of accomplishment and pride in the message, which, as always, is open to interpretation.

*Here I am, again in this city,*
*With a fistful of dollars*
*And you'd better believe . . . I'm back!*
*Back in the New York Groove!*

And a California suntan doesn't suck!
*Awk!*

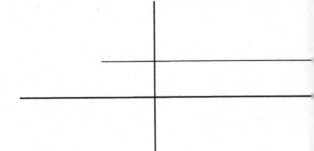

# A SPECIAL THANKS

I would imagine almost everyone who's ever written a book about their life experiences has remembered stories after the fact, thinking, *Shit, I forgot to include this story*, or *I should have told that one differently*. . . .

I'd like to take the opportunity now to thank my publisher, Simon & Schuster and MTV/VH1 Books, for being very patient with me and extending my deadline several months. The additional time allowed me to do some major rewrites with the help of my assistant, John Ostrosky. (Thank you, John.)

Let's face it—my memory isn't what it used to be. Speaking with old friends and coworkers jarred my memory, allowing me to recapture the true flavor of some of the stories within these pages.

I'd also like to thank my fiancée, Rachael, for putting up with all my mood swings at home and while vacationing in the Bahamas.

My manager, Dave Frey, and his assistant, Debi, never stopped believing in me and gave me positive feedback and support when I hit a brick wall mentally.

And last but not least, I'd like to thank my coauthor, Joe Layden!

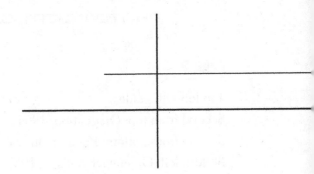

# PHOTO INSERT CAPTIONS

All photos courtesy of the author unless otherwise noted.

### Page 1

Top left: Baby picture, 1951
Top right: 1st grade
Bottom left: Age twelve
Bottom right: My confirmation (Grace Lutheran Church)

### Page 2

Top left: Mom and Dad
Top right: Easter, 1954
Bottom left: The Kids (Mosholu Parkway)
Bottom right: Mom and Dad (Dad looking like a gangster!)

## Page 3

Top left: 4th grade
Second from top: Graduation, 1964
Second from bottom: Photo booth with Billy, 1964
Bottom left: Greenwich Village, 1967
Center top: Wearing my Mr. Freedom shirt, 1969
Top right: Saginaw, Michigan, 1965
Bottom right: Feeding a llama with Mom at Catskill Game Farm, 1963

## Page 4

Top left: Onstage with Magic People, Mount Saint Michael Dance, 1968
Top right: Photo session with Molimo
Bottom left: My bedroom wall, 1967
Bottom right: Graduation, 1964 (Bronx Botanical Gardens)

## Page 5

Top left: Me and my girlfriend Roberta, at Poe Park
Top right: High school award-winning watercolor
Bottom: Molimo playing at the Village Gate

## Page 6

Top: Magic People show, 1969
Bottom left: Philadelphia, 1988
*Chris Ordinsky (Courtesy of the Author)*
Bottom right: Smokin' guitar, on the Just for Fun tour

# PHOTO INSERT CAPTIONS

## Page 7

Top left: At the airport, Boston, 1977
Top right: Party with the crew in Europe, 1975
Bottom: Bill Aucoin and me, 1975

## Page 8

Top left: The boys before takeoff, 1975
Center left: Vacation in Miami, 1977
Bottom left: Alex from Rush, performing "The Bag"
Top right: Bob dressed as an alien (Port Jervis)
Center right: Hunting trip with Bob and Frank, Port Jervis, 1976
Bottom right: Relaxing by the pool

## Page 9

Top left: On the bus, 1977
Top right: With my '59 Les Paul, 1978
*Courtesy of Bob Gruen*
Bottom left: Hangin' with Buddy
Bottom right: In the control room with Anton Fig and Eddie Solan, 1978

## Page 10

Top left: Winter hunting trip with my Uzi, 1981
Top right: Wilton Estate
Center right: Wilton Estate
Center left: On the set of the "Insane" video, 1989
Bottom left: With Lisa and friends
Bottom right: Me and Seamus in Wilton, Connecticut

## Page 11

Top left: DeWitt Clinton High School magazine I designed
Top right: "Spaceman" painting from 1993 (rendered in Infini-D)
Center left: First KISS button I designed, 1973
Right, second from top: An early flyer I designed for the band Honey, 1969
Bottom left: *Anomaly* CD art, designed by me
Bottom right: Anomaly tour VIP laminate I designed

## Page 12

Top left: With my cousins Scott McNeal and Bill Lynch after my accident in Dallas
*Courtesy of Sun Lynch*
Top right: Winning fifty grand in Atlantic City
Right center: With my dear friend, the late Dimebag Darrell (*Guitar World* photo shoot)
*Courtesy of Lorinda Sullivan*
Bottom left: With Paul at the Beacon Theatre after-show party
*Courtesy of Lydia Criss/Sealed with a Kiss*
Bottom right: Me and Anton the day after the Porsche accident

## Page 13

Top left: Mixing with Eddie Kramer and Scott Mabuchi
*Courtesy of Ebet Roberts*
Top right: Gene at our wedding, 1976
Center left: In Wilton, Connecticut
Center right: Gene and me when we appeared on *The Robert Klein Show*
*Courtesy of Ebet Roberts*
Bottom left: The *Tomorrow* show with Tom Snyder

Second from bottom, right: KISS horsing around in drag with Billy and Eddie
Bottom right: Me, Jeanette, and Hanna in wigs!

## Page 14

Top left: With Jeff Beck at a Les Paul tribute concert
*Courtesy of Getty*
Top right: With my buddy Slash at VH1 Rock Honors
*Courtesy of Getty*
Center left: Ace Frehley Band, Australian Tour 2010
*Courtesy of John Raptis*
Center: Vacationing in the Bahamas with Rachael
Center right: At a New York Dolls show, Halloween 1973
Bottom: With Monique at the House of Blues, for a Dimebag Darrell fund-raiser

## Page 15

Top: At Bob Gruen's apartment, 2004
*Courtesy of Bob Gruen*
Bottom left: Vacationing with Rachael in Puerto Vallarta
*Courtesy Jessica Marlo Croce*
Bottom center: Monument Valley, Utah
Bottom right: Jamming with Les Paul at the Iridium
*Courtesy of Bob Gruen*

## Page 16

Top: Jamming with Charlie and Cousin John in New Bern, North Carolina, 1957
Bottom: Ace Frehley Band at Sweden Rock Festival, 2009
*Courtesy of Henry Smith*